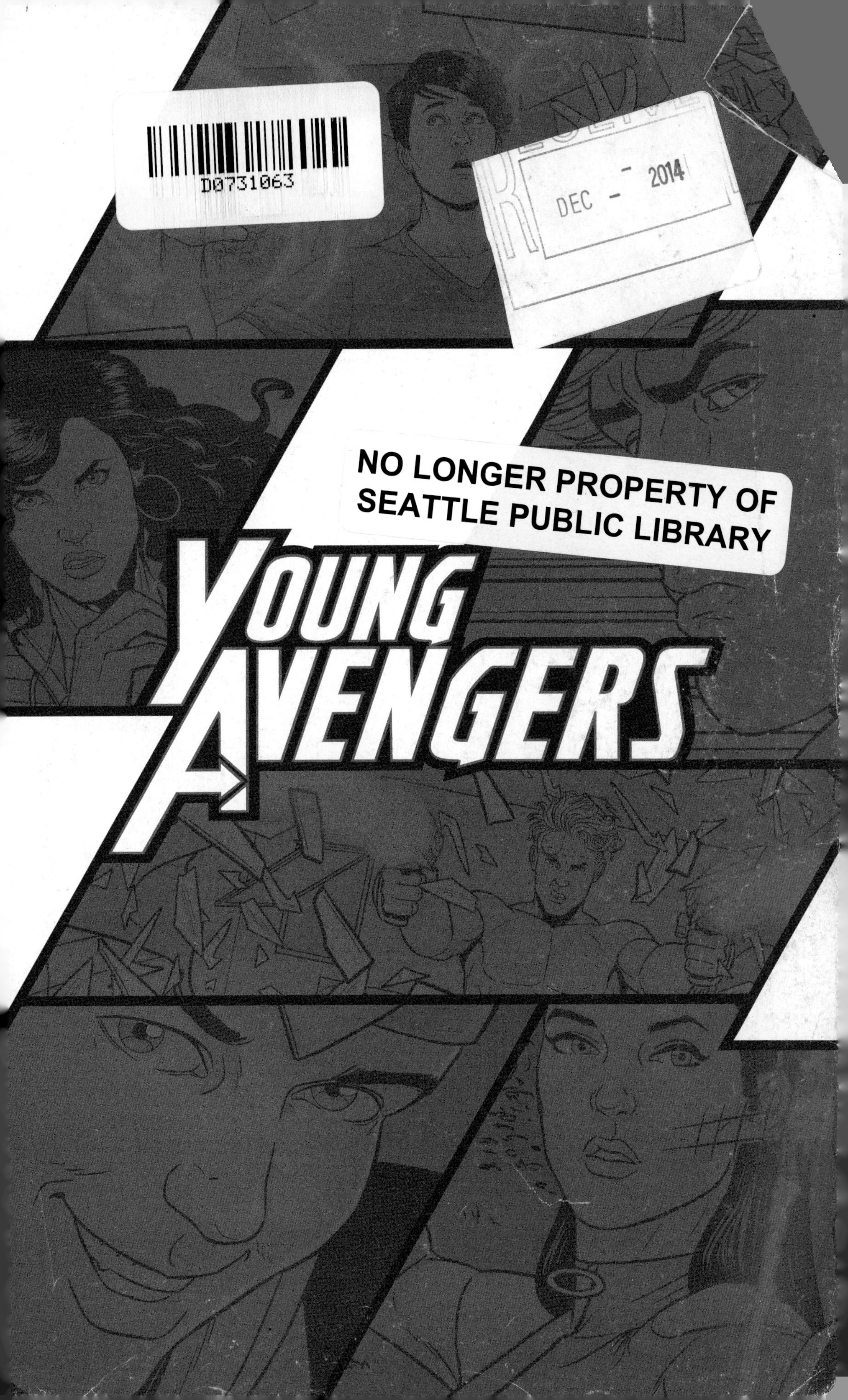
YOUNG
AVENGERS

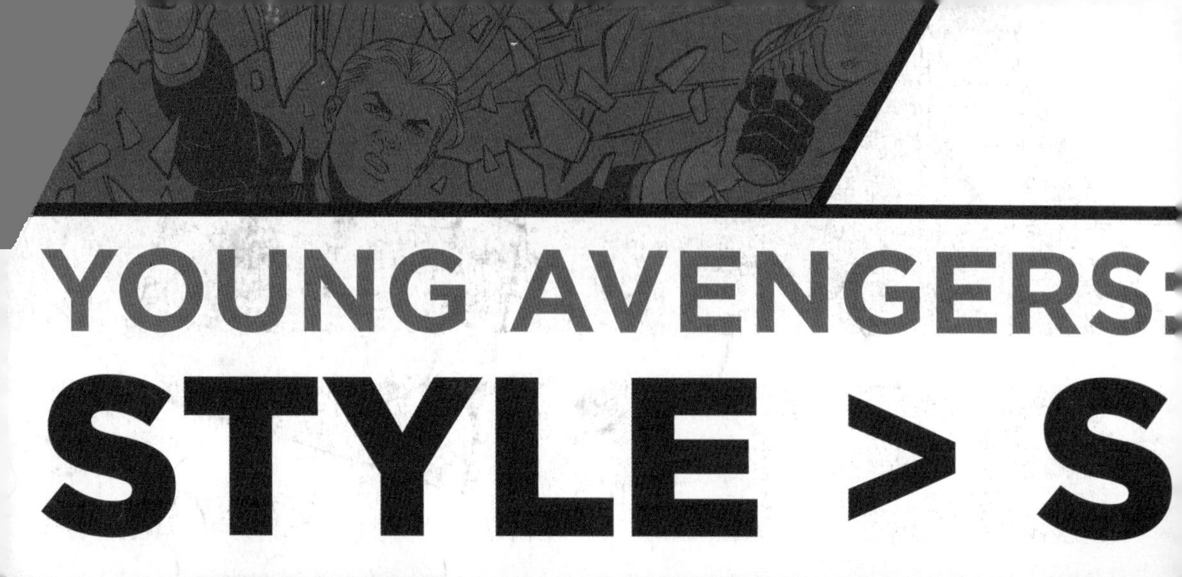

# YOUNG AVENGERS:
# STYLE > S

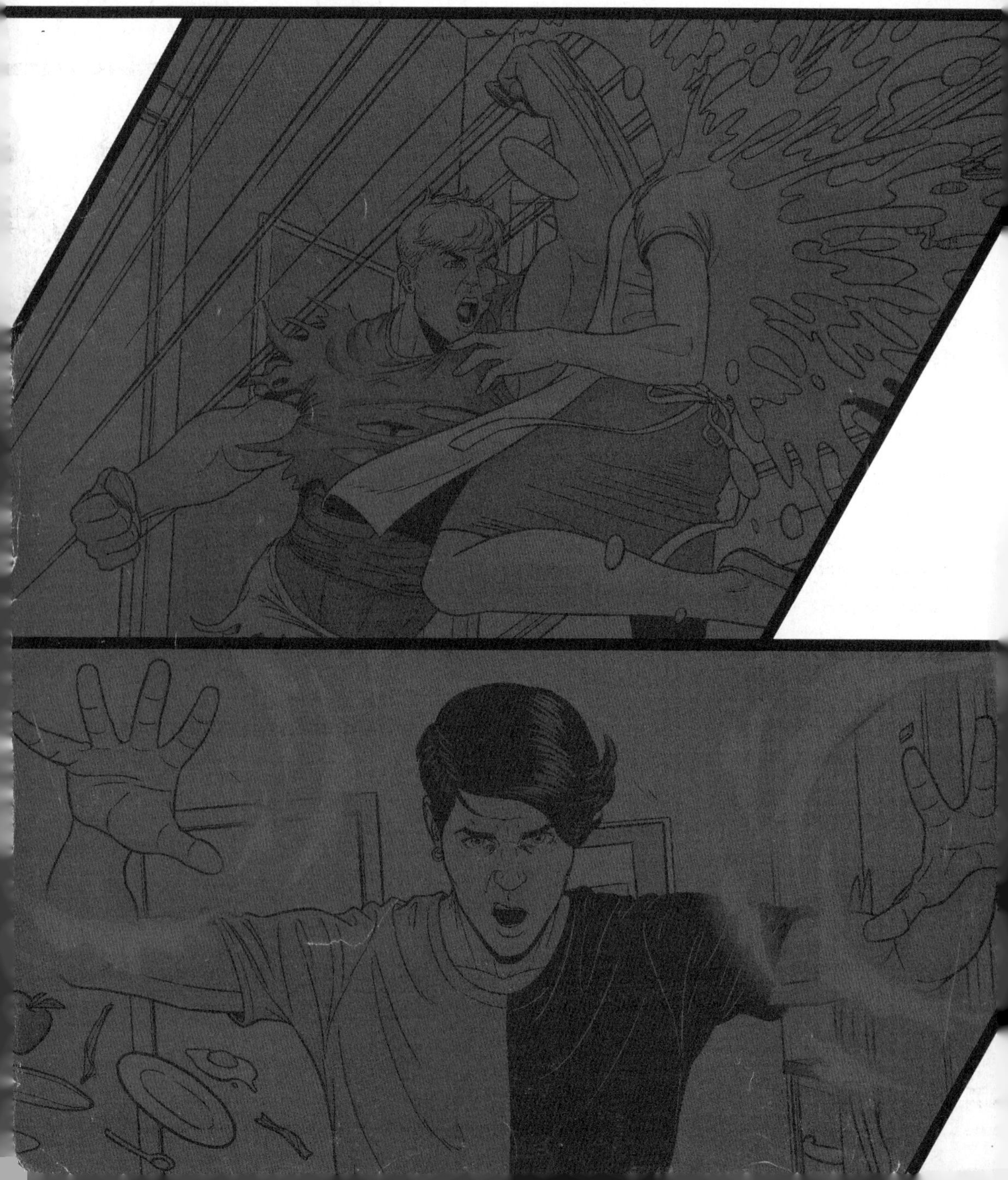

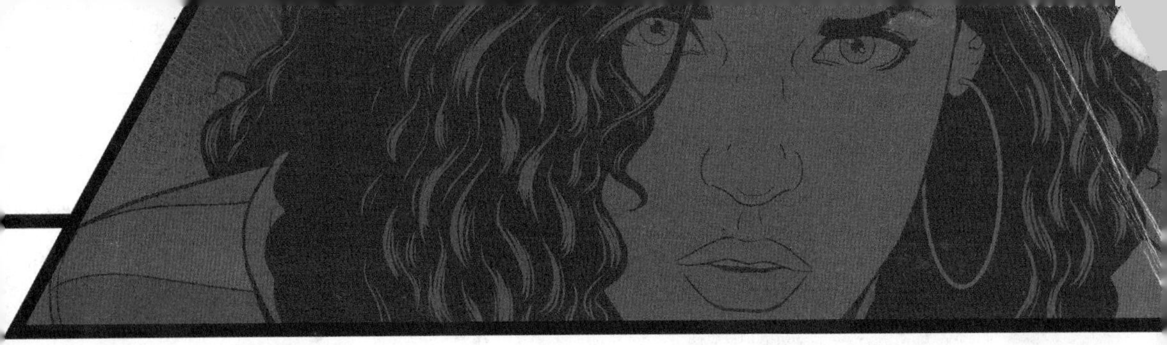

# BSTANCE

writer: **KIERON GILLEN**
artist: **JAMIE McKELVIE** with **MIKE NORTON**
color artist: **MATTHEW WILSON**
letterer: **VC'S CLAYTON COWLES**
cover art: **JAMIE MCKELVIE & MATTHEW WILSON**
assistant editor: **JACOB THOMAS**
editor: **LAUREN SANKOVITCH**

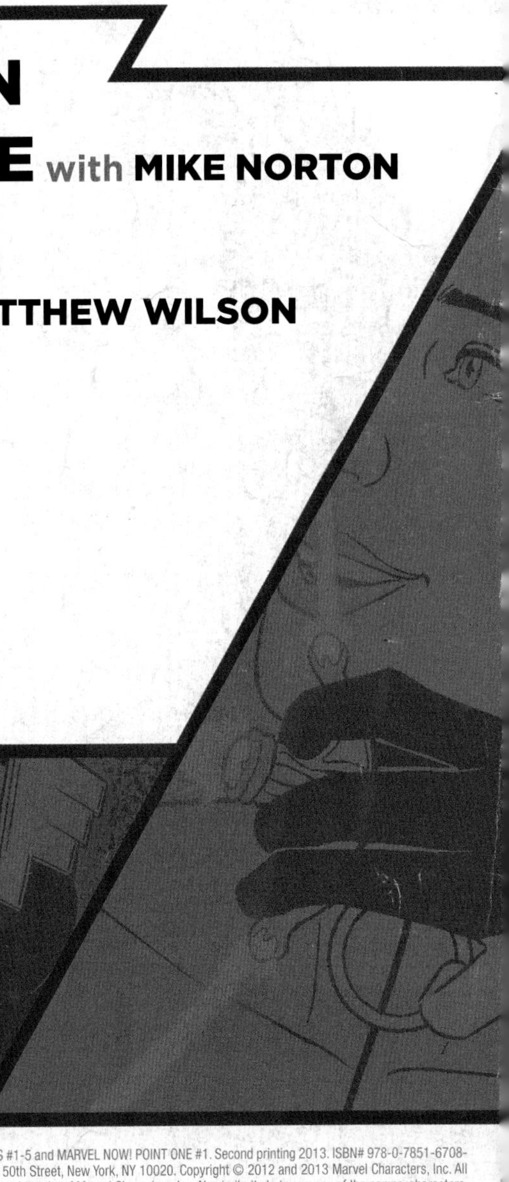

collection editor: JENNIFER GRÜNWALD
assistant editors: ALEX STARBUCK & NELSON RIBEIRO
editor, special projects: MARK D. BEAZLEY
senior editor, special projects: JEFF YOUNGQUIST
svp of print & digital publishing sales: DAVID GABRIEL
book design: JEFF POWELL

editor in chief: AXEL ALONSO
chief creative officer: JOE QUESADA
publisher: DAN BUCKLEY
executive producer: ALAN FINE

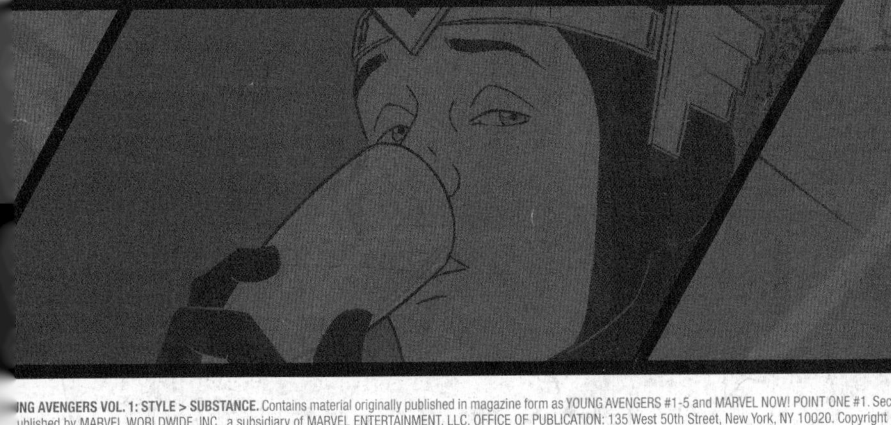

**ING AVENGERS VOL. 1: STYLE > SUBSTANCE.** Contains material originally published in magazine form as YOUNG AVENGERS #1-5 and MARVEL NOW! POINT ONE #1. Second printing 2013. ISBN# 978-0-7851-6708- ublished by MARVEL WORLDWIDE, INC., a subsidiary of MARVEL ENTERTAINMENT, LLC. OFFICE OF PUBLICATION: 135 West 50th Street, New York, NY 10020.  **Printed in the U.S.A.** ALAN FINE, EVP - Office ne President, Marvel Worldwide, Inc. and EVP & CMO Marvel Characters B.V.; DAN BUCKLEY, Publisher & President - Print, Animation & Digital Divisions; JOE QUESADA, Chief Creative Officer; TOM BREVOORT, SVP of lishing; DAVID BOGART, SVP of Operations & Procurement, Publishing; C.B. CEBULSKI, SVP of Creator & Content Development; DAVID GABRIEL, SVP of Print & Digital Publishing Sales; JIM O'KEEFE, VP of Operations & istics; DAN CARR, Executive Director of Publishing Technology; SUSAN CRESPI, Editorial Operations Manager; ALEX MORALES, Publishing Operations Manager; STAN LEE, Chairman Emeritus. For information regarding ertising in Marvel Comics or on Marvel.com, please contact Niza Disla, Director of Marvel Partnerships, at ndisla@marvel.com. For Marvel subscription inquiries, please call 800-217-9158. **Manufactured between 16/2013 and 11/18/13 by QUAD/GRAPHICS, VERSAILLES, KY, USA.**

98765432

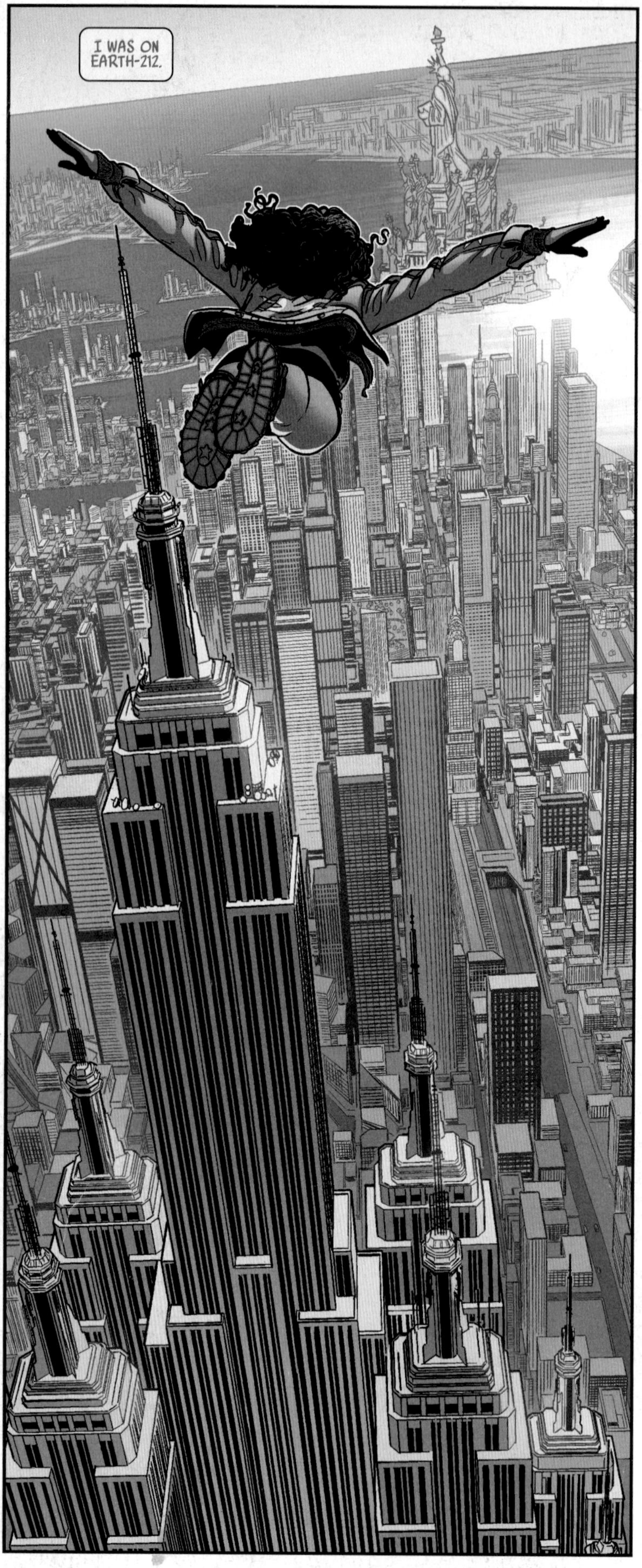
I WAS ON EARTH-212.

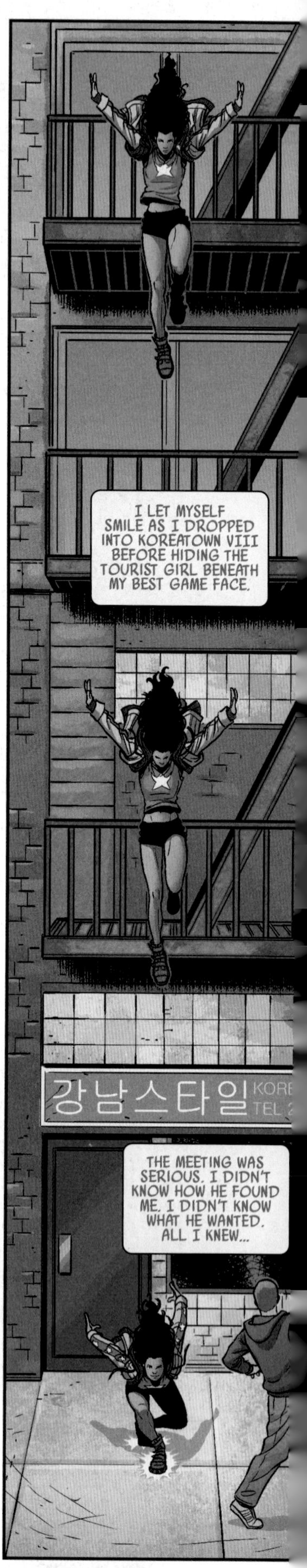
I LET MYSELF SMILE AS I DROPPED INTO KOREATOWN VIII BEFORE HIDING THE TOURIST GIRL BENEATH MY BEST GAME FACE.
강남스타일
THE MEETING WAS SERIOUS. I DIDN'T KNOW HOW HE FOUND ME. I DIDN'T KNOW WHAT HE WANTED. ALL I KNEW...

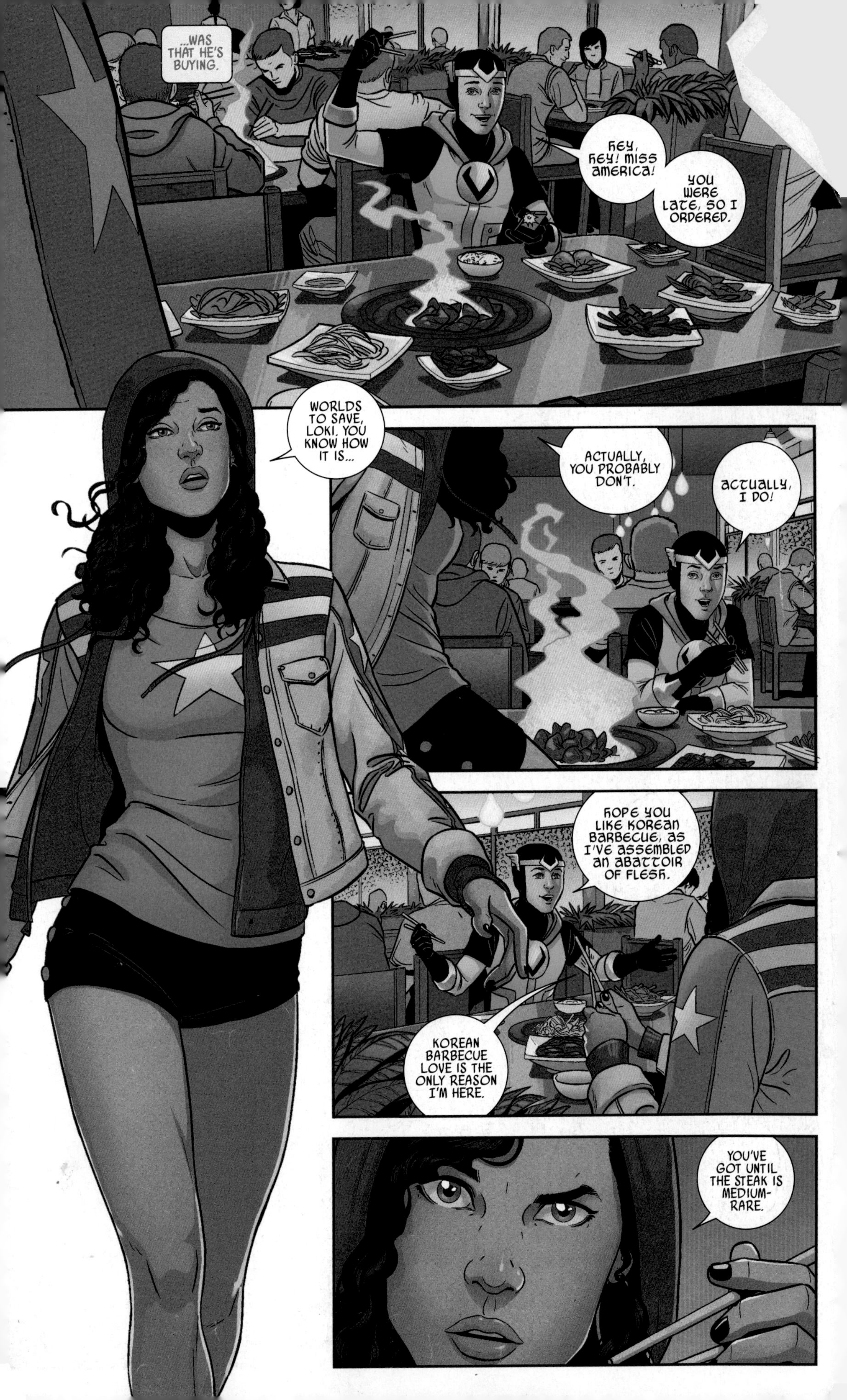
...WAS THAT HE'S BUYING.
HEY, HEY! MISS AMERICA!
YOU WERE LATE, SO I ORDERED.
WORLDS TO SAVE, LOKI. YOU KNOW HOW IT IS...
ACTUALLY, YOU PROBABLY DON'T.
ACTUALLY, I DO!
HOPE YOU LIKE KOREAN BARBECUE, AS I'VE ASSEMBLED AN ABATTOIR OF FLESH.
KOREAN BARBECUE LOVE IS THE ONLY REASON I'M HERE.
YOU'VE GOT UNTIL THE STEAK IS MEDIUM-RARE.

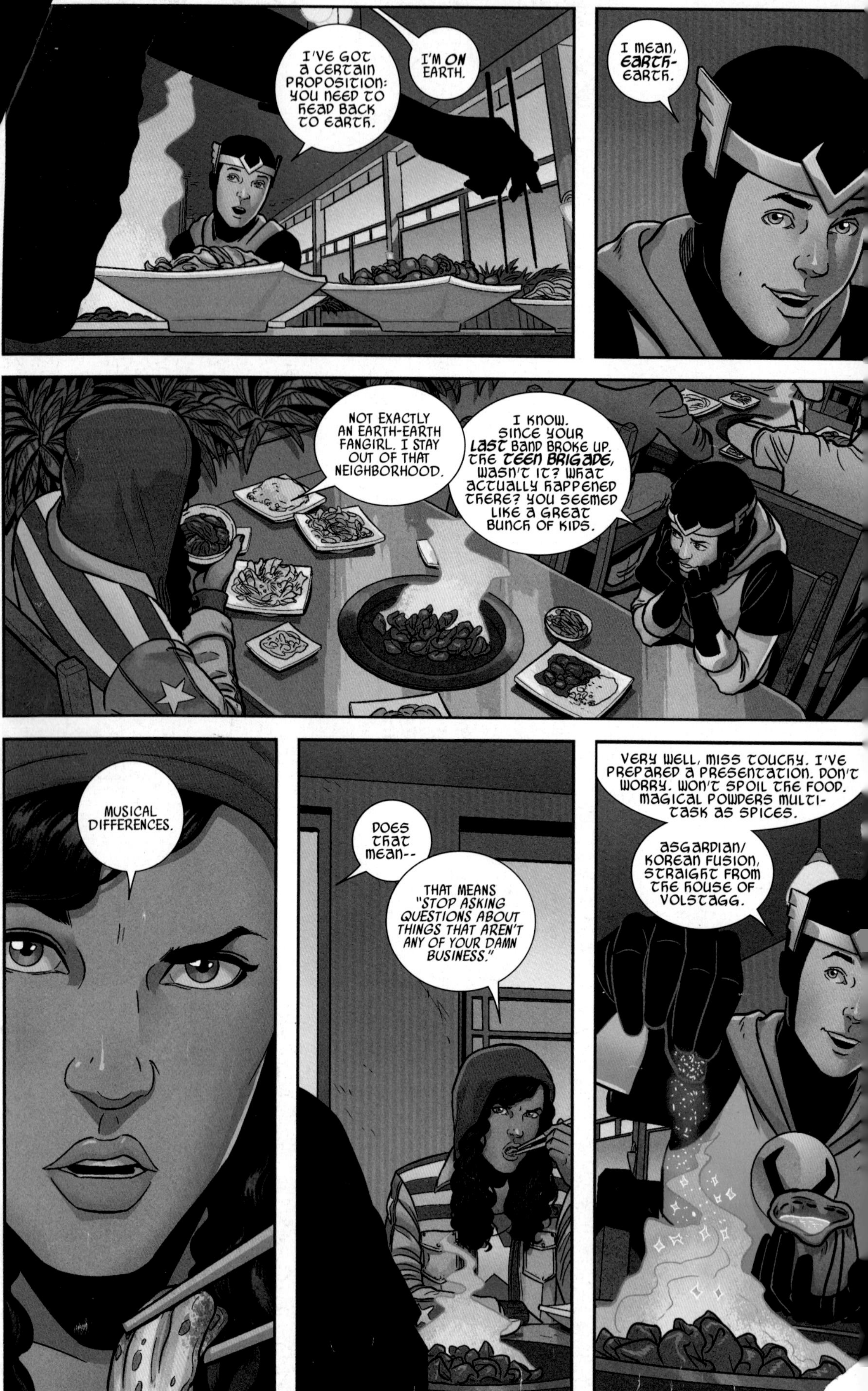
I'VE GOT A CERTAIN PROPOSITION: YOU NEED TO HEAD BACK TO EARTH.
I'M ON EARTH.
I MEAN, EARTH-EARTH.
NOT EXACTLY AN EARTH-EARTH FANGIRL. I STAY OUT OF THAT NEIGHBORHOOD.
I KNOW. SINCE YOUR LAST BAND BROKE UP. THE TEEN BRIGADE, WASN'T IT? WHAT ACTUALLY HAPPENED THERE? YOU SEEMED LIKE A GREAT BUNCH OF KIDS.
MUSICAL DIFFERENCES.
DOES THAT MEAN--
THAT MEANS "STOP ASKING QUESTIONS ABOUT THINGS THAT AREN'T ANY OF YOUR DAMN BUSINESS."
VERY WELL, MISS TOUCHY. I'VE PREPARED A PRESENTATION. DON'T WORRY. WON'T SPOIL THE FOOD. MAGICAL POWDERS MULTI-TASK AS SPICES.
ASGARDIAN/KOREAN FUSION, STRAIGHT FROM THE HOUSE OF VOLSTAGG.

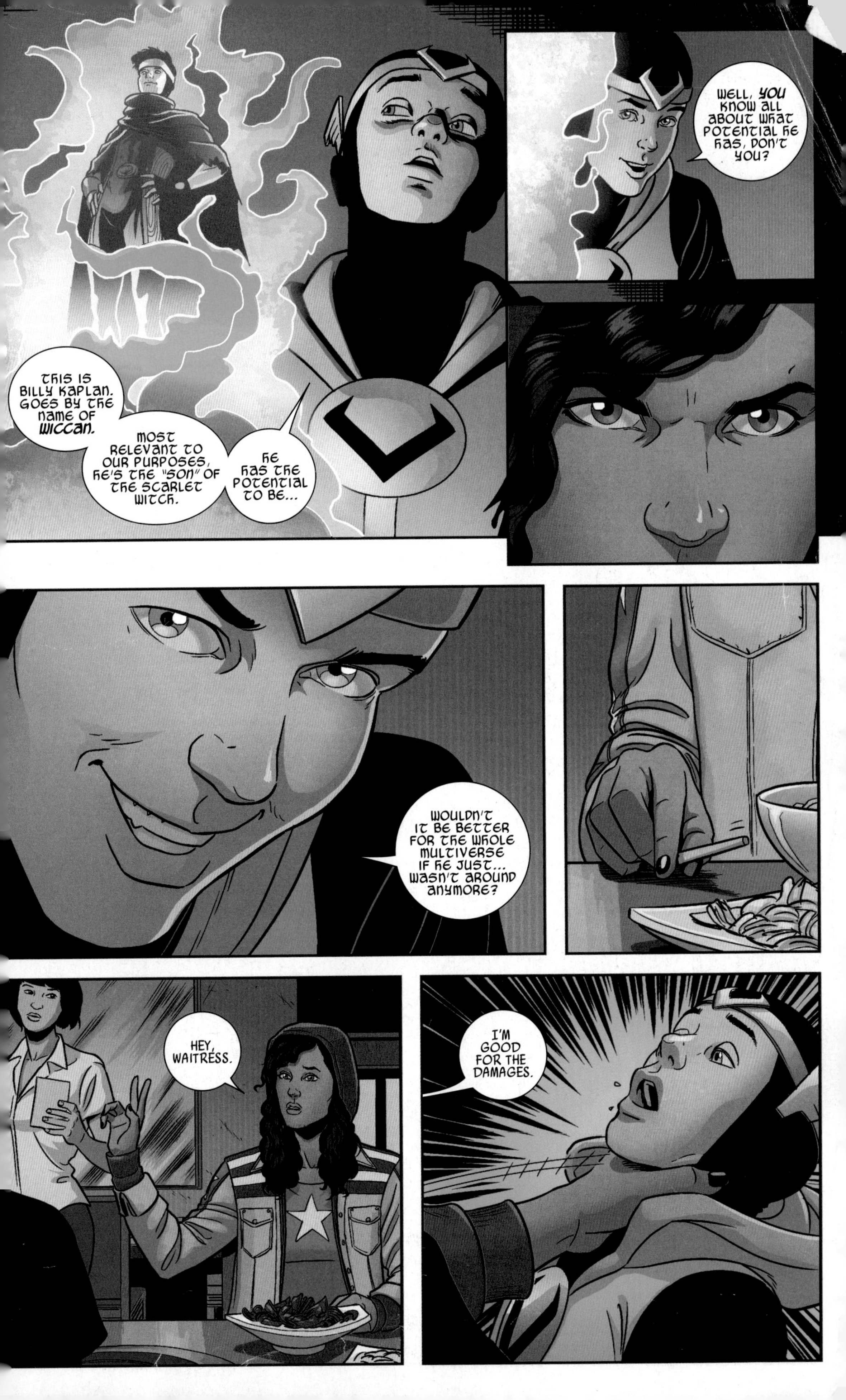
THIS IS BILLY KAPLAN. GOES BY THE NAME OF WICCAN.
MOST RELEVANT TO OUR PURPOSES, HE'S THE "SON" OF THE SCARLET WITCH.
HE HAS THE POTENTIAL TO BE...
WELL, YOU KNOW ALL ABOUT WHAT POTENTIAL HE HAS, DON'T YOU?
WOULDN'T IT BE BETTER FOR THE WHOLE MULTIVERSE IF HE JUST... WASN'T AROUND ANYMORE?
HEY, WAITRESS.
I'M GOOD FOR THE DAMAGES.

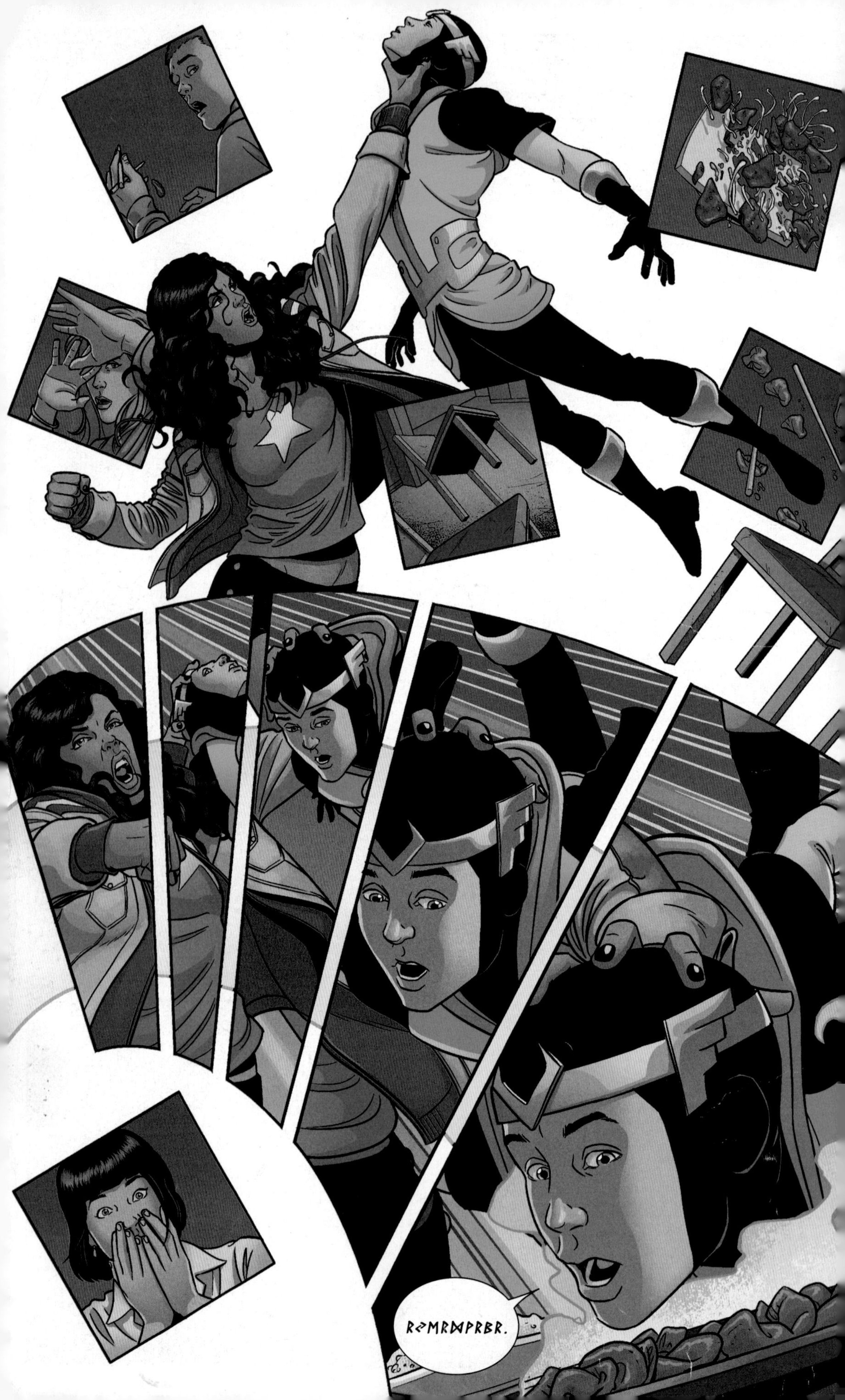
ᚱᛜᛗᚱᛞᚹᚱᛒᚱ.

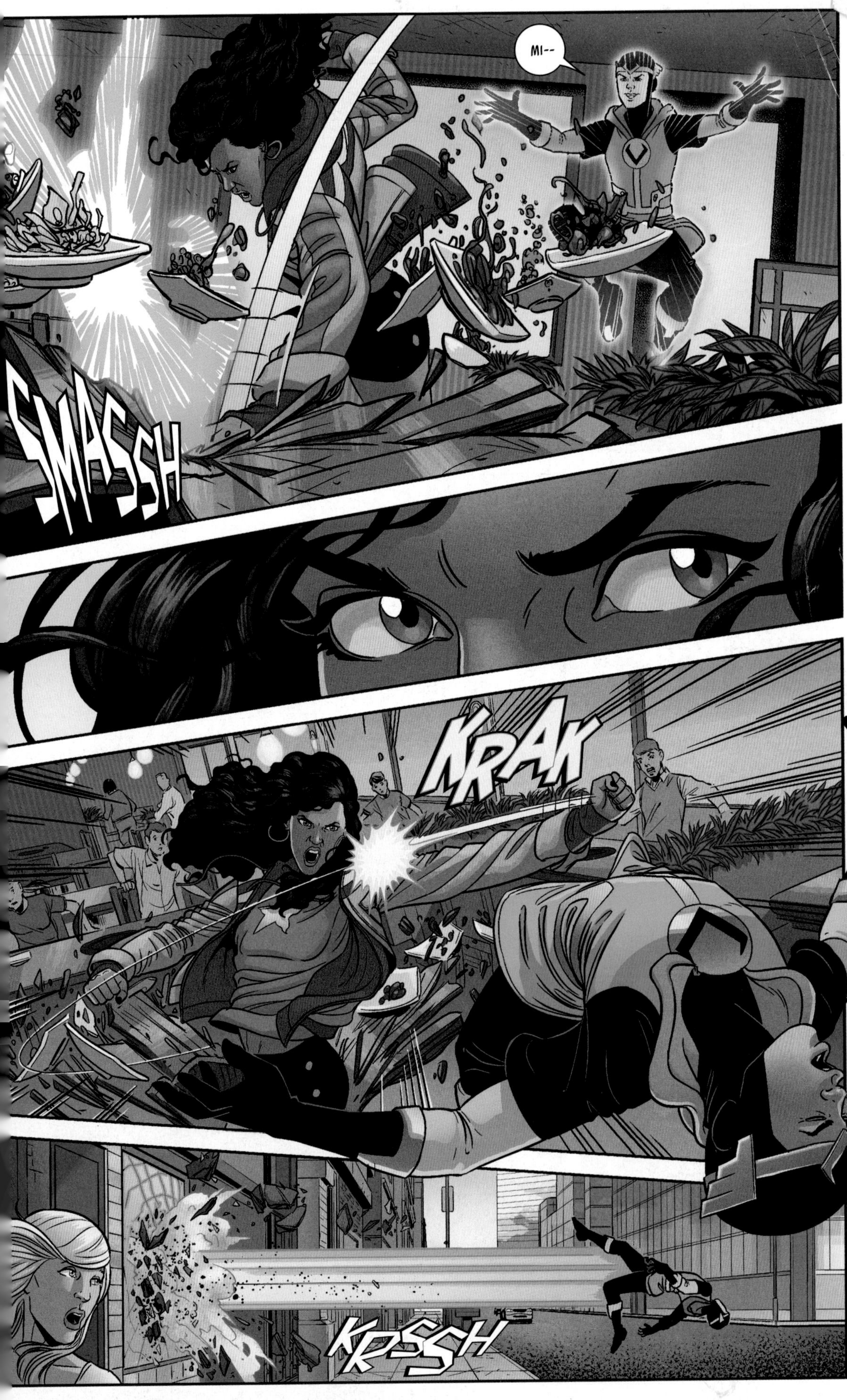

MI--
SMASSH
KRAK
KRSSH

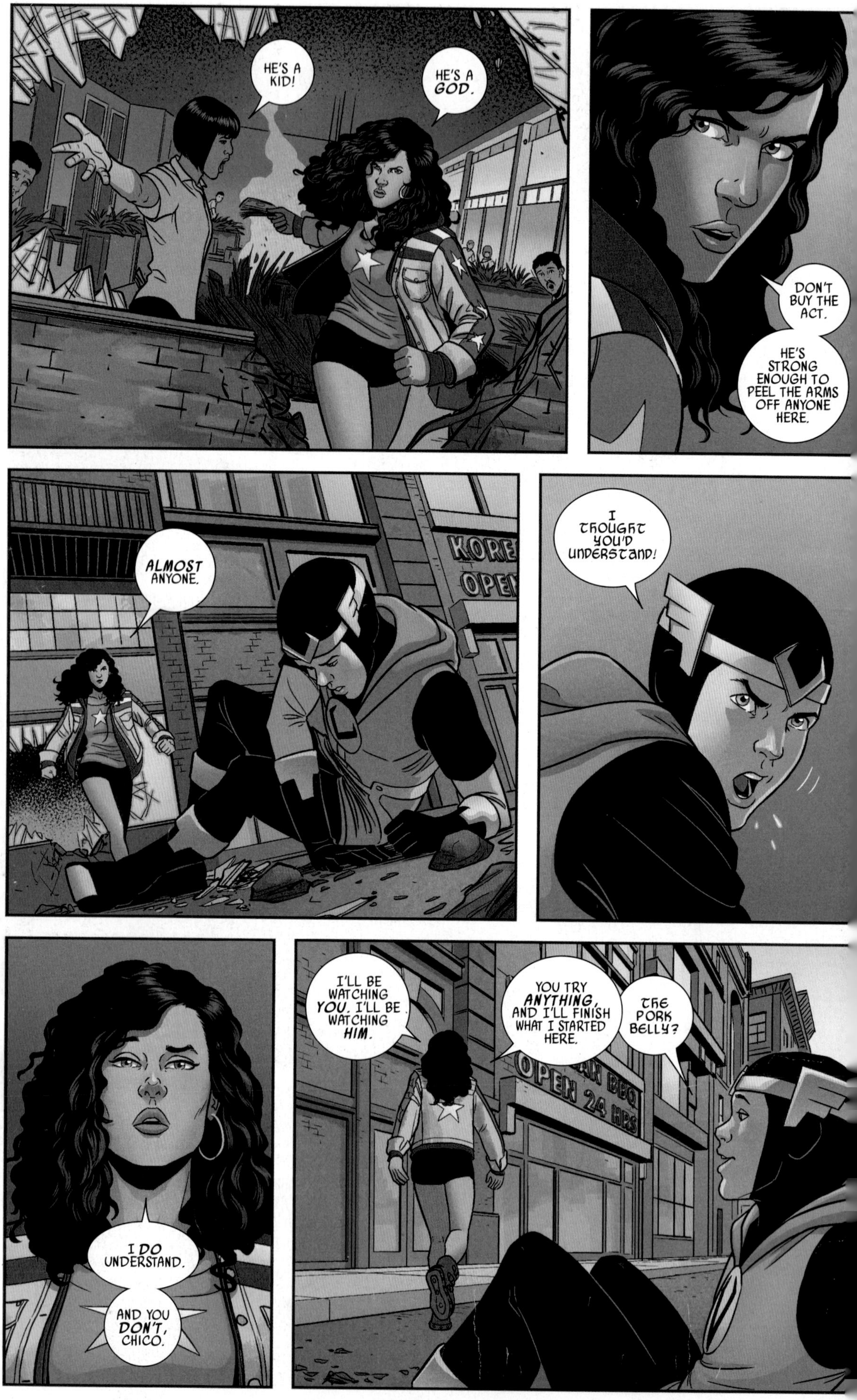
HE'S A KID!
HE'S A GOD.
DON'T BUY THE ACT.
HE'S STRONG ENOUGH TO PEEL THE ARMS OFF ANYONE HERE.
ALMOST ANYONE.
I THOUGHT YOU'D UNDERSTAND!
I DO UNDERSTAND.
AND YOU DON'T, CHICO.
I'LL BE WATCHING YOU. I'LL BE WATCHING HIM.
YOU TRY ANYTHING, AND I'LL FINISH WHAT I STARTED HERE.
THE PORK BELLY?
OPEN 24 HRS

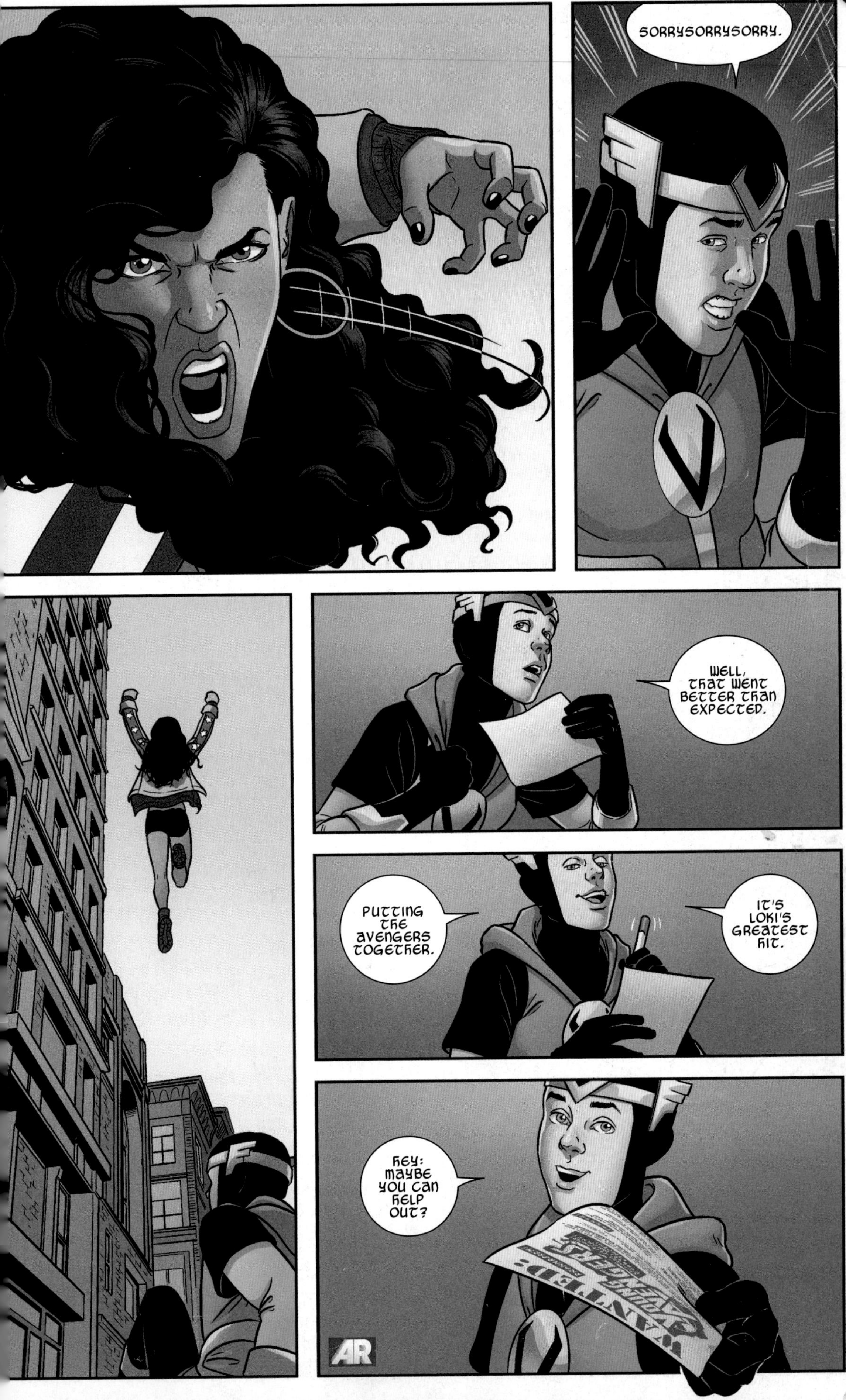
SORRYSORRYSORRY.
WELL, THAT WENT BETTER THAN EXPECTED.
PUTTING THE AVENGERS TOGETHER.
IT'S LOKI'S GREATEST HIT.
HEY: MAYBE YOU CAN HELP OUT?

# WANTED:

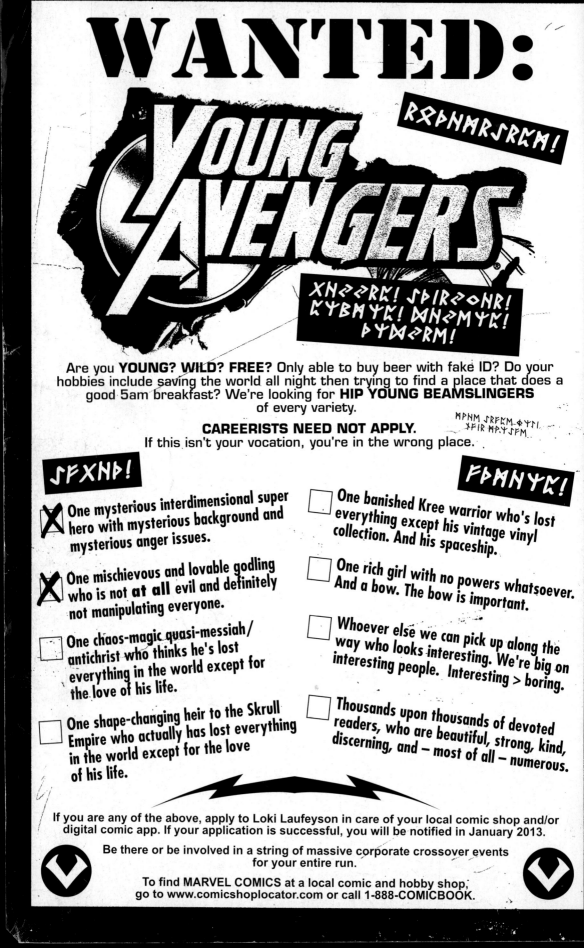

**YOUNG AVENGERS**

Are you **YOUNG? WILD? FREE?** Only able to buy beer with fake ID? Do your hobbies include saving the world all night then trying to find a place that does a good 5am breakfast? We're looking for **HIP YOUNG BEAMSLINGERS** of every variety.

## CAREERISTS NEED NOT APPLY.
If this isn't your vocation, you're in the wrong place.

**X** One mysterious interdimensional super hero with mysterious background and mysterious anger issues.

**X** One mischievous and lovable godling who is not **at all** evil and definitely not manipulating everyone.

One chaos-magic quasi-messiah/ antichrist who thinks he's lost everything in the world except for the love of his life.

One shape-changing heir to the Skrull Empire who actually has lost everything in the world except for the love of his life.

One banished Kree warrior who's lost everything except his vintage vinyl collection. And his spaceship.

One rich girl with no powers whatsoever. And a bow. The bow is important.

Whoever else we can pick up along the way who looks interesting. We're big on interesting people. Interesting > boring.

Thousands upon thousands of devoted readers, who are beautiful, strong, kind, discerning, and – most of all – numerous.

If you are any of the above, apply to Loki Laufeyson in care of your local comic shop and/or digital comic app. If your application is successful, you will be notified in January 2013.

Be there or be involved in a string of massive corporate crossover events for your entire run.

To find MARVEL COMICS at a local comic and hobby shop, go to www.comicshoplocator.com or call 1-888-COMICBOOK.

**#1 VARIANT**
BY BRYAN LEE O'MALLEY

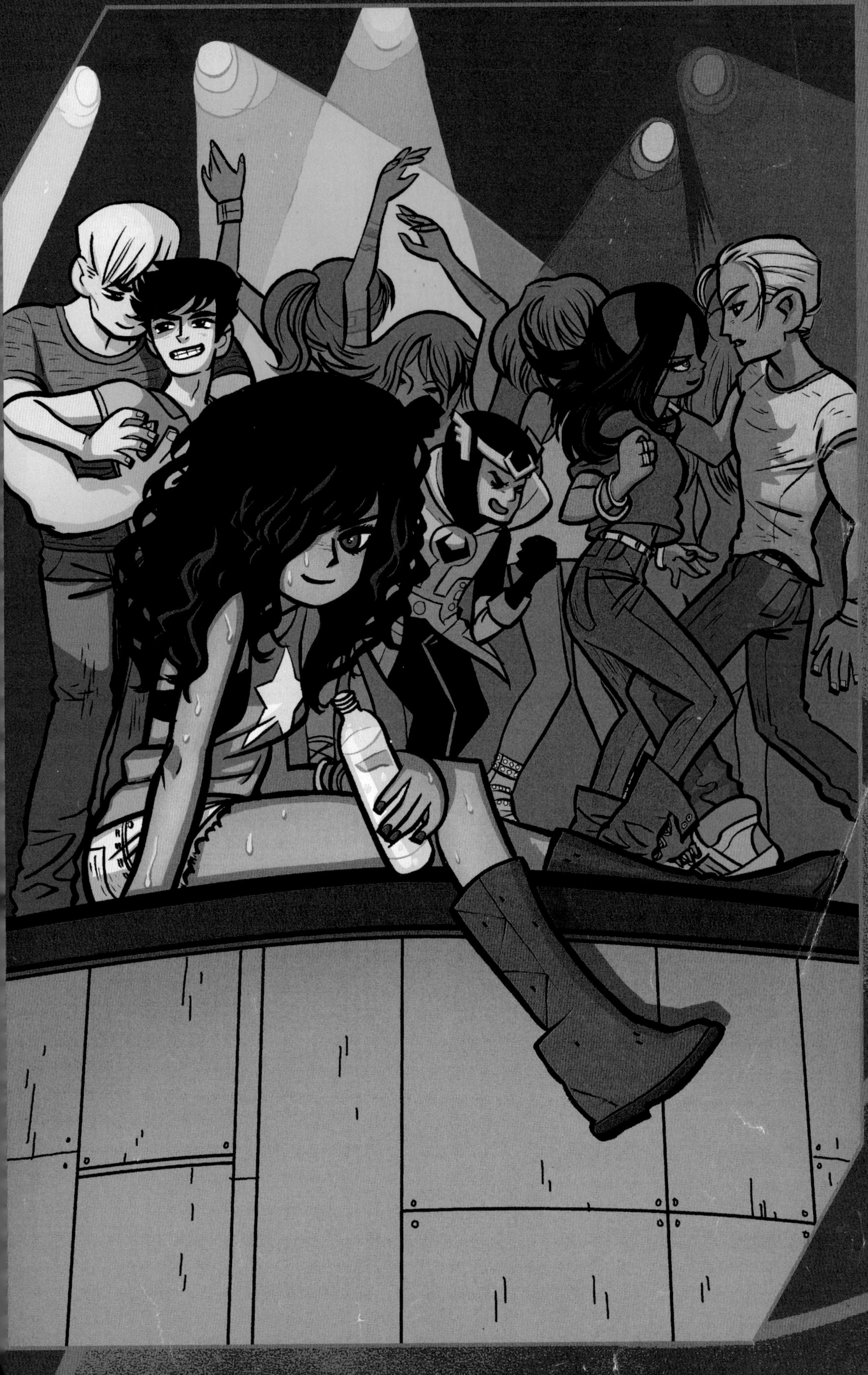

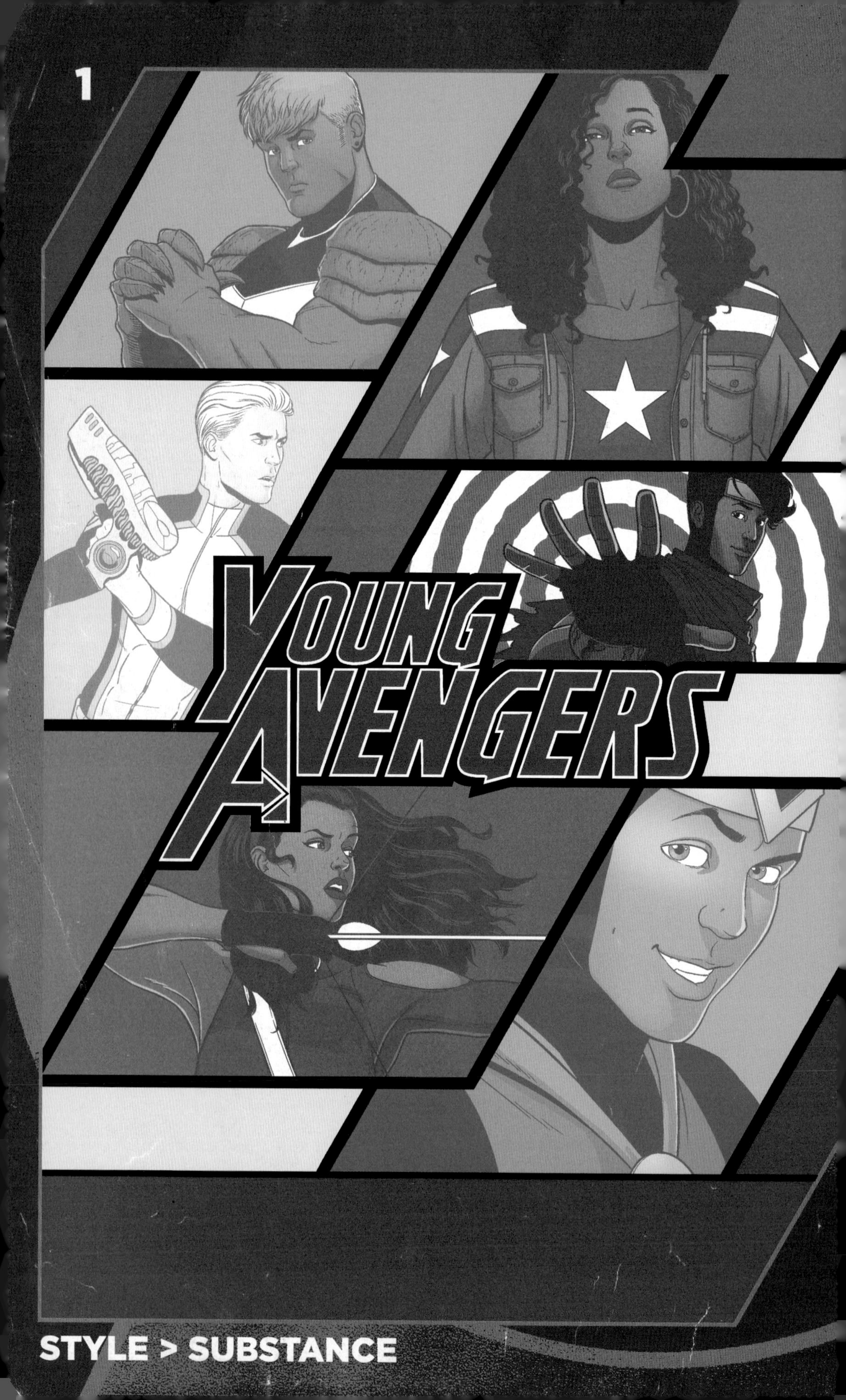
1
YOUNG AVENGERS
STYLE > SUBSTANCE

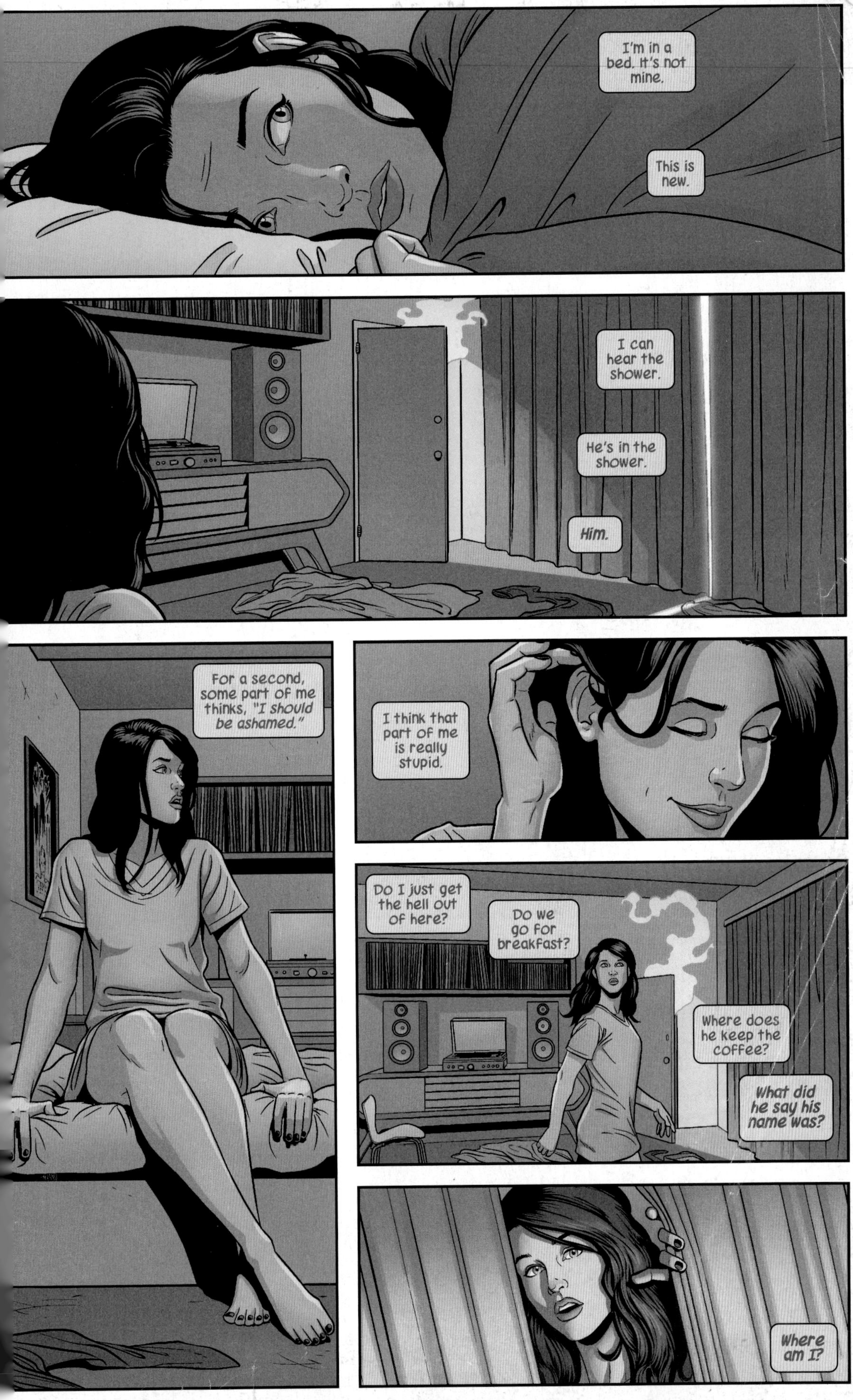
I'm in a bed. It's not mine.
This is new.
I can hear the shower.
He's in the shower.
*Him.*
For a second, some part of me thinks, "*I should be ashamed.*"
I think that part of me is really stupid.
Do I just get the hell out of here?
Do we go for breakfast?
Where does he keep the coffee?
*What did he say his name was?*
*Where am I?*

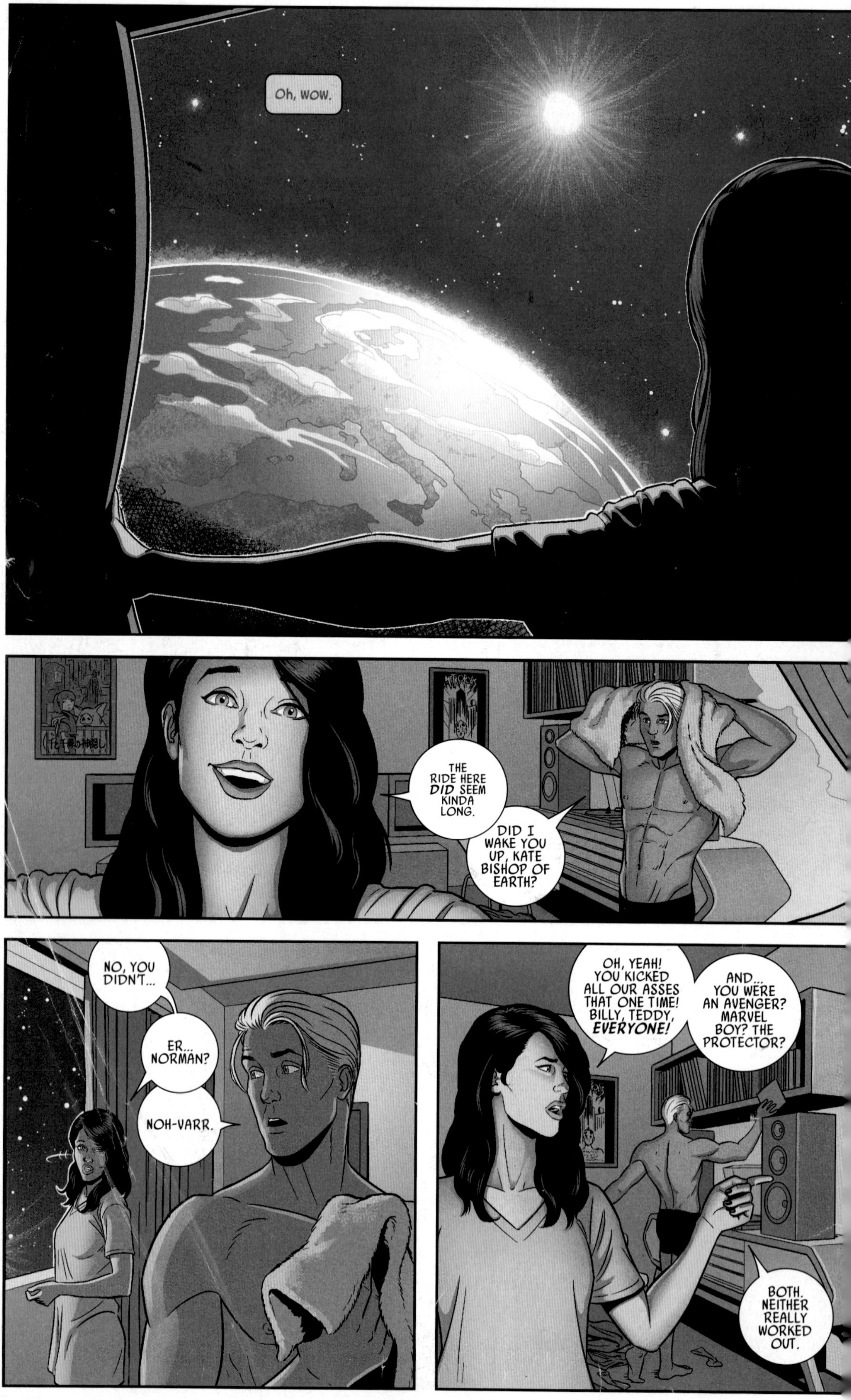

Oh, WOW.
THE RIDE HERE DID SEEM KINDA LONG.
DID I WAKE YOU UP, KATE BISHOP OF EARTH?
NO, YOU DIDN'T...
ER... NORMAN?
NOH-VARR.
OH, YEAH! YOU KICKED ALL OUR ASSES THAT ONE TIME! BILLY, TEDDY, EVERYONE!
AND... YOU WERE AN AVENGER? MARVEL BOY? THE PROTECTOR?
BOTH. NEITHER REALLY WORKED OUT.

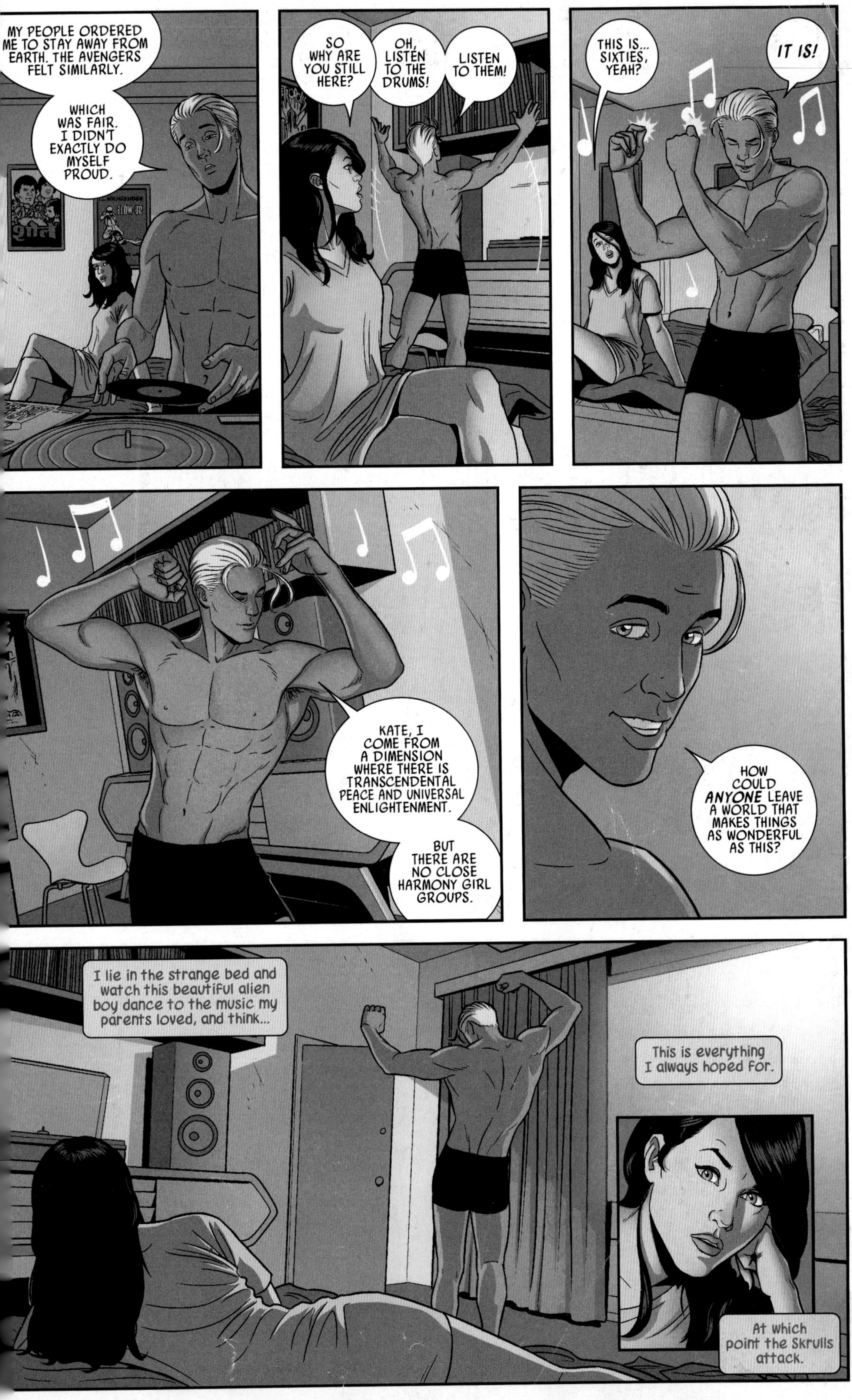

MY PEOPLE ORDERED ME TO STAY AWAY FROM EARTH. THE AVENGERS FELT SIMILARLY.
WHICH WAS FAIR. I DIDN'T EXACTLY DO MYSELF PROUD.
SO WHY ARE YOU STILL HERE?
OH, LISTEN TO THE DRUMS!
LISTEN TO THEM!
THIS IS... SIXTIES, YEAH?
IT IS!
KATE, I COME FROM A DIMENSION WHERE THERE IS TRANSCENDENTAL PEACE AND UNIVERSAL ENLIGHTENMENT.
BUT THERE ARE NO CLOSE HARMONY GIRL GROUPS.
HOW COULD ANYONE LEAVE A WORLD THAT MAKES THINGS AS WONDERFUL AS THIS?
I lie in the strange bed and watch this beautiful alien boy dance to the music my parents loved, and think...
This is everything I always hoped for.
At which point the Skrulls attack.

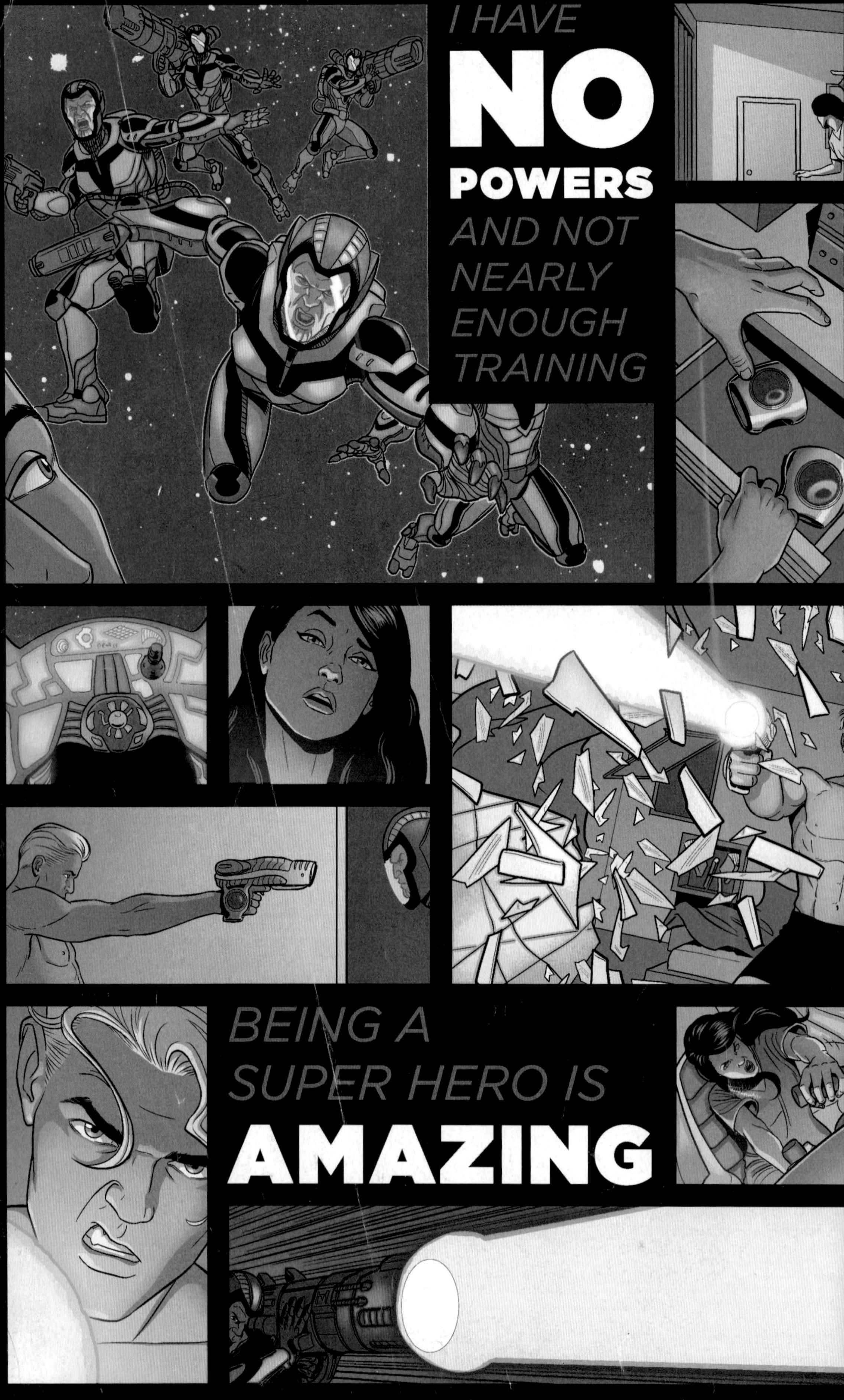
I HAVE
NO
POWERS
AND NOT
NEARLY
ENOUGH
TRAINING
BEING A
SUPER HERO IS
AMAZING

BUT I'M
DOING THIS
**ANYWAY**

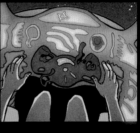

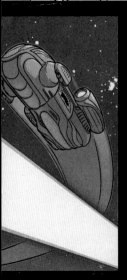

EVERYONE
SHOULD
**TRY IT**

# YOUNG AVENGERS:
# STYLE > S

UBSTANCE

AR

# NEW YORK.

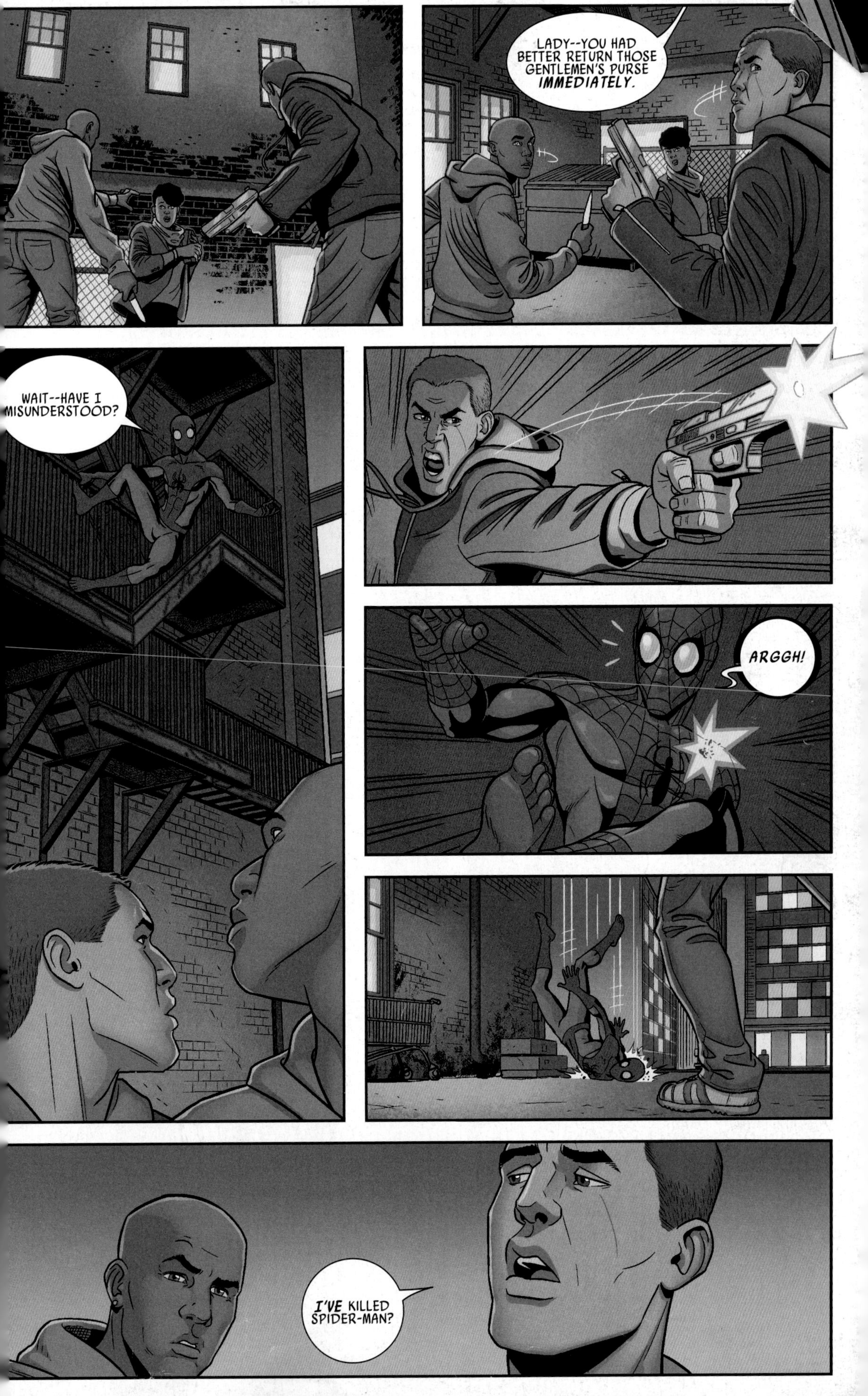
LADY--YOU HAD BETTER RETURN THOSE GENTLEMEN'S PURSE *IMMEDIATELY.*
WAIT--HAVE I MISUNDERSTOOD?
ARGGH!
*I'VE* KILLED SPIDER-MAN?

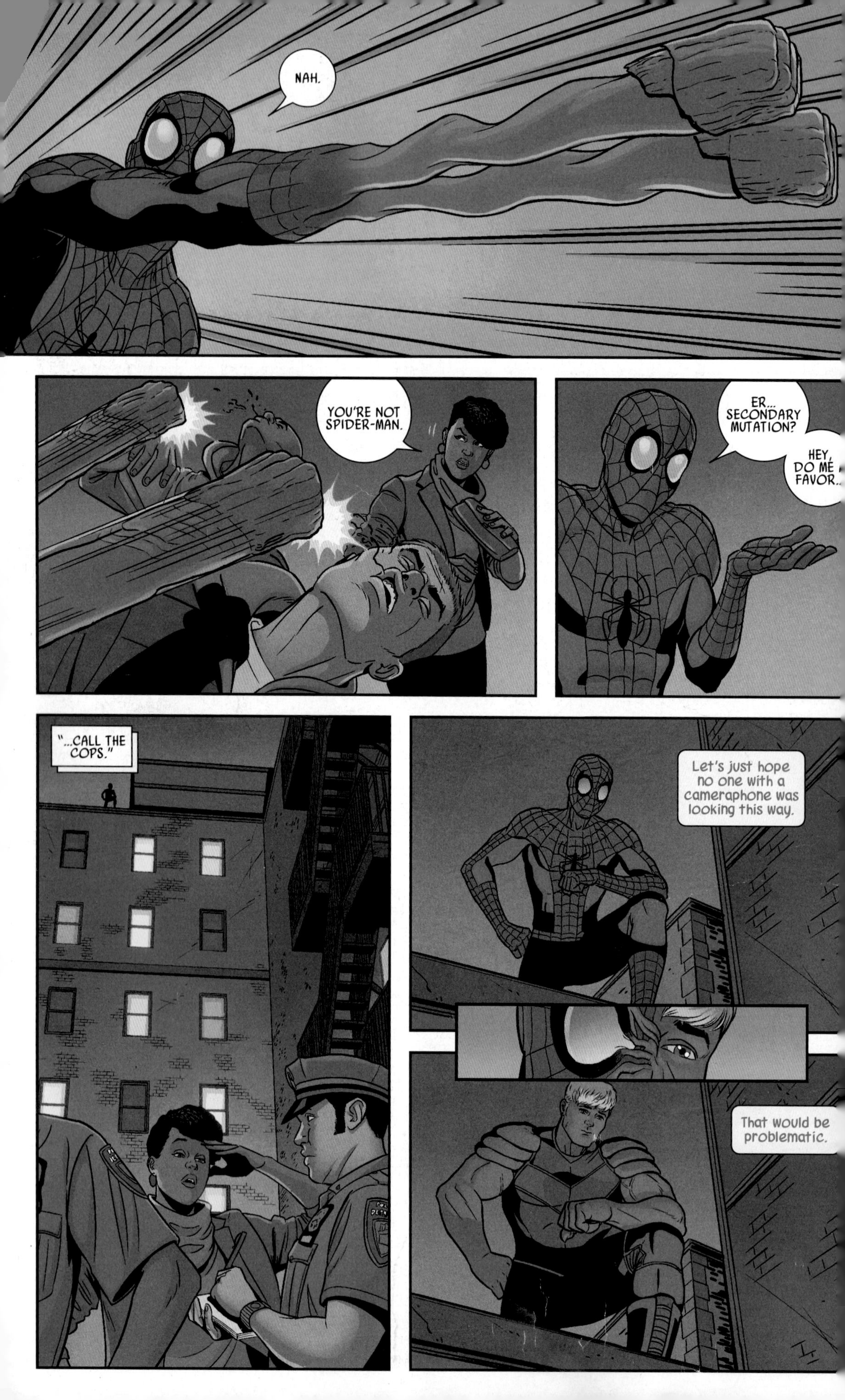
NAH.
YOU'RE NOT SPIDER-MAN.
ER... SECONDARY MUTATION?
HEY, DO ME FAVOR...
"...CALL THE COPS."
Let's just hope no one with a cameraphone was looking this way.
That would be problematic.

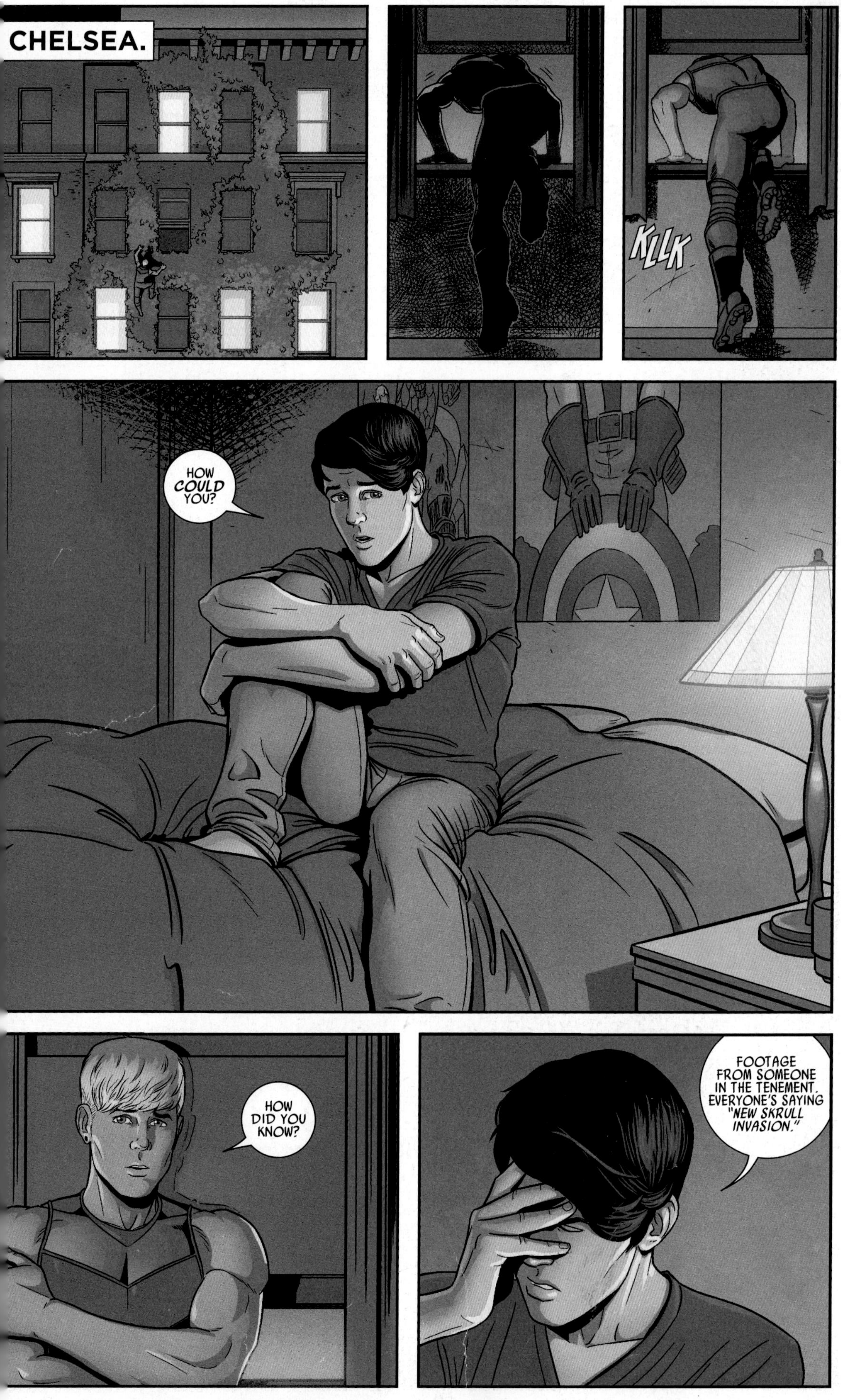
CHELSEA.
KLLK
HOW COULD YOU?
HOW DID YOU KNOW?
FOOTAGE FROM SOMEONE IN THE TENEMENT. EVERYONE'S SAYING "NEW SKRULL INVASION."

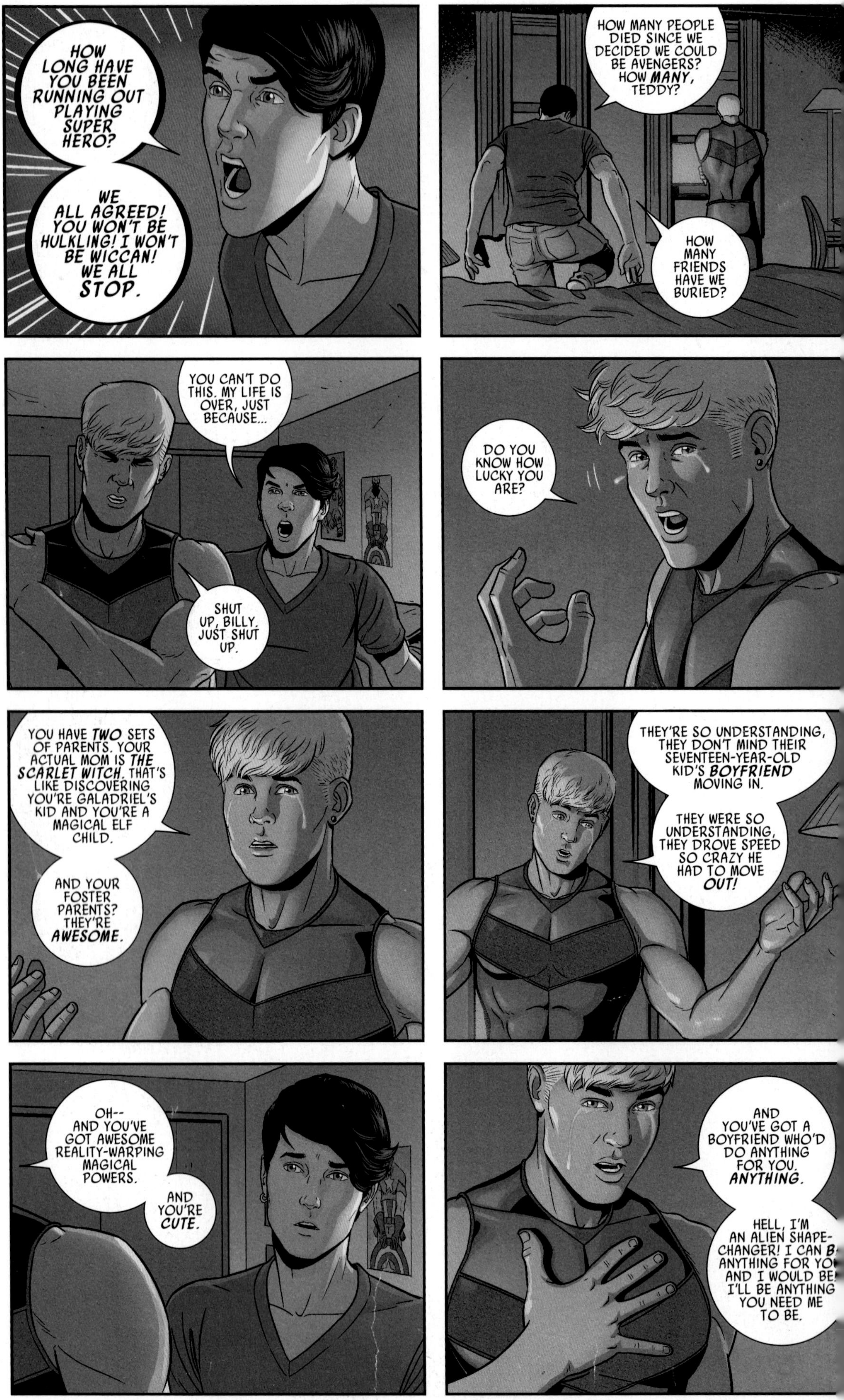
HOW LONG HAVE YOU BEEN RUNNING OUT PLAYING SUPER HERO?
WE ALL AGREED! YOU WON'T BE HULKLING! I WON'T BE WICCAN! WE ALL STOP.
HOW MANY PEOPLE DIED SINCE WE DECIDED WE COULD BE AVENGERS? HOW MANY, TEDDY?
HOW MANY FRIENDS HAVE WE BURIED?
YOU CAN'T DO THIS. MY LIFE IS OVER, JUST BECAUSE...
SHUT UP, BILLY. JUST SHUT UP.
DO YOU KNOW HOW LUCKY YOU ARE?
YOU HAVE TWO SETS OF PARENTS. YOUR ACTUAL MOM IS THE SCARLET WITCH. THAT'S LIKE DISCOVERING YOU'RE GALADRIEL'S KID AND YOU'RE A MAGICAL ELF CHILD.
AND YOUR FOSTER PARENTS? THEY'RE AWESOME.
THEY'RE SO UNDERSTANDING, THEY DON'T MIND THEIR SEVENTEEN-YEAR-OLD KID'S BOYFRIEND MOVING IN.
THEY WERE SO UNDERSTANDING, THEY DROVE SPEED SO CRAZY HE HAD TO MOVE OUT!
OH-- AND YOU'VE GOT AWESOME REALITY-WARPING MAGICAL POWERS.
AND YOU'RE CUTE.
AND YOU'VE GOT A BOYFRIEND WHO'D DO ANYTHING FOR YOU. ANYTHING.
HELL, I'M AN ALIEN SHAPE-CHANGER! I CAN B ANYTHING FOR YO AND I WOULD BE I'LL BE ANYTHING YOU NEED ME TO BE.

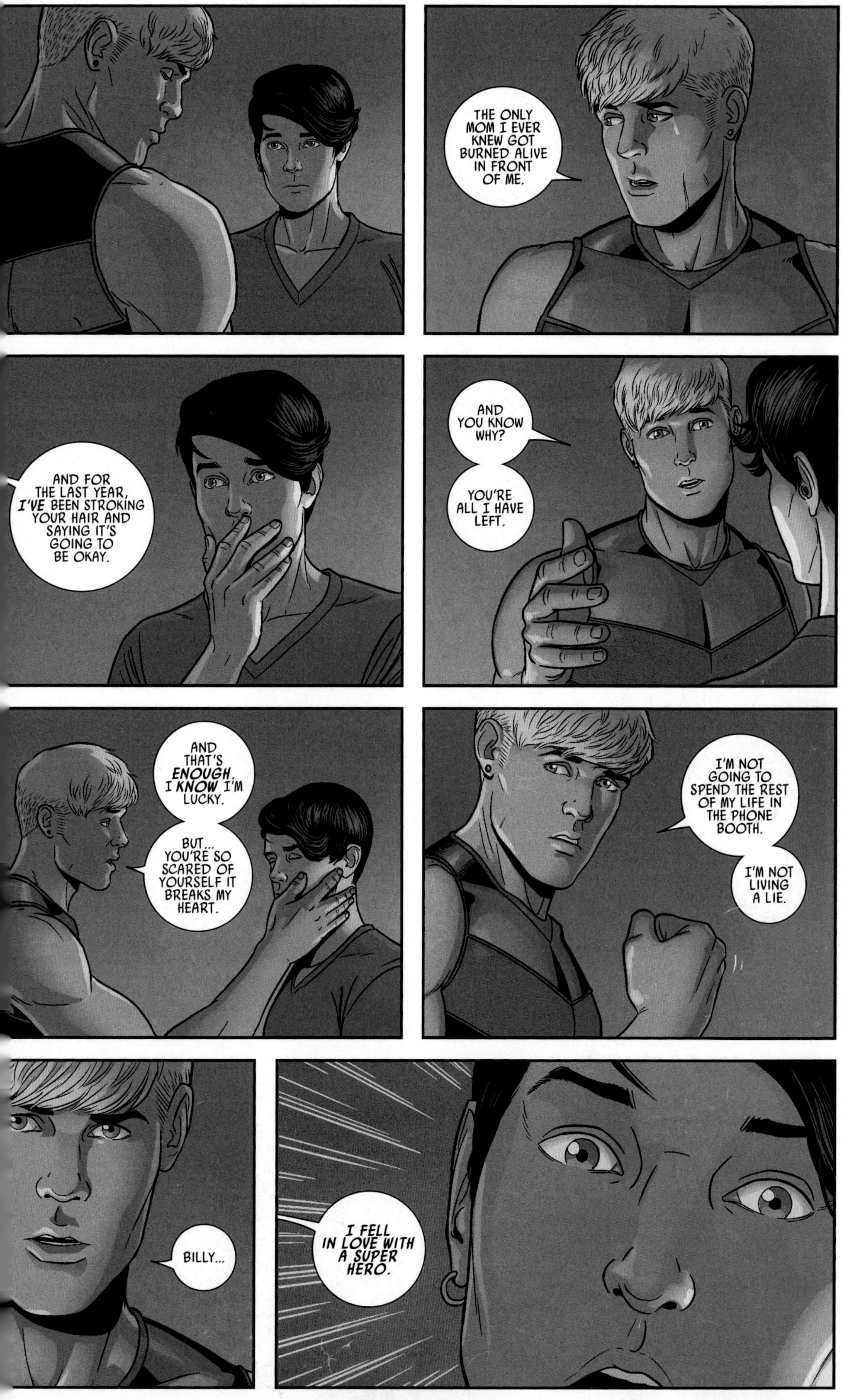
THE ONLY MOM I EVER KNEW GOT BURNED ALIVE IN FRONT OF ME.
AND FOR THE LAST YEAR, *I'VE* BEEN STROKING YOUR HAIR AND SAYING IT'S GOING TO BE OKAY.
AND YOU KNOW WHY?
YOU'RE ALL I HAVE LEFT.
AND THAT'S *ENOUGH*. I *KNOW* I'M LUCKY.
BUT... YOU'RE SO SCARED OF YOURSELF IT BREAKS MY HEART.
I'M NOT GOING TO SPEND THE REST OF MY LIFE IN THE PHONE BOOTH.
I'M NOT LIVING A LIE.
BILLY...
*I FELL IN LOVE WITH A SUPER HERO.*

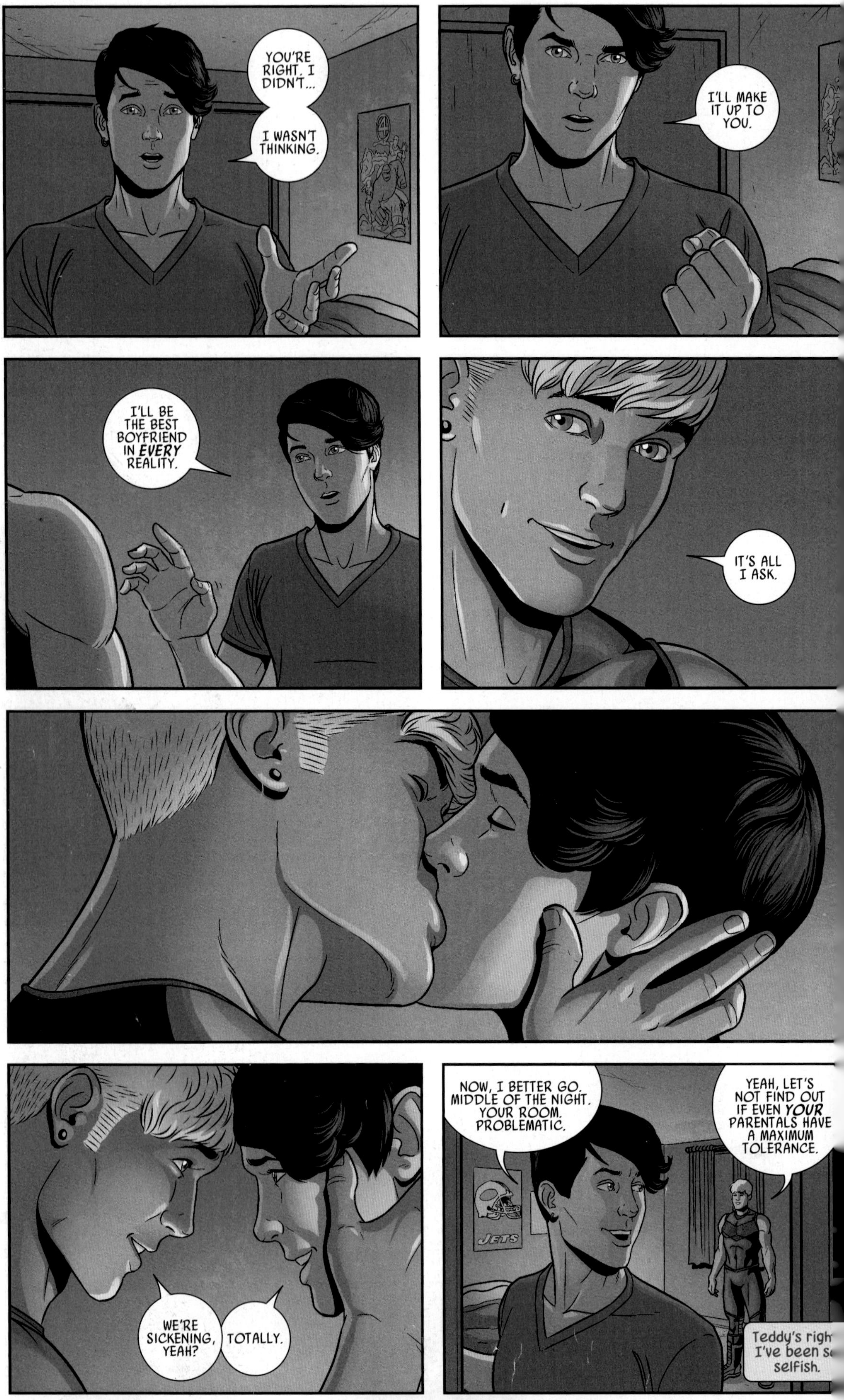
YOU'RE RIGHT. I DIDN'T...
I WASN'T THINKING.
I'LL MAKE IT UP TO YOU.
I'LL BE THE BEST BOYFRIEND IN EVERY REALITY.
IT'S ALL I ASK.
WE'RE SICKENING, YEAH?
TOTALLY.
NOW, I BETTER GO. MIDDLE OF THE NIGHT. YOUR ROOM. PROBLEMATIC.
YEAH, LET'S NOT FIND OUT IF EVEN YOUR PARENTALS HAVE A MAXIMUM TOLERANCE.
JETS
Teddy's righ
I've been s
selfish.

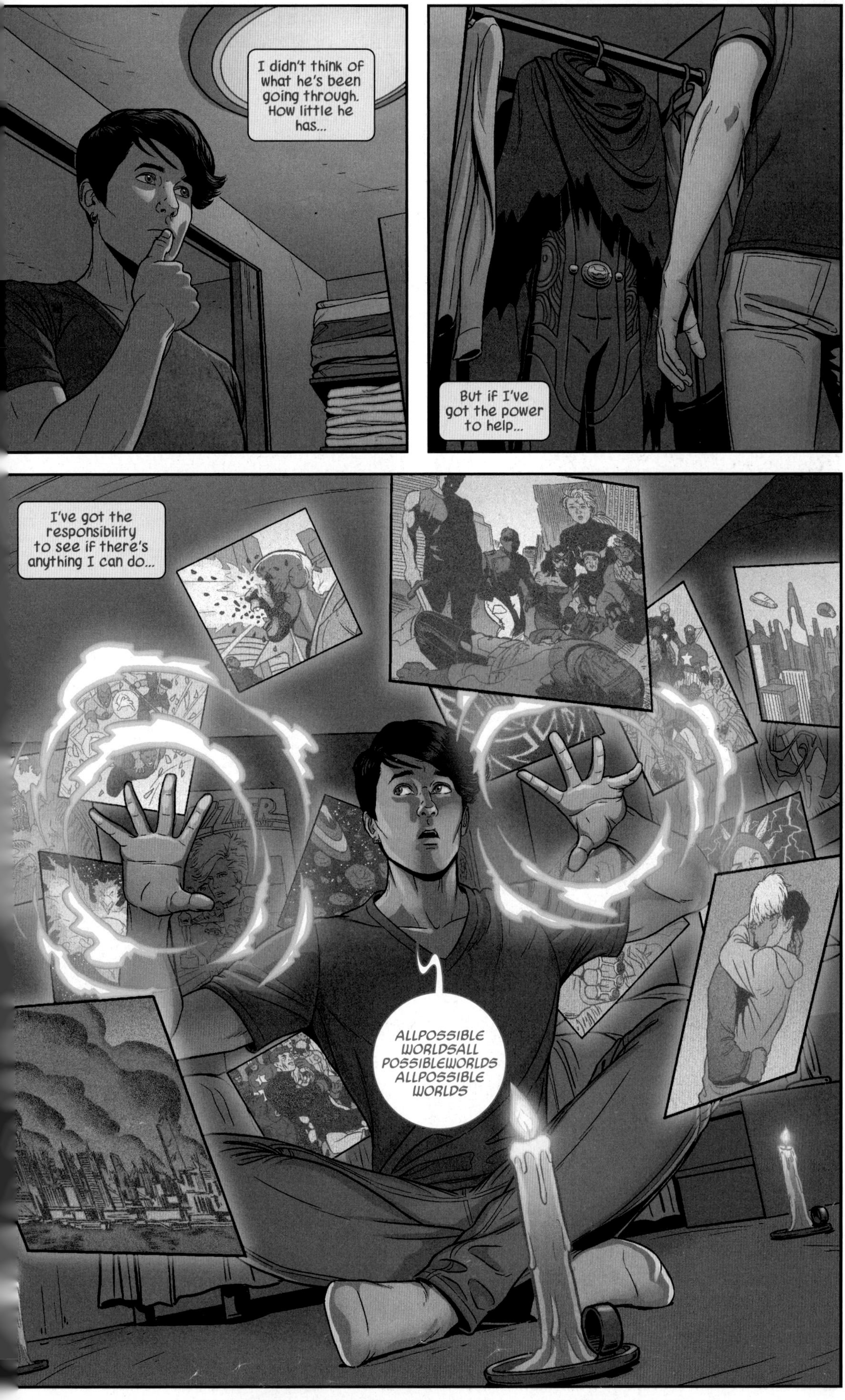
I didn't think of what he's been going through. How little he has...
But if I've got the power to help...
I've got the responsibility to see if there's anything I can do...
ALLPOSSIBLE WORLDSALL POSSIBLEWORLDS ALLPOSSIBLE WORLDS

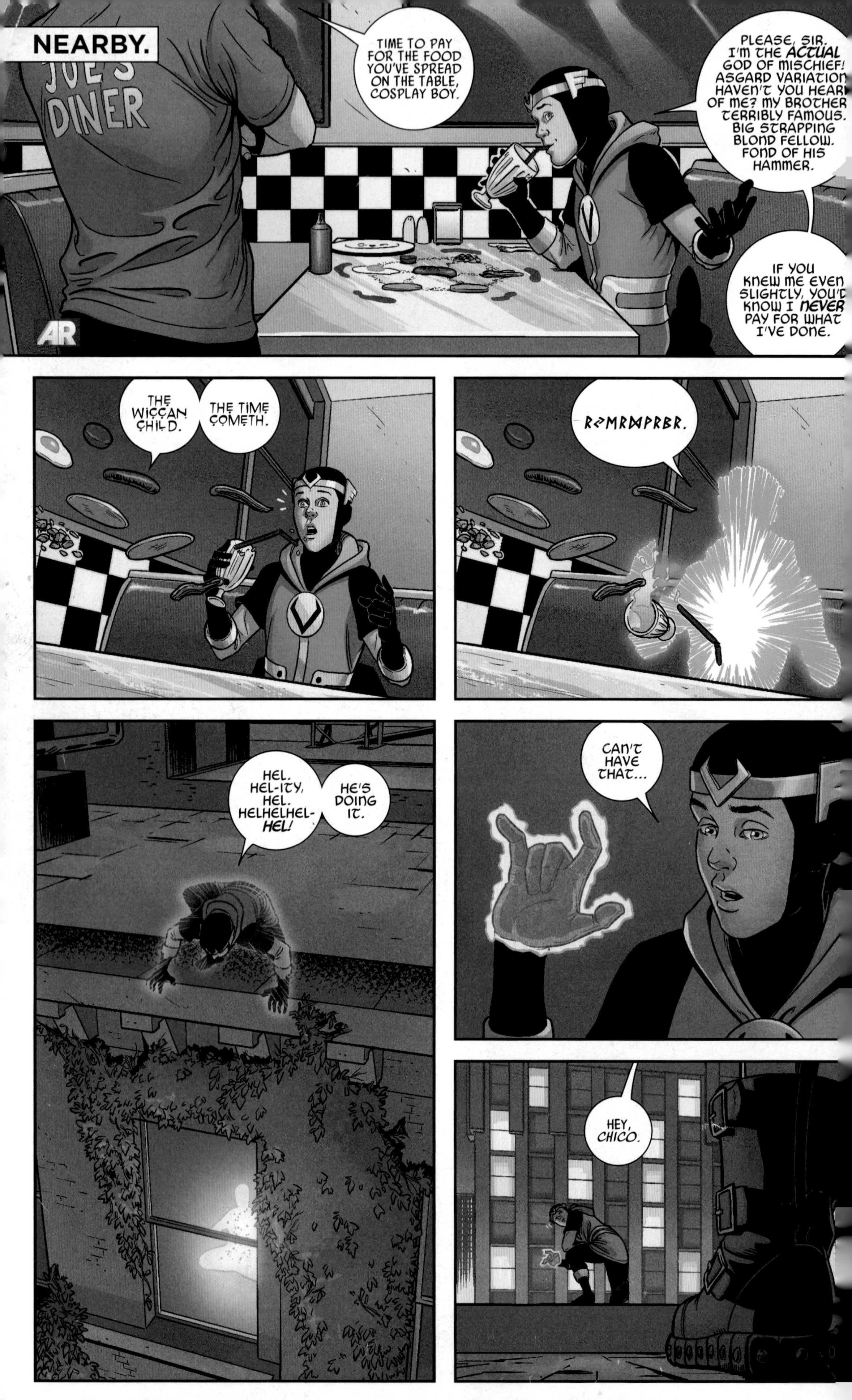
NEARBY.
JOE'S DINER
TIME TO PAY FOR THE FOOD YOU'VE SPREAD ON THE TABLE, COSPLAY BOY.
PLEASE, SIR. I'M THE *ACTUAL* GOD OF MISCHIEF! ASGARD VARIATION HAVEN'T YOU HEAR OF ME? MY BROTHER TERRIBLY FAMOUS. BIG STRAPPING BLOND FELLOW. FOND OF HIS HAMMER.
IF YOU KNEW ME EVEN SLIGHTLY, YOU'D KNOW I *NEVER* PAY FOR WHAT I'VE DONE.
THE WICCAN CHILD.
THE TIME COMETH.
HEL. HEL-ITY, HEL. HELHELHEL-*HEL!*
HE'S DOING IT.
CAN'T HAVE THAT...
HEY, CHICO.

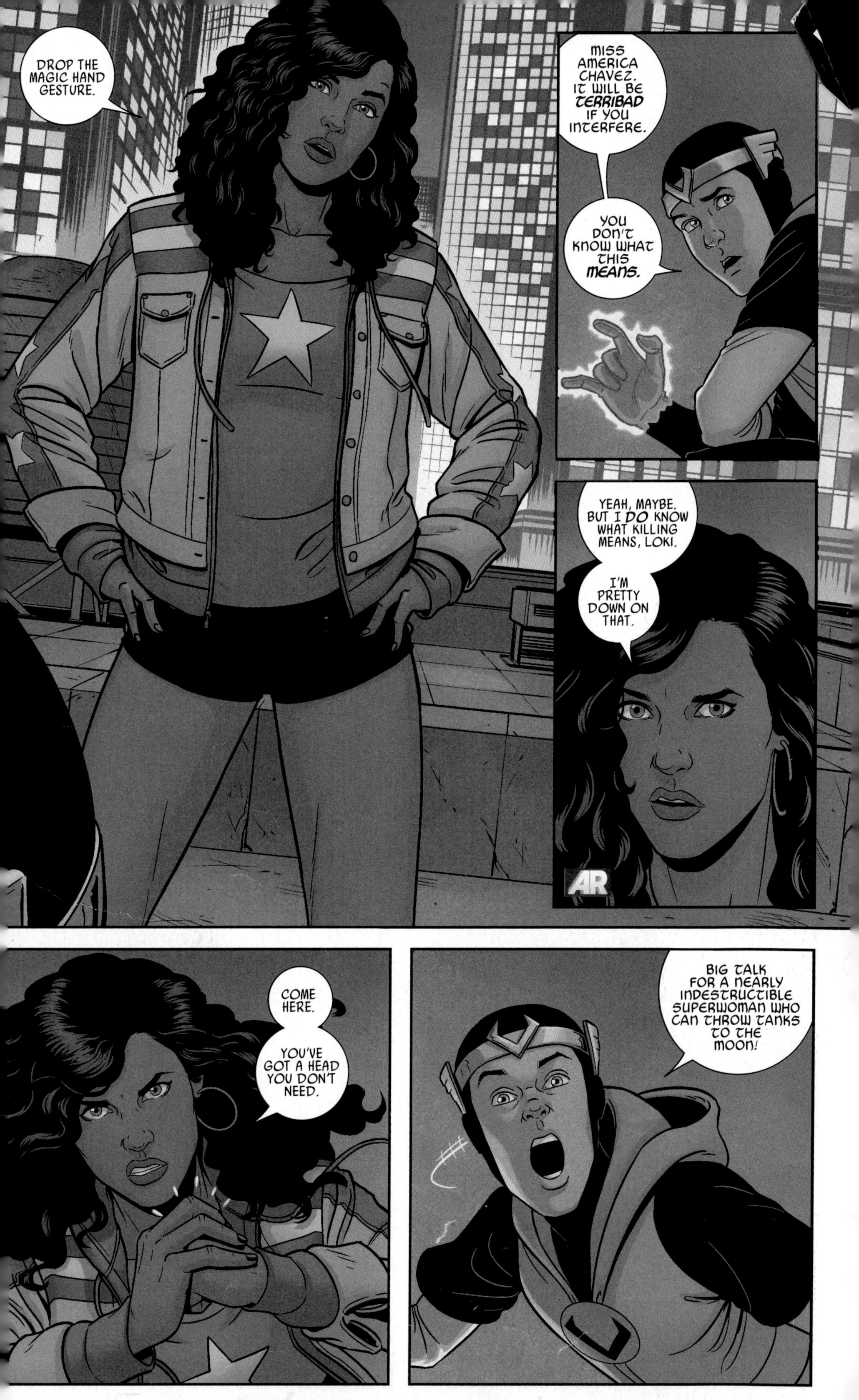
DROP THE MAGIC HAND GESTURE.
MISS AMERICA CHAVEZ. IT WILL BE TERRIBAD IF YOU INTERFERE.
YOU DON'T KNOW WHAT THIS MEANS.
YEAH, MAYBE. BUT I DO KNOW WHAT KILLING MEANS, LOKI.
I'M PRETTY DOWN ON THAT.
AR
COME HERE.
YOU'VE GOT A HEAD YOU DON'T NEED.
BIG TALK FOR A NEARLY INDESTRUCTIBLE SUPERWOMAN WHO CAN THROW TANKS TO THE MOON!

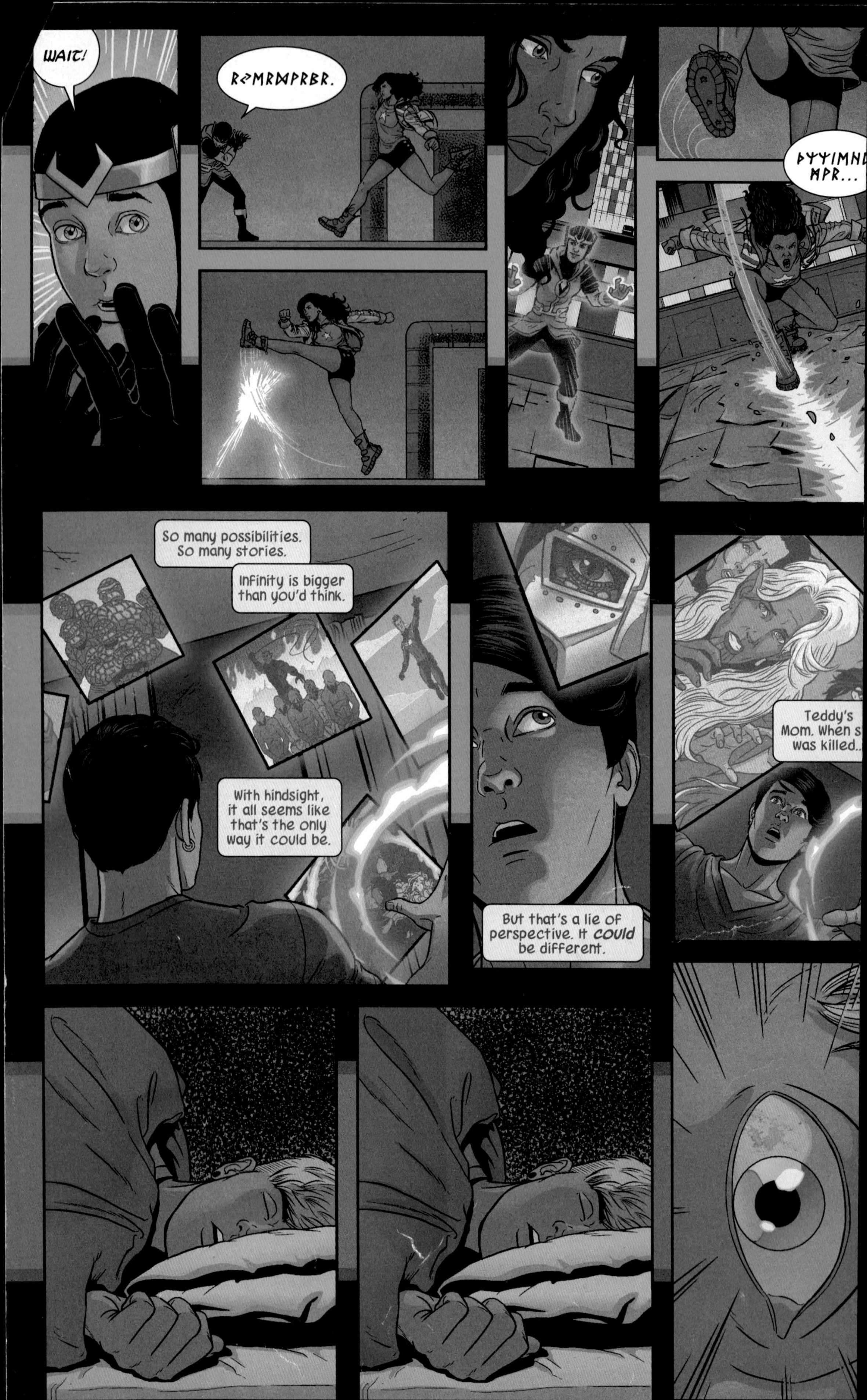
WAIT!
So many possibilities. So many stories.
Infinity is bigger than you'd think.
With hindsight, it all seems like that's the only way it could be.
But that's a lie of perspective. It could be different.
Teddy's Mom. When s was killed..

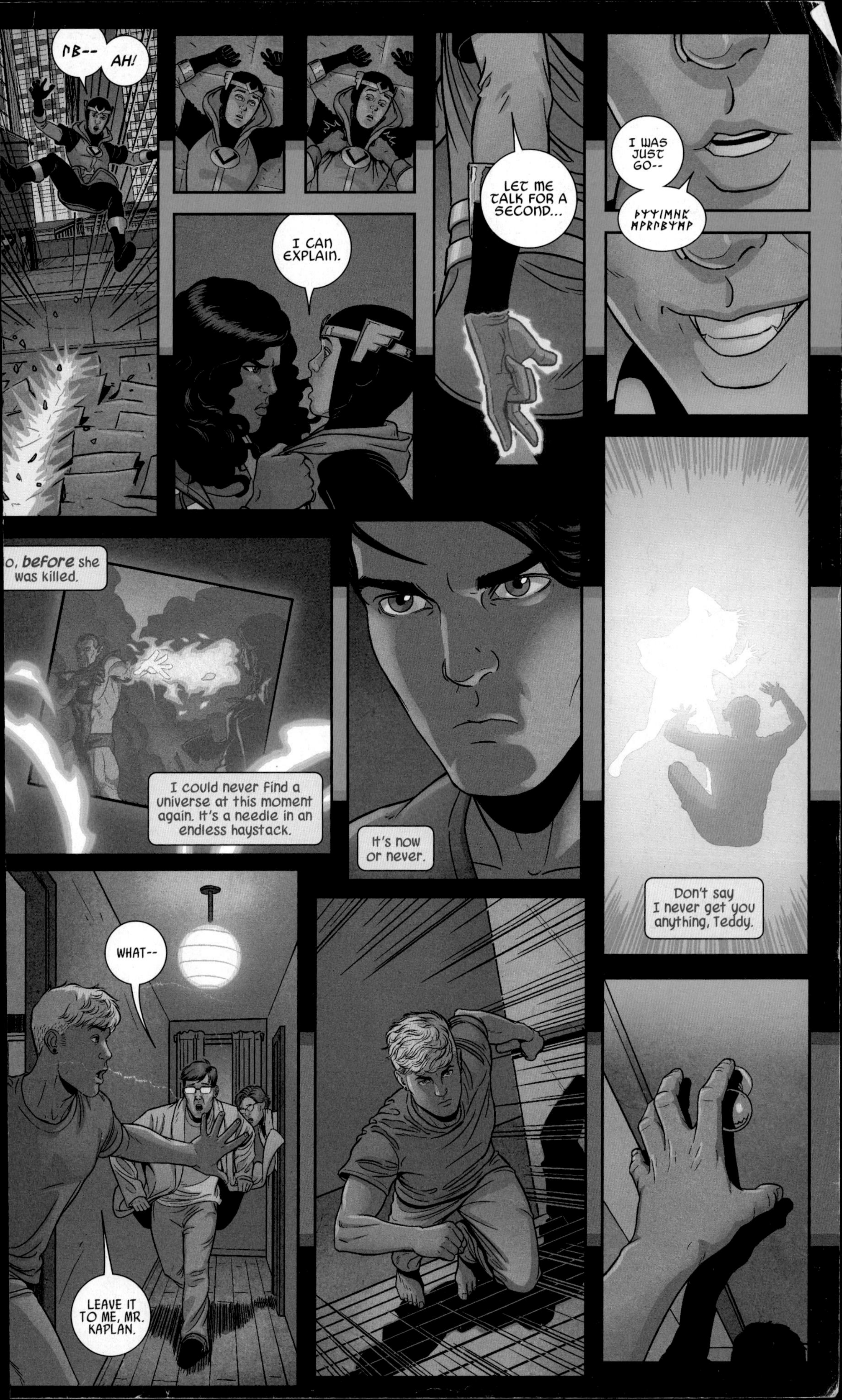
AH!
I CAN EXPLAIN.
LET ME TALK FOR A SECOND...
I WAS JUST GO--
o, *before* she was killed.
I could never find a universe at this moment again. It's a needle in an endless haystack.
It's now or never.
Don't say I never get you anything, Teddy.
WHAT--
LEAVE IT TO ME, MR. KAPLAN.

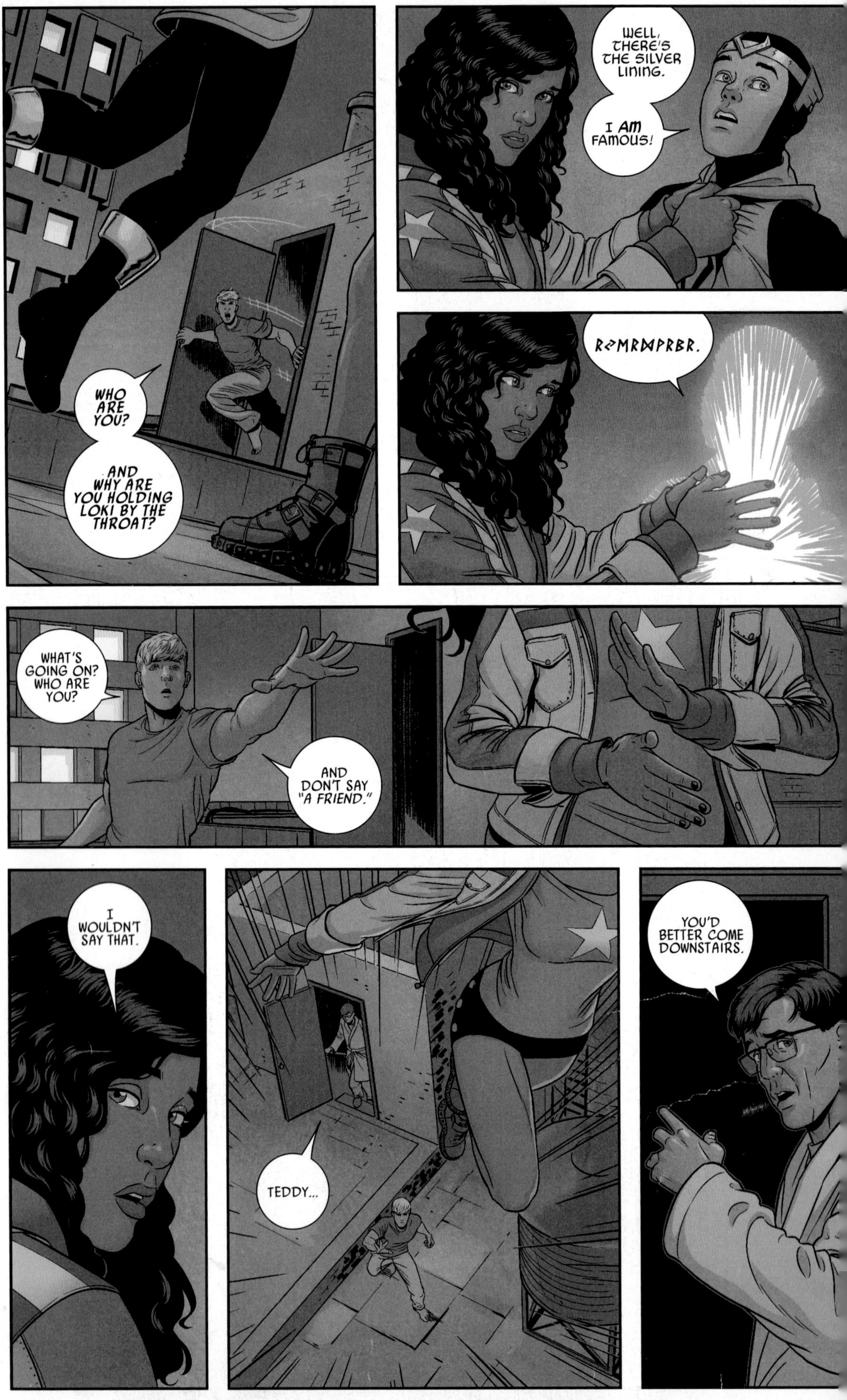
WHO ARE YOU?
AND WHY ARE YOU HOLDING LOKI BY THE THROAT?
WELL, THERE'S THE SILVER LINING.
I AM FAMOUS!
WHAT'S GOING ON? WHO ARE YOU?
AND DON'T SAY "A FRIEND."
I WOULDN'T SAY THAT.
TEDDY...
YOU'D BETTER COME DOWNSTAIRS.

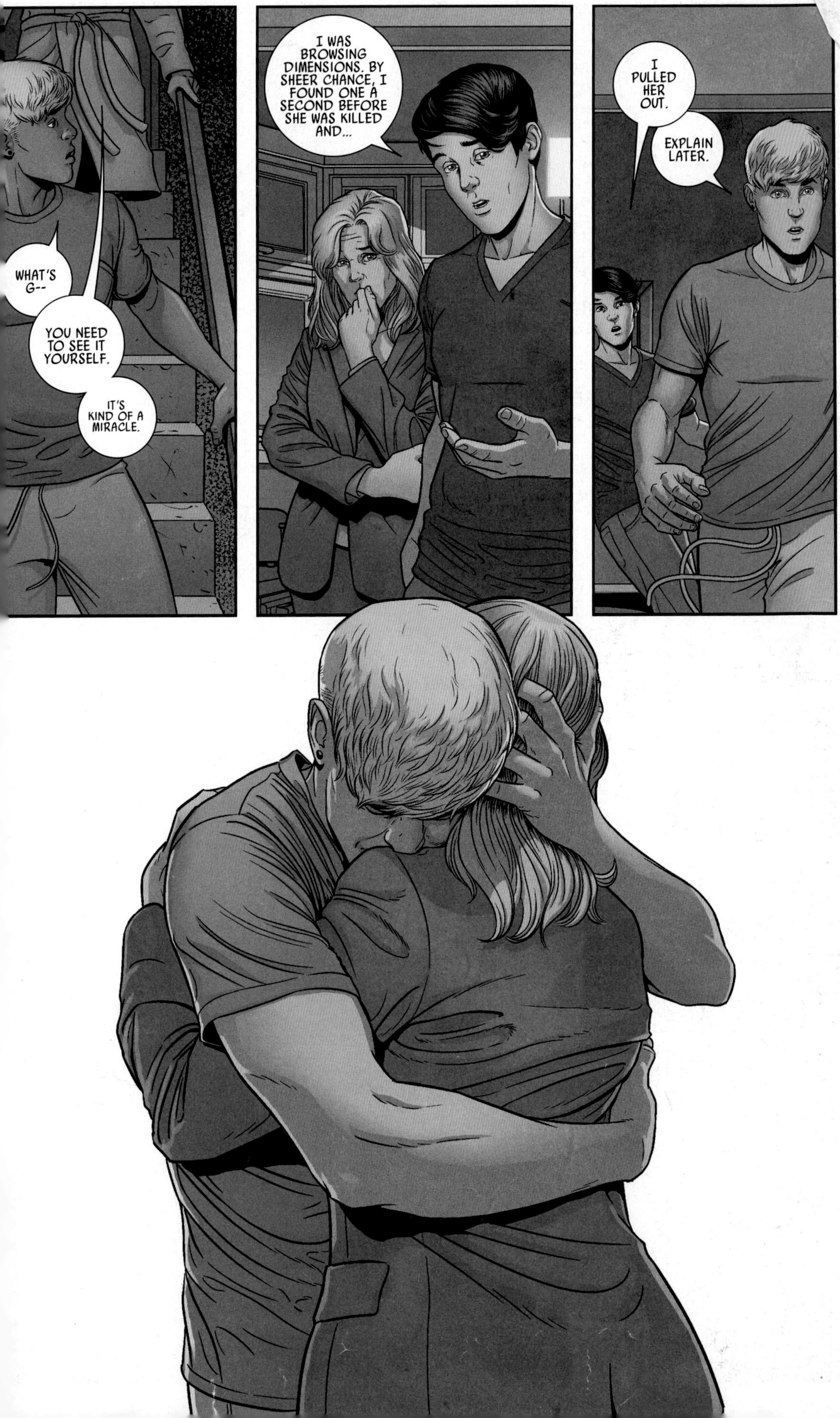
WHAT'S G--
YOU NEED TO SEE IT YOURSELF.
IT'S KIND OF A MIRACLE.
I WAS BROWSING DIMENSIONS. BY SHEER CHANCE, I FOUND ONE A SECOND BEFORE SHE WAS KILLED AND...
I PULLED HER OUT.
EXPLAIN LATER.

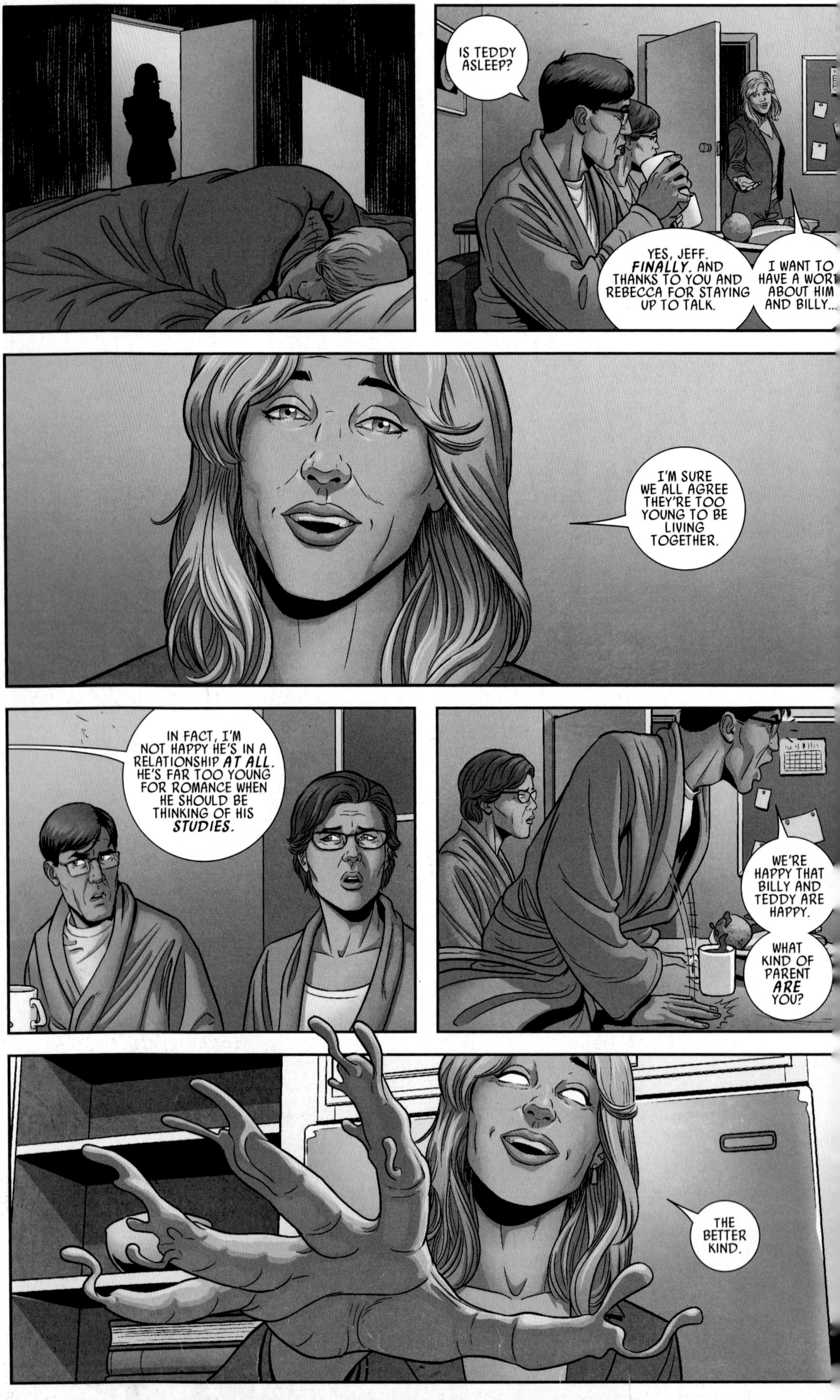
IS TEDDY ASLEEP?
YES, JEFF. FINALLY. AND THANKS TO YOU AND REBECCA FOR STAYING UP TO TALK.
I WANT TO HAVE A WOR ABOUT HIM AND BILLY...
I'M SURE WE ALL AGREE THEY'RE TOO YOUNG TO BE LIVING TOGETHER.
IN FACT, I'M NOT HAPPY HE'S IN A RELATIONSHIP AT ALL. HE'S FAR TOO YOUNG FOR ROMANCE WHEN HE SHOULD BE THINKING OF HIS STUDIES.
WE'RE HAPPY THAT BILLY AND TEDDY ARE HAPPY.
WHAT KIND OF PARENT ARE YOU?
THE BETTER KIND.

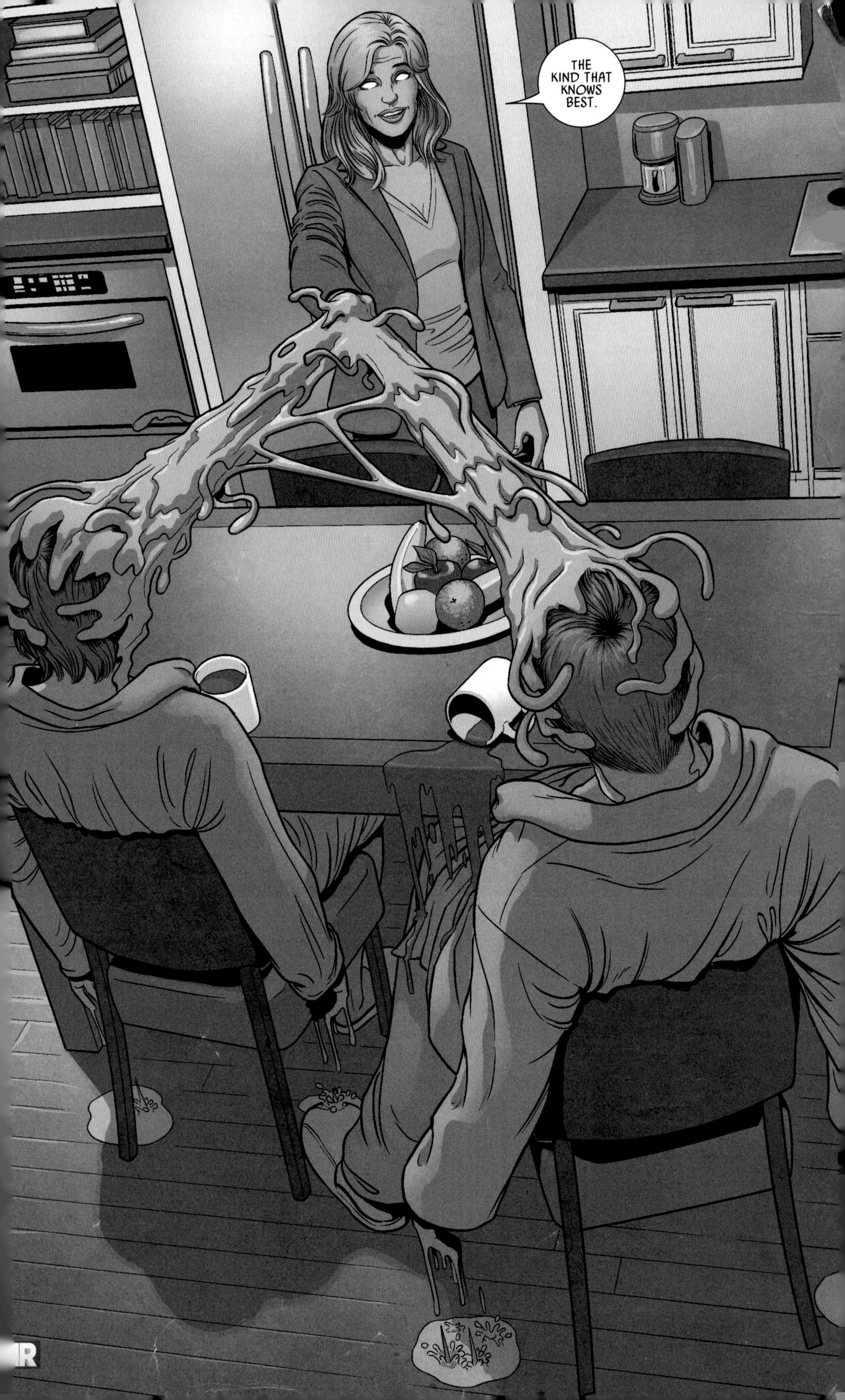
THE KIND THAT KNOWS BEST.

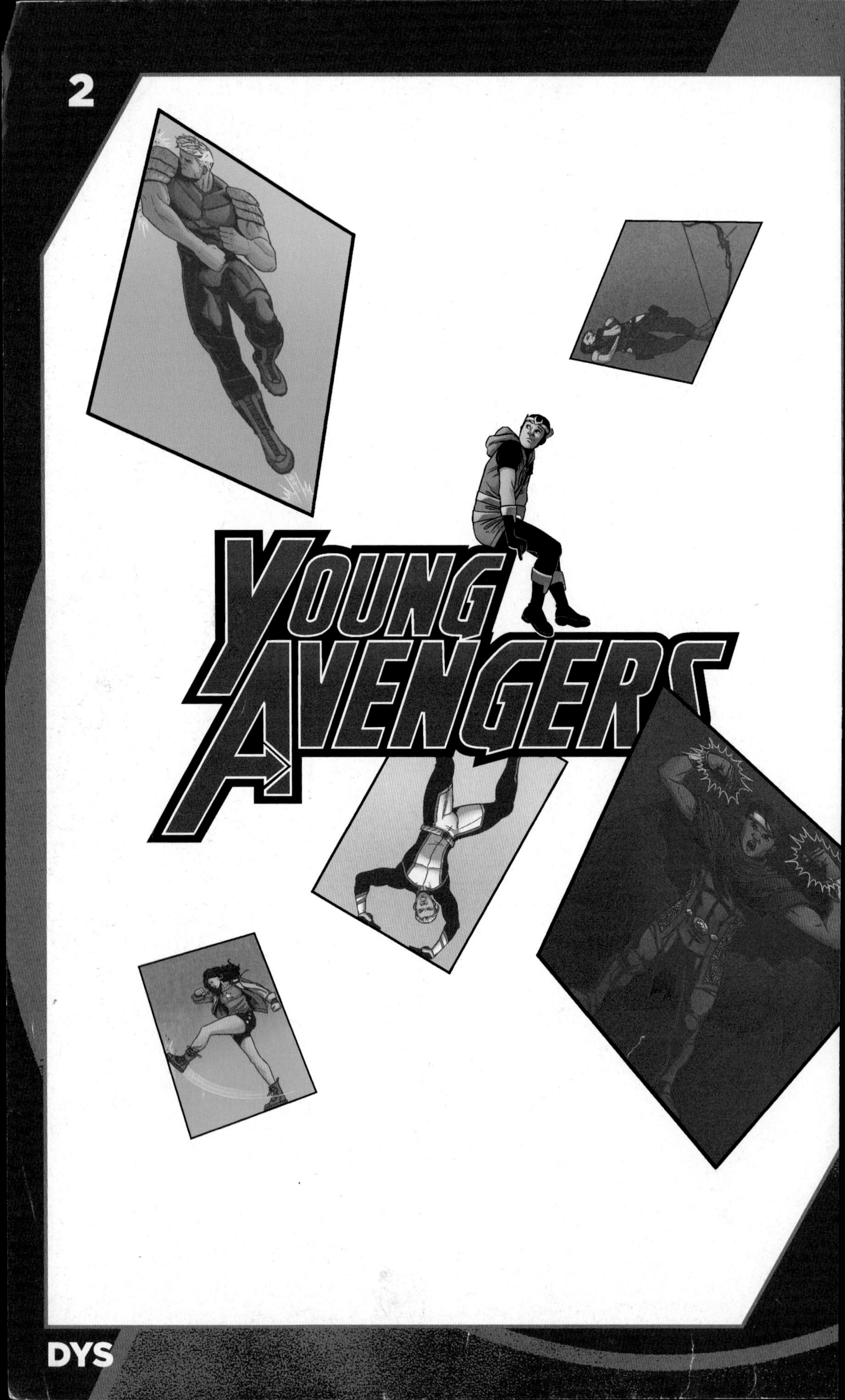
2
YOUNG AVENGERS
DYS

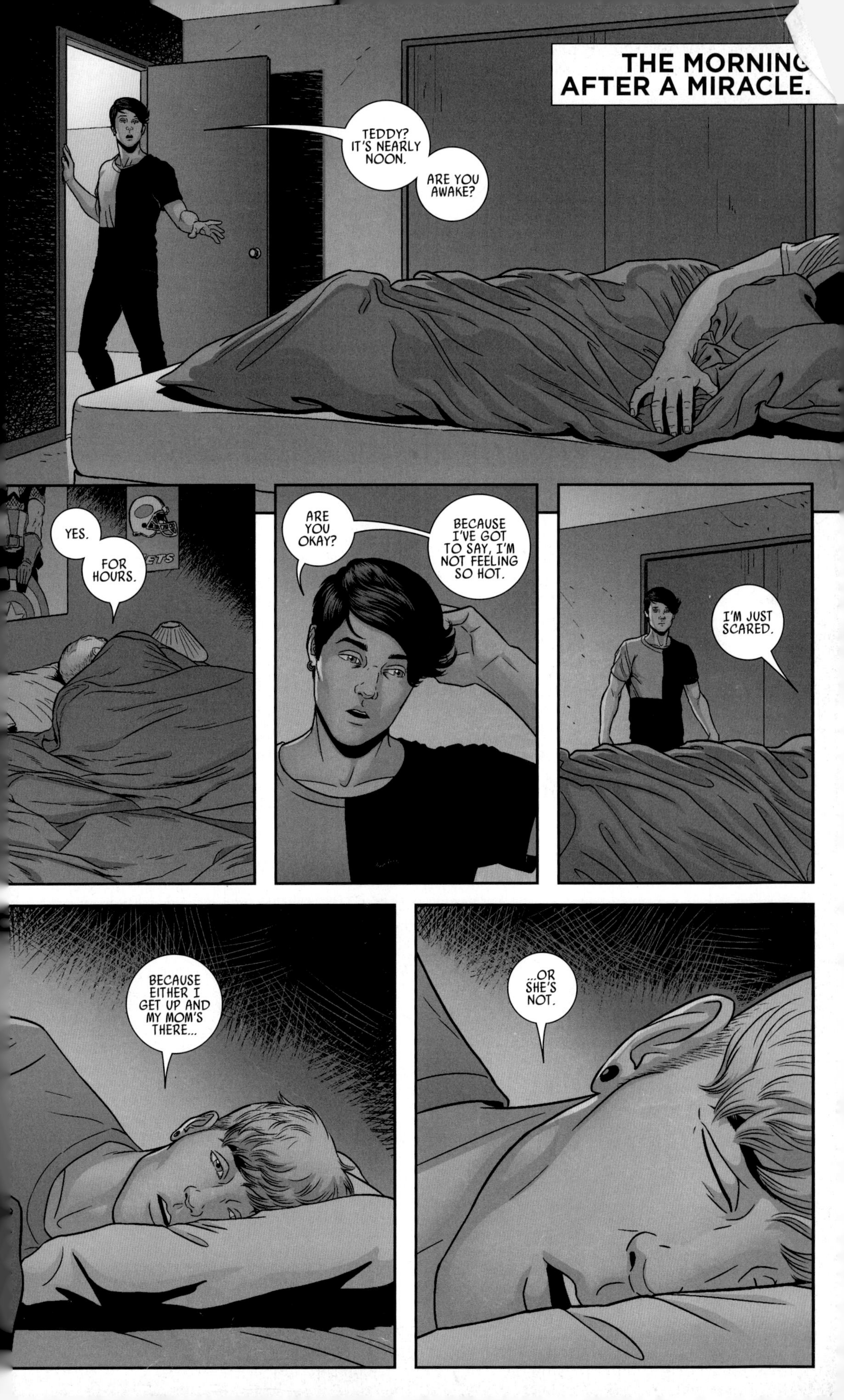
THE MORNING AFTER A MIRACLE.
TEDDY? IT'S NEARLY NOON.
ARE YOU AWAKE?
YES.
FOR HOURS.
ARE YOU OKAY?
BECAUSE I'VE GOT TO SAY, I'M NOT FEELING SO HOT.
I'M JUST SCARED.
BECAUSE EITHER I GET UP AND MY MOM'S THERE...
...OR SHE'S NOT.

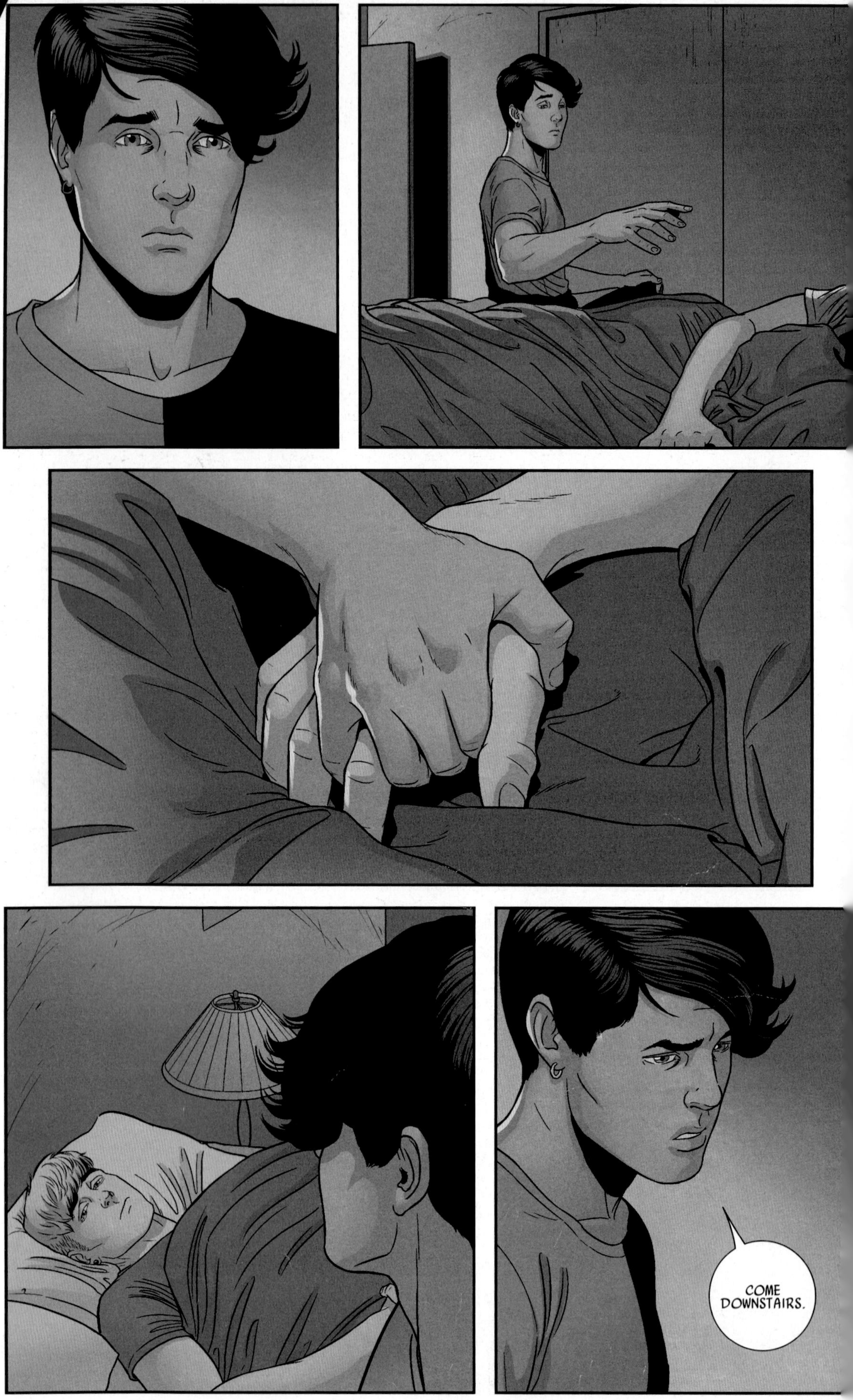
COME DOWNSTAIRS.

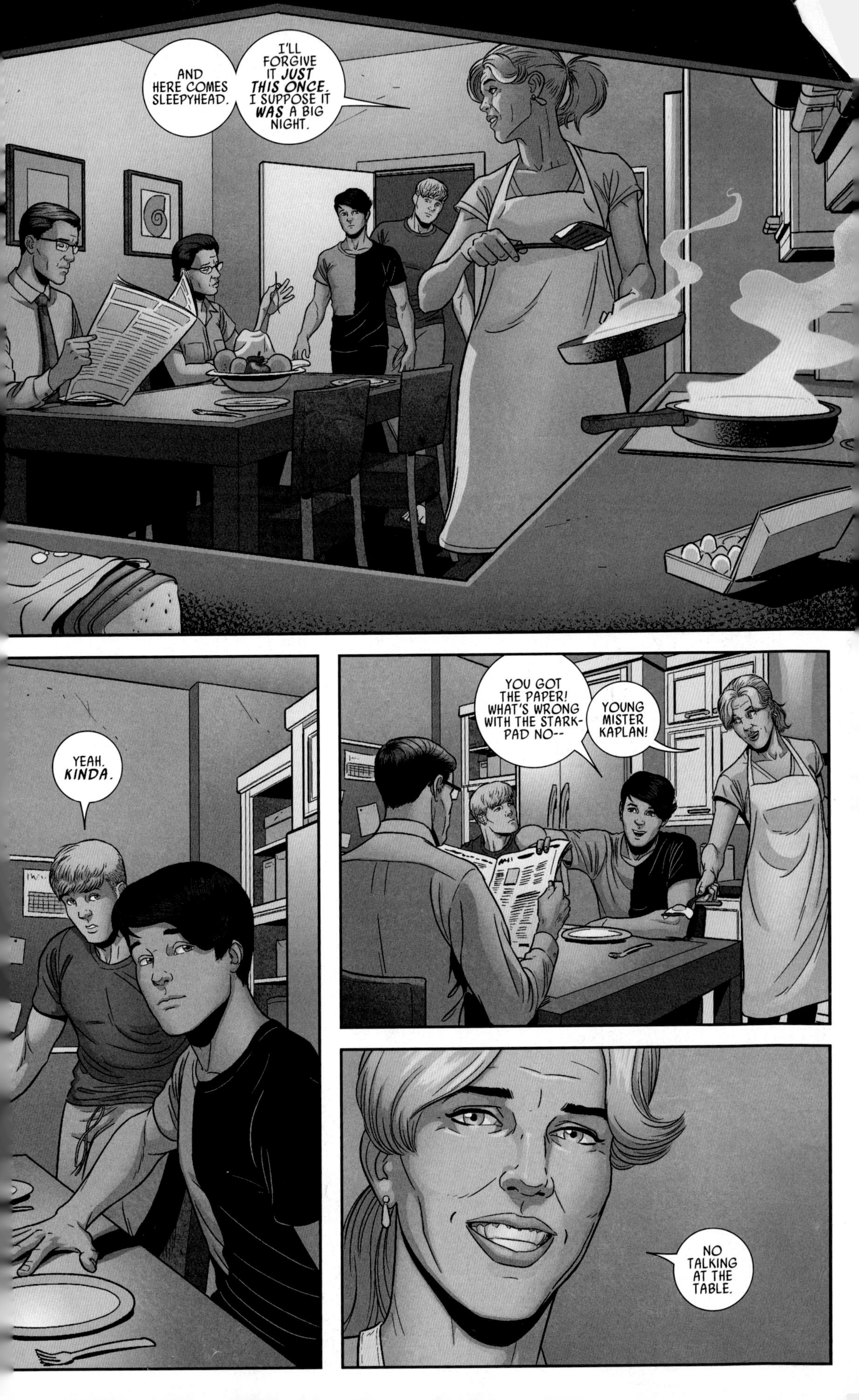
AND HERE COMES SLEEPYHEAD.
I'LL FORGIVE IT JUST THIS ONCE. I SUPPOSE IT WAS A BIG NIGHT.
YEAH. KINDA.
YOU GOT THE PAPER! WHAT'S WRONG WITH THE STARK-PAD NO--
YOUNG MISTER KAPLAN!
NO TALKING AT THE TABLE.

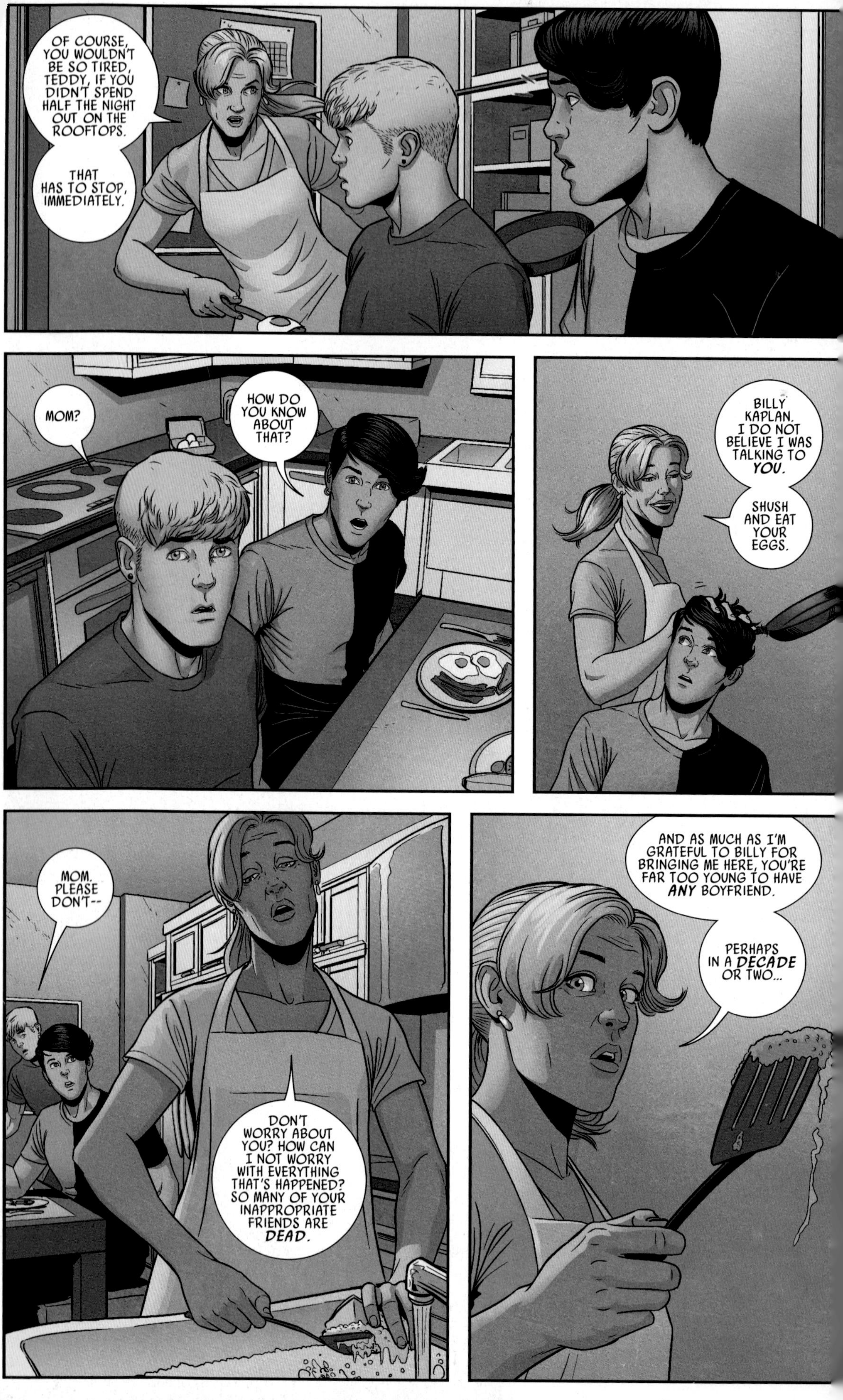
OF COURSE, YOU WOULDN'T BE SO TIRED, TEDDY, IF YOU DIDN'T SPEND HALF THE NIGHT OUT ON THE ROOFTOPS.
THAT HAS TO STOP, IMMEDIATELY.
MOM?
HOW DO YOU KNOW ABOUT THAT?
BILLY KAPLAN. I DO NOT BELIEVE I WAS TALKING TO YOU.
SHUSH AND EAT YOUR EGGS.
MOM. PLEASE DON'T--
DON'T WORRY ABOUT YOU? HOW CAN I NOT WORRY WITH EVERYTHING THAT'S HAPPENED? SO MANY OF YOUR INAPPROPRIATE FRIENDS ARE DEAD.
AND AS MUCH AS I'M GRATEFUL TO BILLY FOR BRINGING ME HERE, YOU'RE FAR TOO YOUNG TO HAVE ANY BOYFRIEND.
PERHAPS IN A DECADE OR TWO...

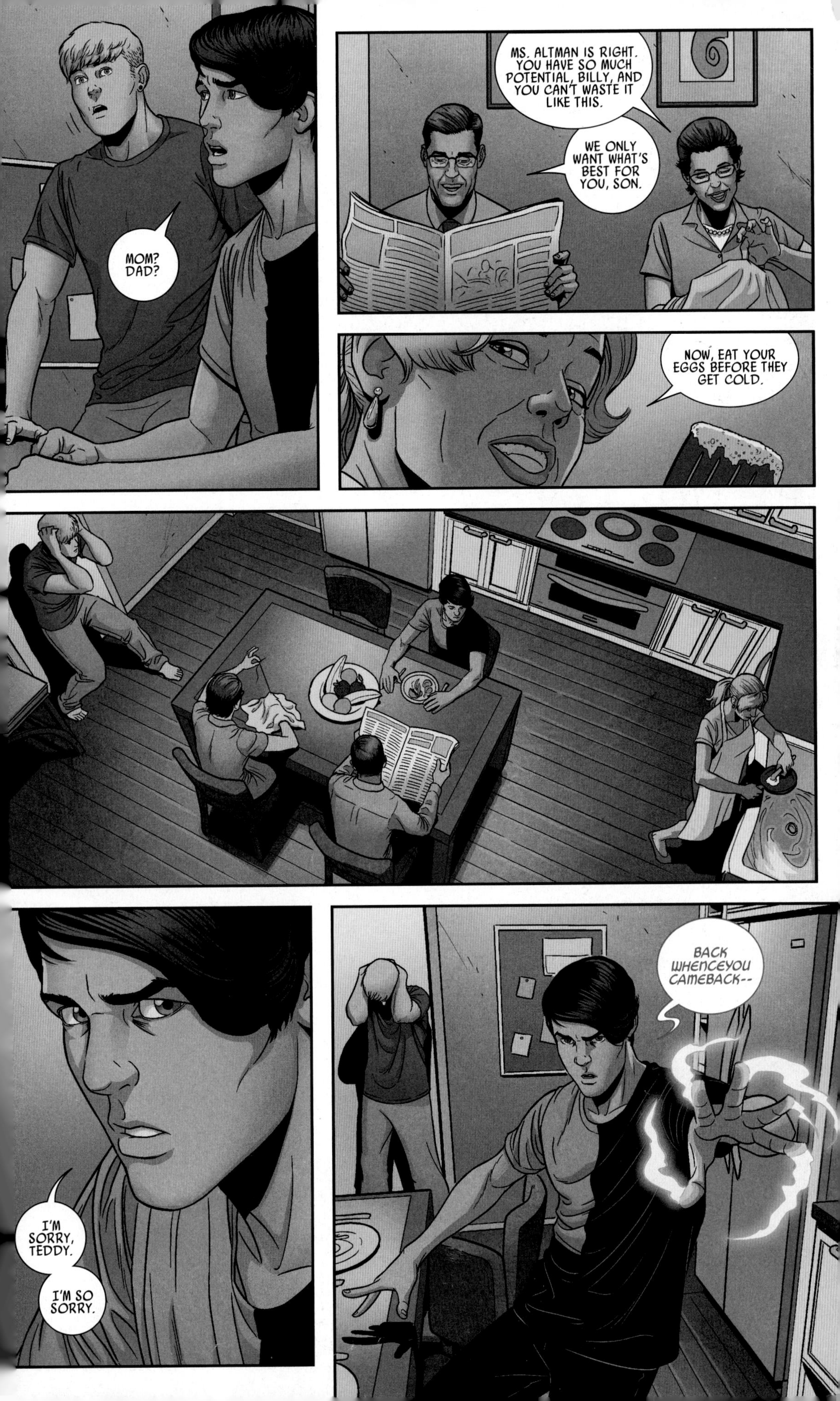
MOM? DAD?
MS. ALTMAN IS RIGHT. YOU HAVE SO MUCH POTENTIAL, BILLY, AND YOU CAN'T WASTE IT LIKE THIS.
WE ONLY WANT WHAT'S BEST FOR YOU, SON.
NOW, EAT YOUR EGGS BEFORE THEY GET COLD.
I'M SORRY, TEDDY.
I'M SO SORRY.
BACK WHENCEYOU CAMEBACK--

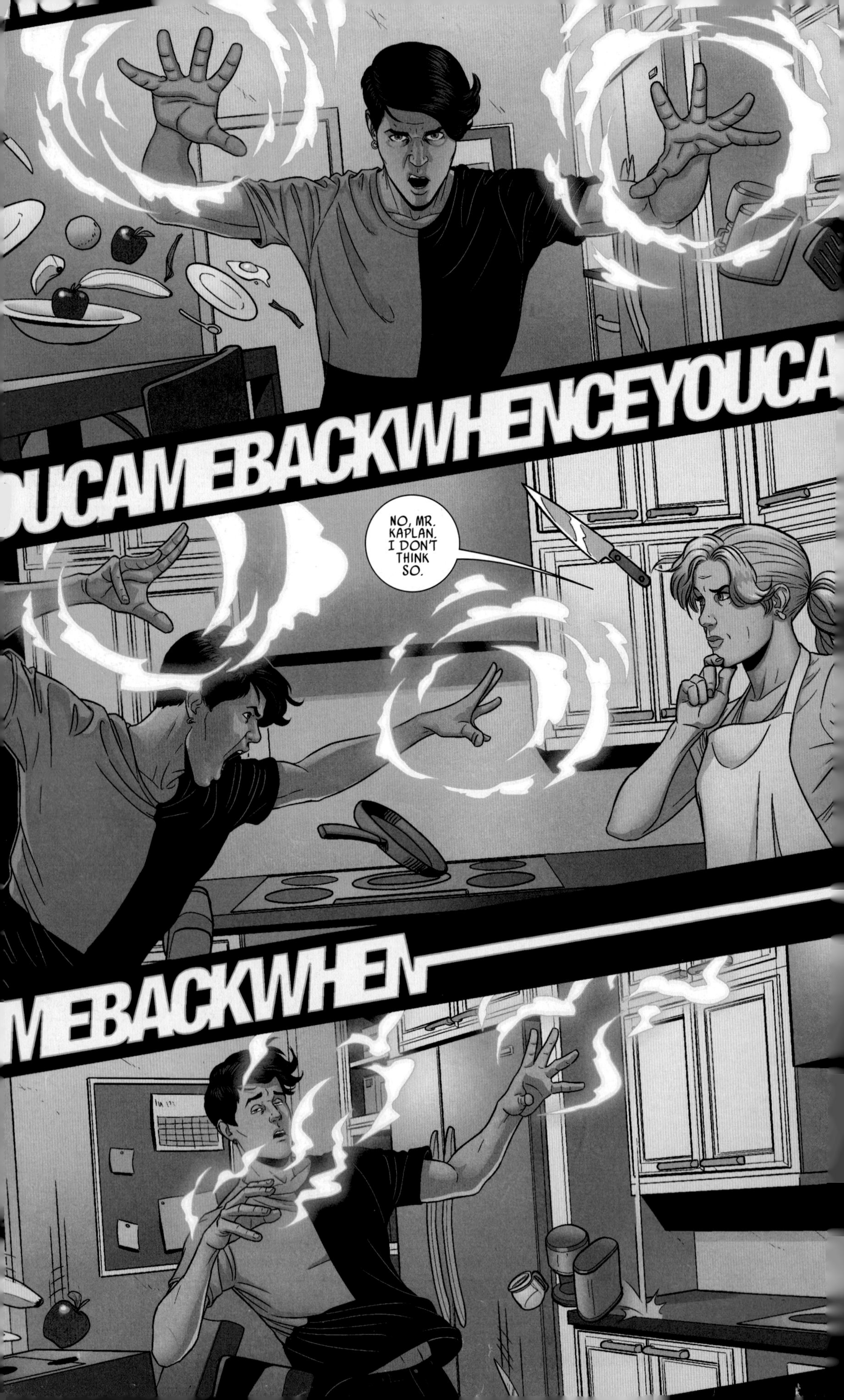
YOUCAMEBACKWHENCEYOUCA
OUCAMEBACKWHENCEYOUCA
NO, MR. KAPLAN. I DON'T THINK SO.
MEBACKWHEN

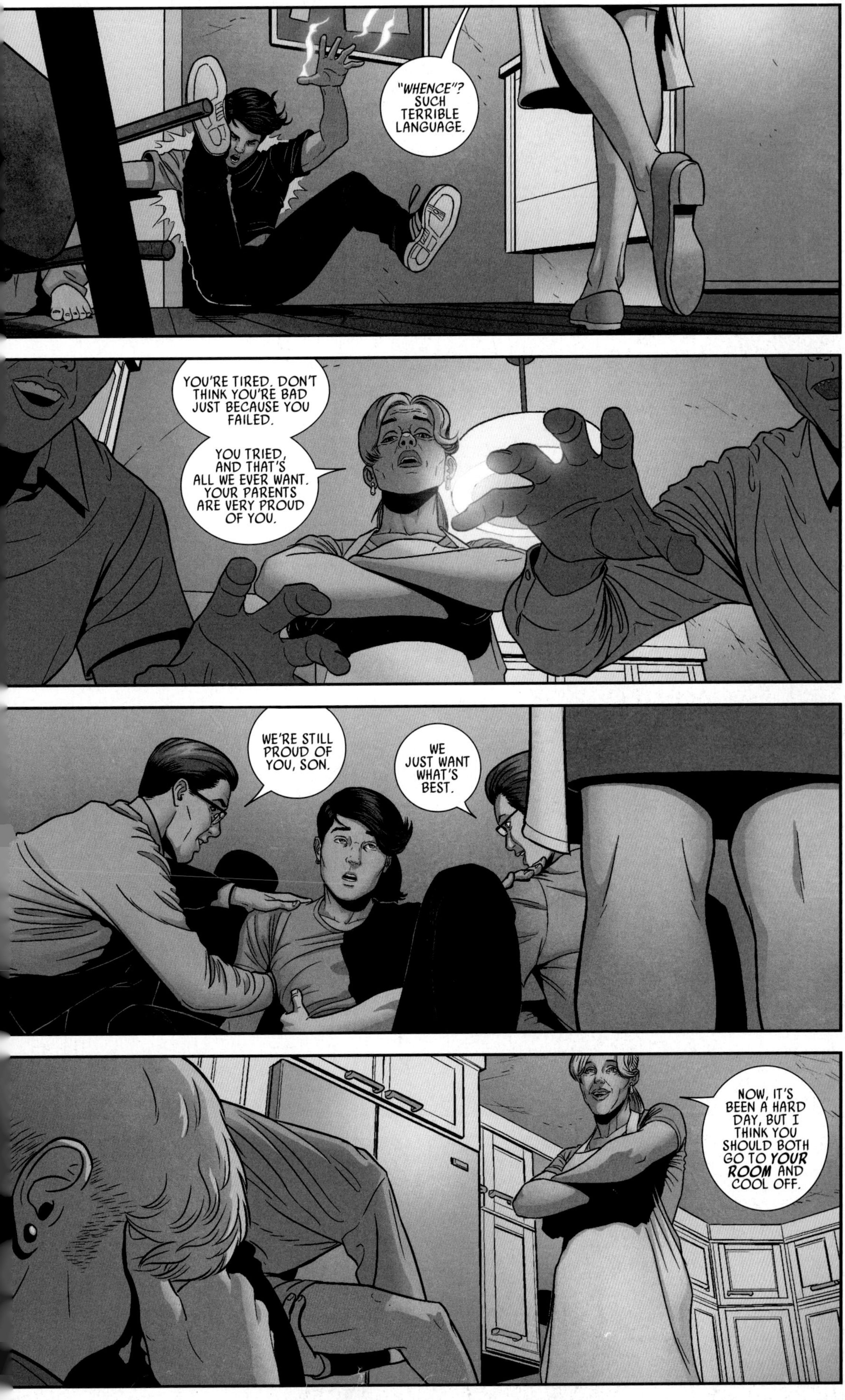
"WHENCE"? SUCH TERRIBLE LANGUAGE.
YOU'RE TIRED. DON'T THINK YOU'RE BAD JUST BECAUSE YOU FAILED.
YOU TRIED, AND THAT'S ALL WE EVER WANT. YOUR PARENTS ARE VERY PROUD OF YOU.
WE'RE STILL PROUD OF YOU, SON.
WE JUST WANT WHAT'S BEST.
NOW, IT'S BEEN A HARD DAY, BUT I THINK YOU SHOULD BOTH GO TO YOUR ROOM AND COOL OFF.

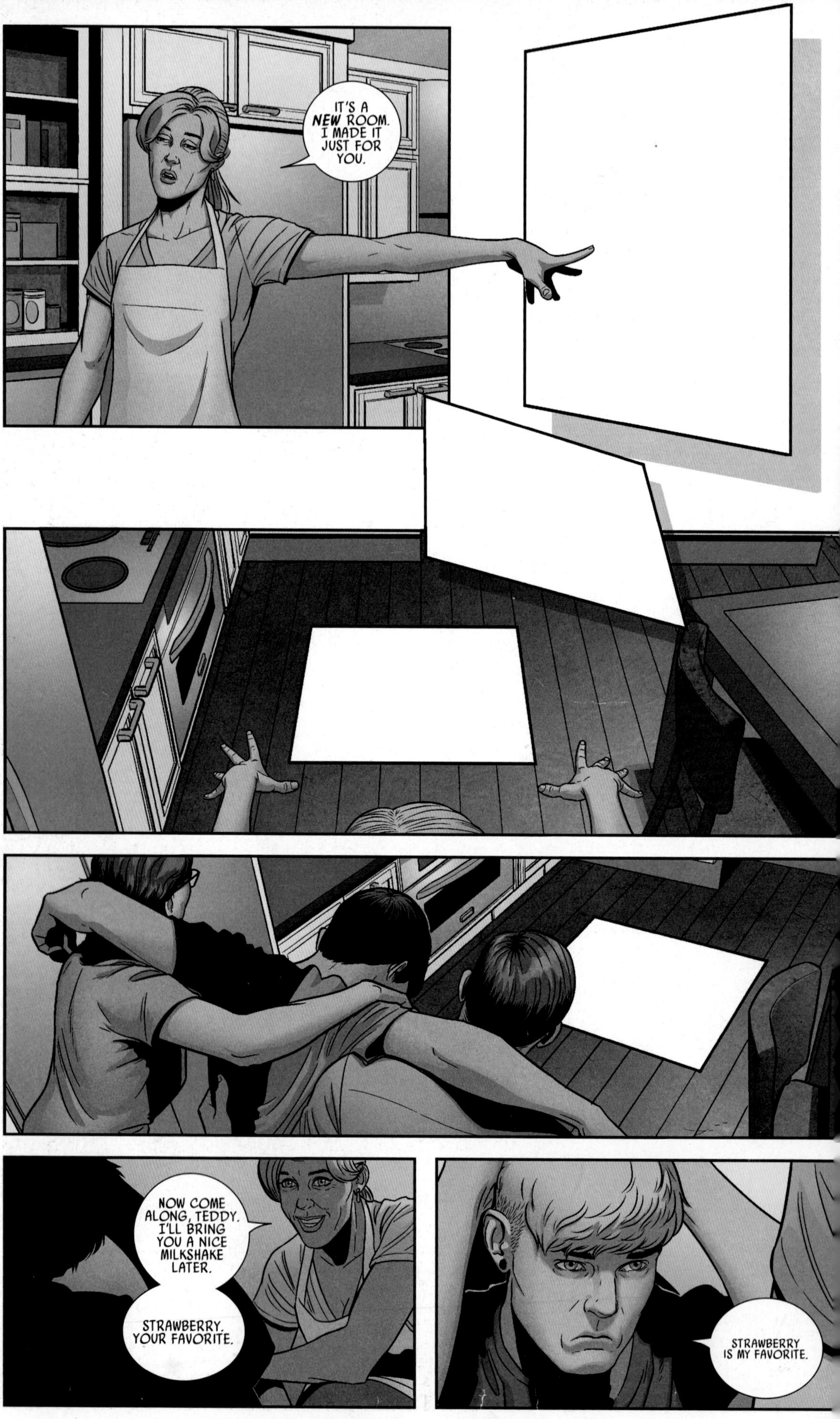
IT'S A NEW ROOM. I MADE IT JUST FOR YOU.
NOW COME ALONG, TEDDY. I'LL BRING YOU A NICE MILKSHAKE LATER.
STRAWBERRY. YOUR FAVORITE.
STRAWBERRY IS MY FAVORITE.

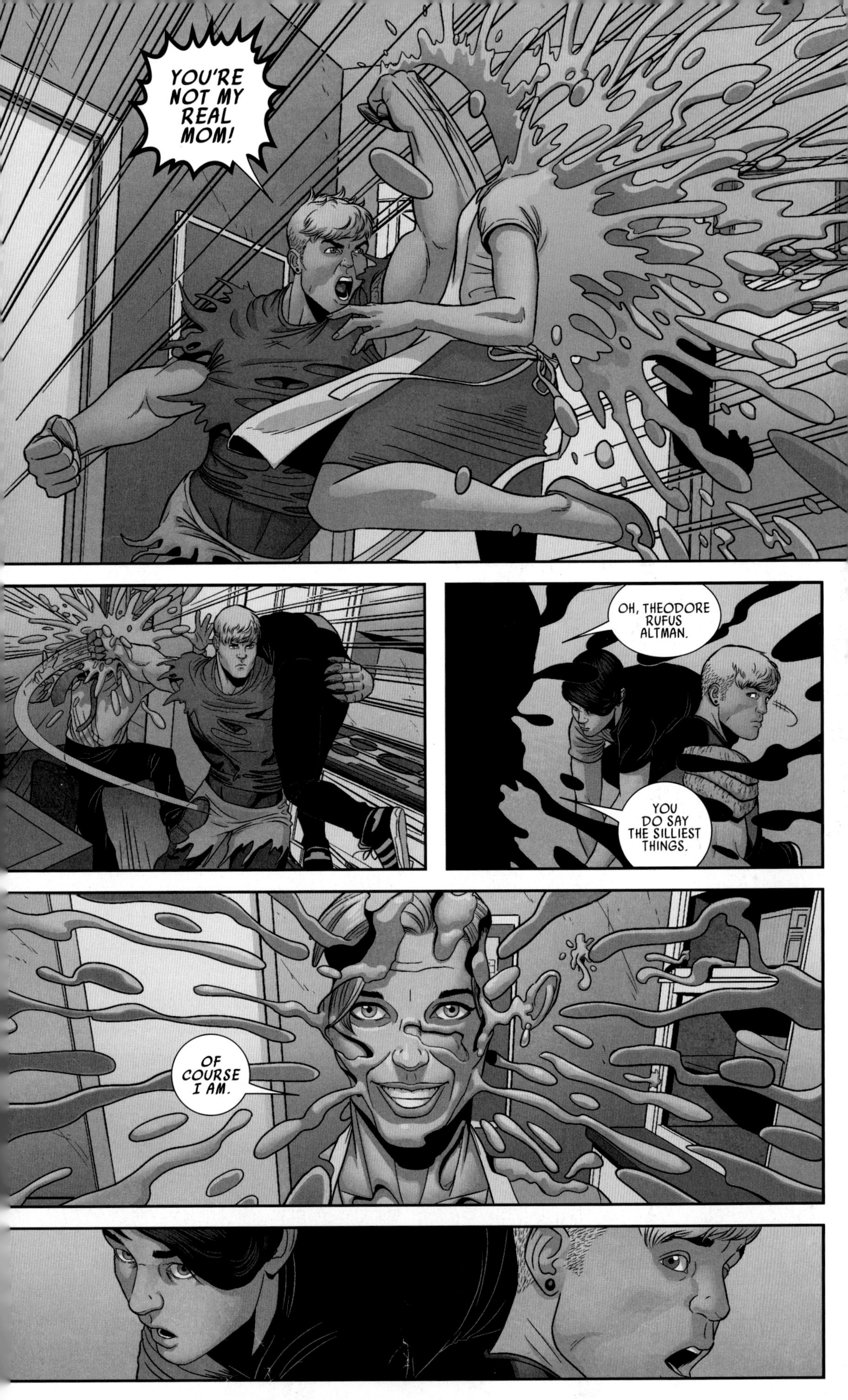
YOU'RE NOT MY REAL MOM!
OH, THEODORE RUFUS ALTMAN.
YOU DO SAY THE SILLIEST THINGS.
OF COURSE I AM.

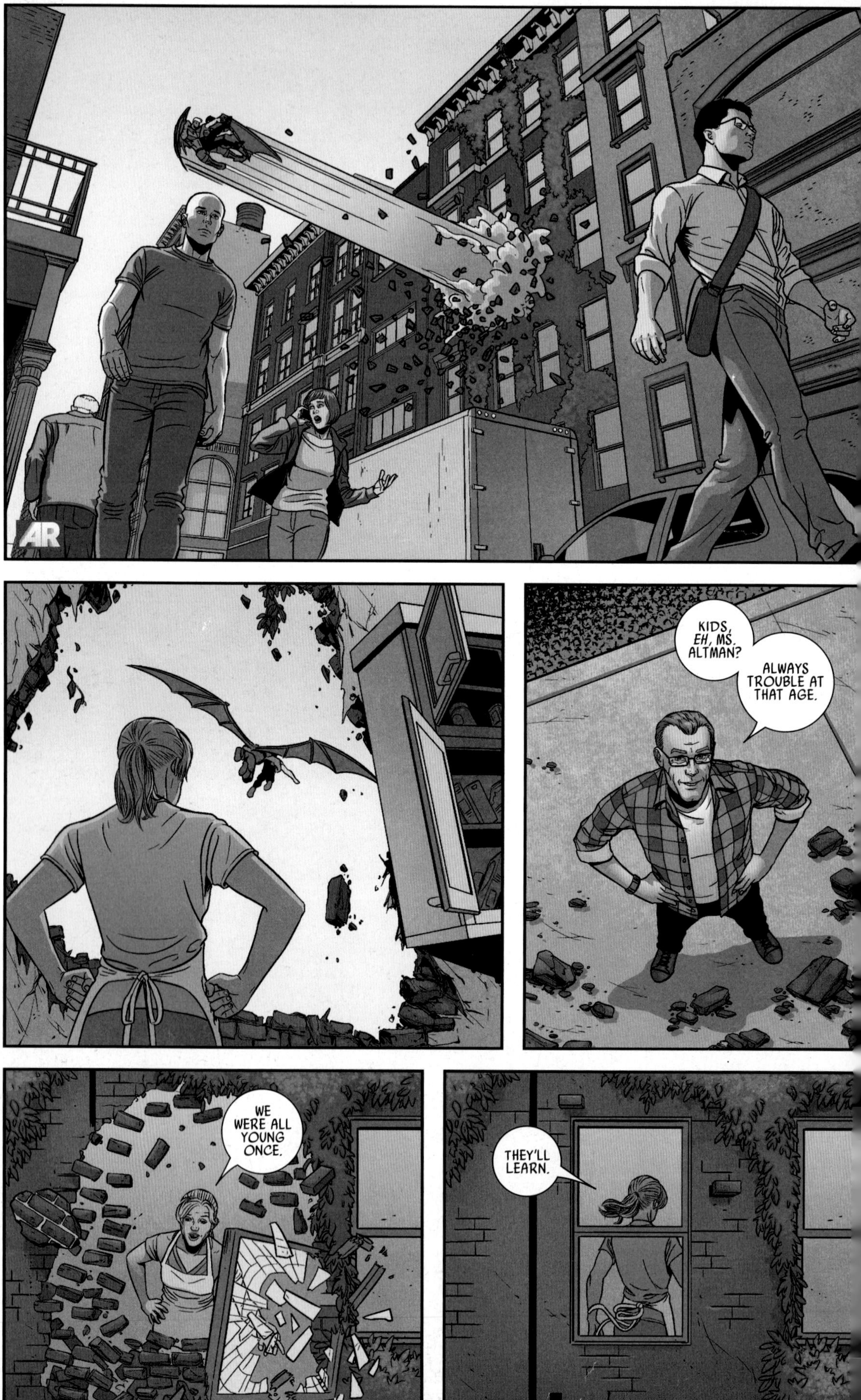
AR
KIDS, EH, MS. ALTMAN?
ALWAYS TROUBLE AT THAT AGE.
WE WERE ALL YOUNG ONCE.
THEY'LL LEARN.

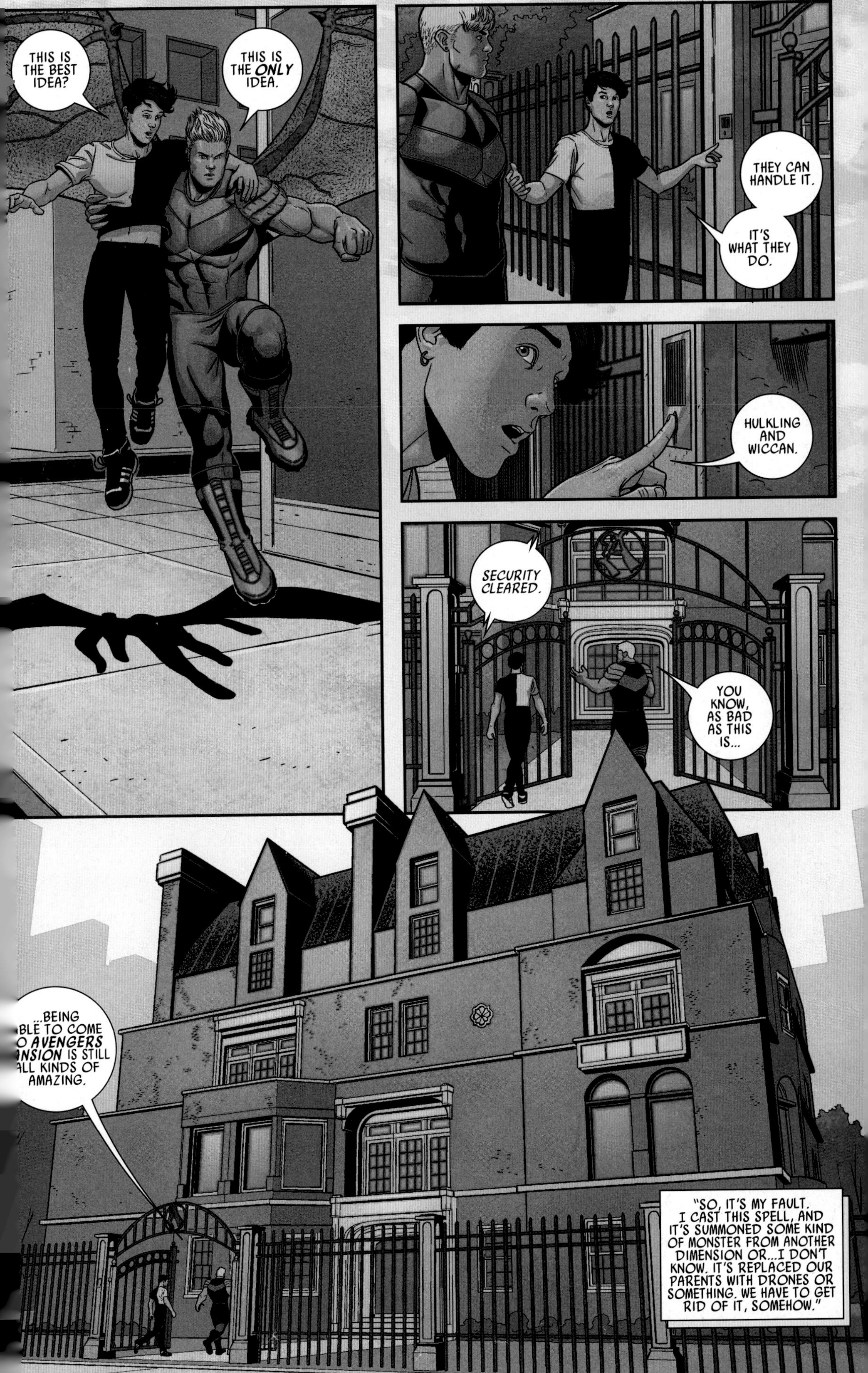
THIS IS THE BEST IDEA?
THIS IS THE *ONLY* IDEA.
THEY CAN HANDLE IT.
IT'S WHAT THEY DO.
HULKLING AND WICCAN.
SECURITY CLEARED.
YOU KNOW, AS BAD AS THIS IS...
...BEING BLE TO COME O *AVENGERS* *ANSION* IS STILL LL KINDS OF AMAZING.
"SO, IT'S MY FAULT. I CAST THIS SPELL, AND IT'S SUMMONED SOME KIND OF MONSTER FROM ANOTHER DIMENSION OR...I DON'T KNOW. IT'S REPLACED OUR PARENTS WITH DRONES OR SOMETHING. WE HAVE TO GET RID OF IT, SOMEHOW."

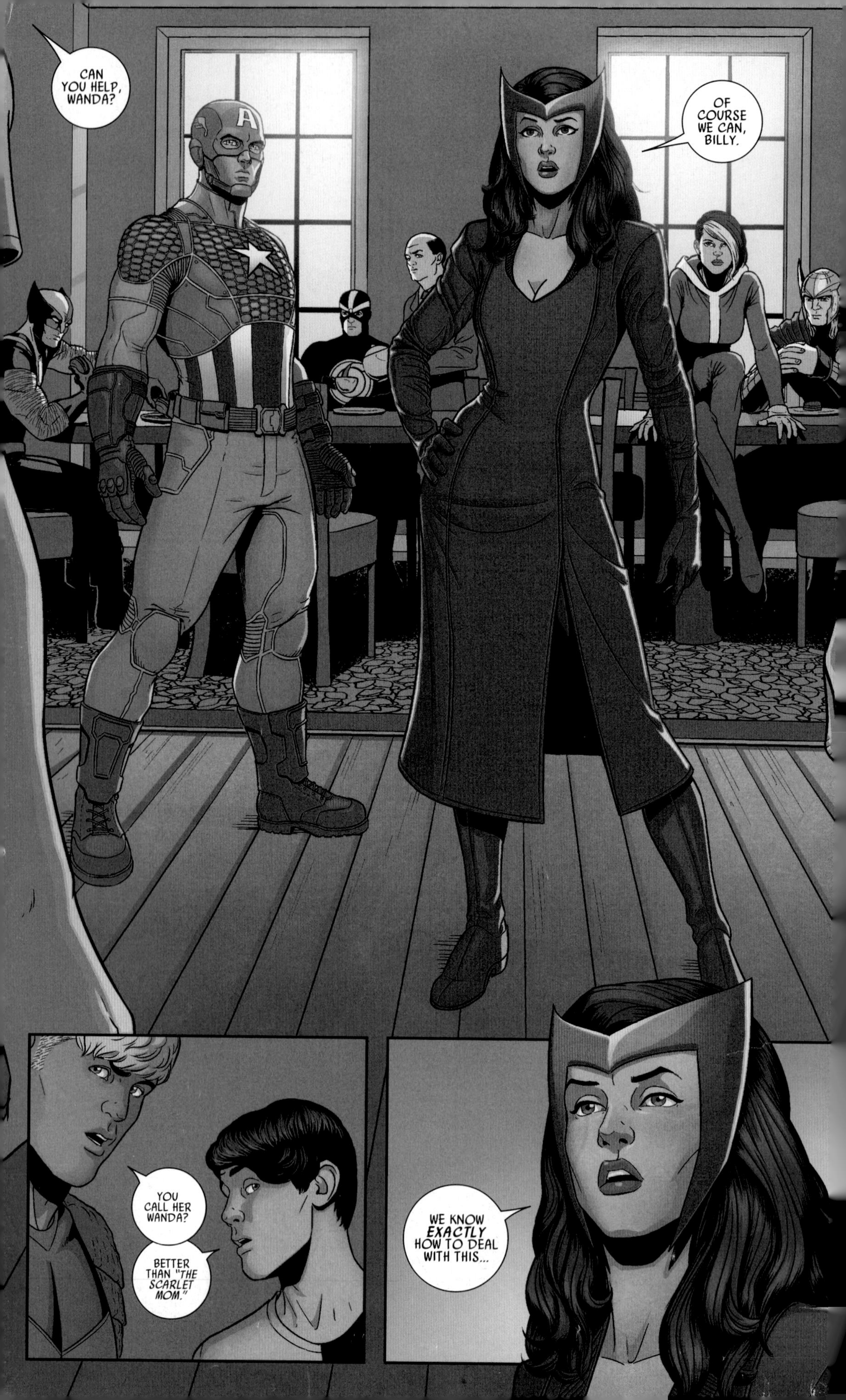
CAN YOU HELP, WANDA?
OF COURSE WE CAN, BILLY.
YOU CALL HER WANDA?
BETTER THAN "THE SCARLET MOM."
WE KNOW *EXACTLY* HOW TO DEAL WITH THIS...

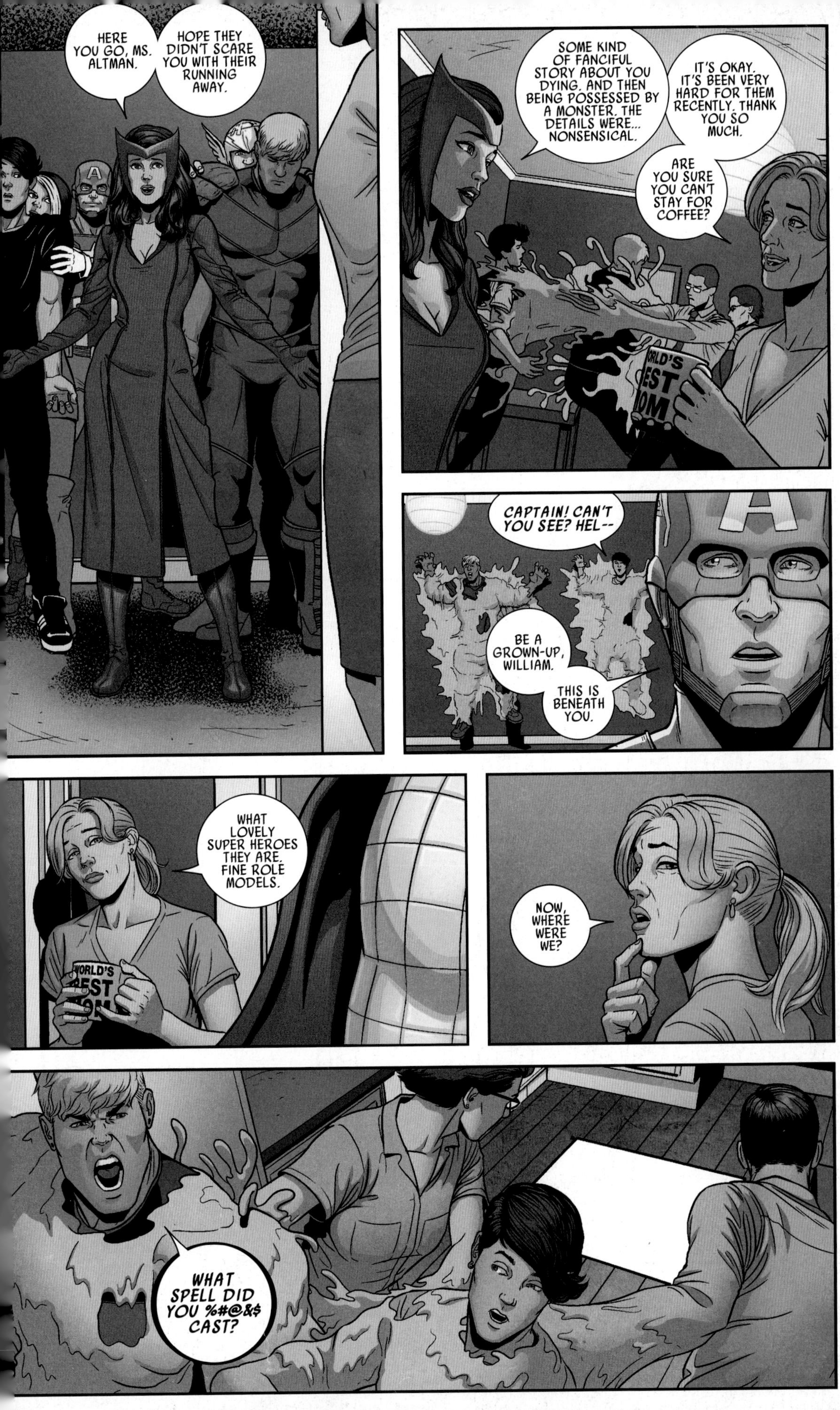
HERE YOU GO, MS. ALTMAN.
HOPE THEY DIDN'T SCARE YOU WITH THEIR RUNNING AWAY.
SOME KIND OF FANCIFUL STORY ABOUT YOU DYING. AND THEN BEING POSSESSED BY A MONSTER. THE DETAILS WERE... NONSENSICAL.
IT'S OKAY. IT'S BEEN VERY HARD FOR THEM RECENTLY. THANK YOU SO MUCH.
ARE YOU SURE YOU CAN'T STAY FOR COFFEE?
WORLD'S BEST MOM
CAPTAIN! CAN'T YOU SEE? HEL--
BE A GROWN-UP, WILLIAM.
THIS IS BENEATH YOU.
WHAT LOVELY SUPER HEROES THEY ARE. FINE ROLE MODELS.
NOW, WHERE WERE WE?
WHAT SPELL DID YOU %#@&$ CAST?

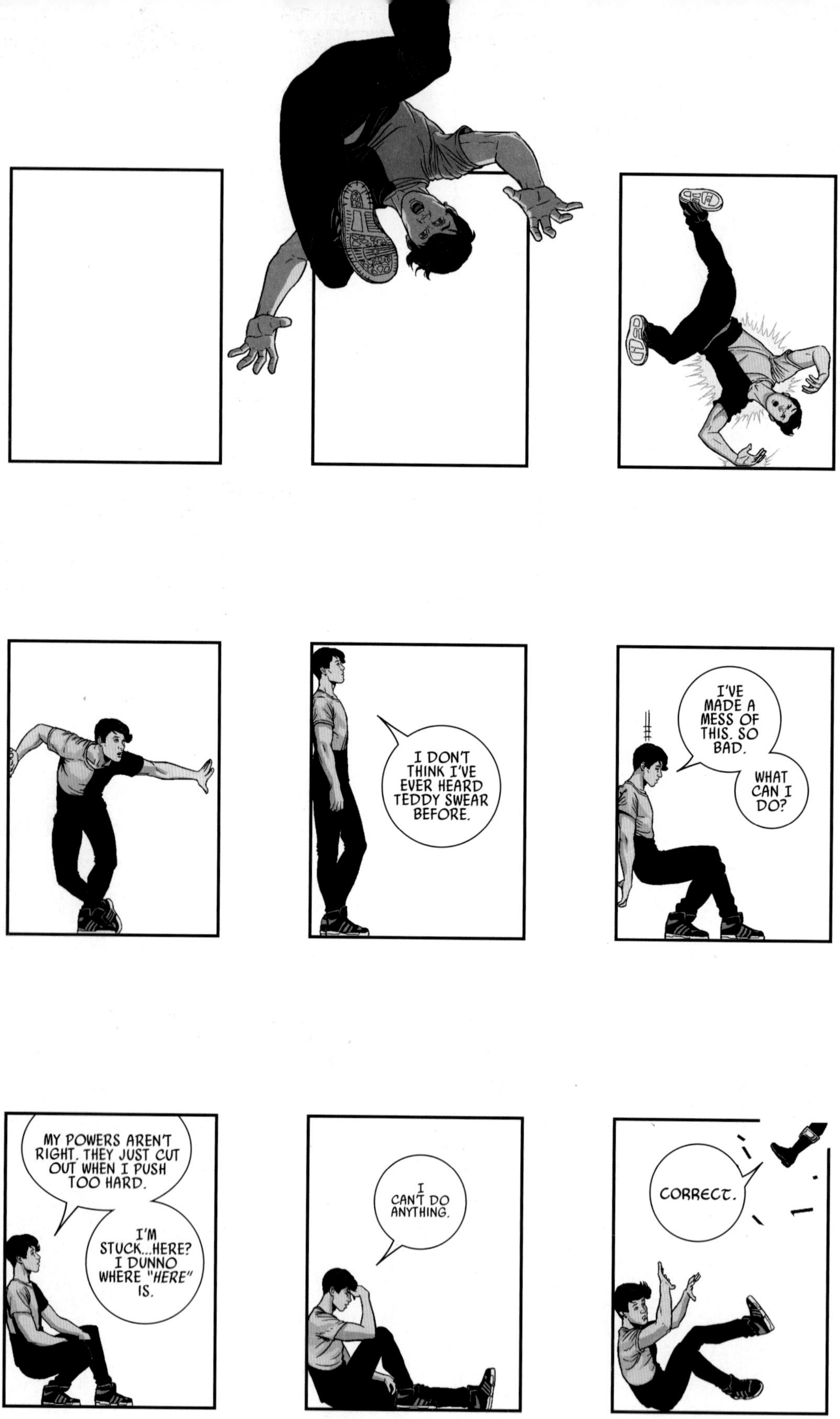
I DON'T THINK I'VE EVER HEARD TEDDY SWEAR BEFORE.
I'VE MADE A MESS OF THIS. SO BAD.
WHAT CAN I DO?
MY POWERS AREN'T RIGHT. THEY JUST CUT OUT WHEN I PUSH TOO HARD.
I'M STUCK...HERE? I DUNNO WHERE "*HERE*" IS.
I CAN'T DO ANYTHING.
CORRECT.

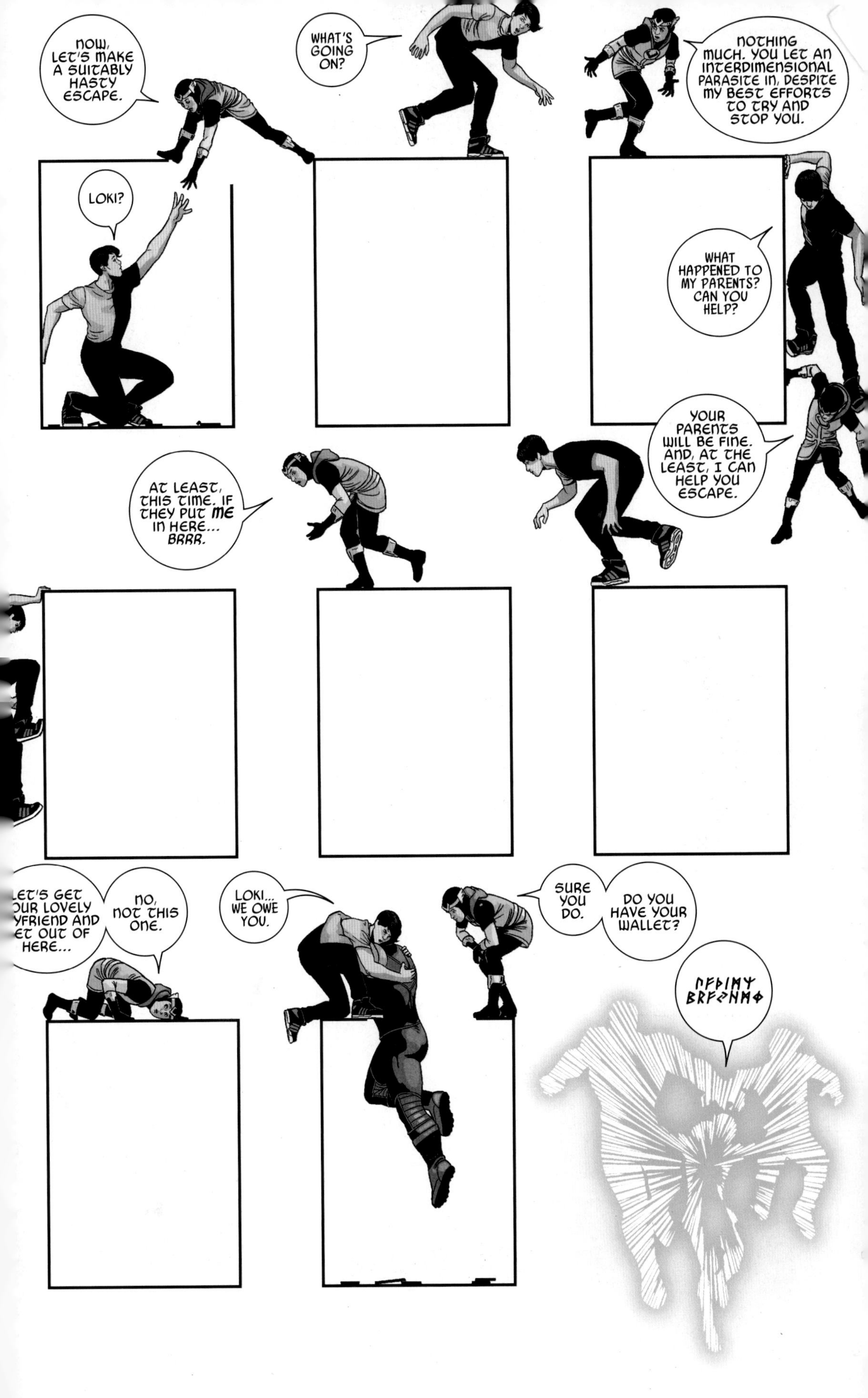
NOW, LET'S MAKE A SUITABLY HASTY ESCAPE.
LOKI?
WHAT'S GOING ON?
NOTHING MUCH. YOU LET AN INTERDIMENSIONAL PARASITE IN, DESPITE MY BEST EFFORTS TO TRY AND STOP YOU.
WHAT HAPPENED TO MY PARENTS? CAN YOU HELP?
YOUR PARENTS WILL BE FINE. AND, AT THE LEAST, I CAN HELP YOU ESCAPE.
AT LEAST, THIS TIME. IF THEY PUT *ME* IN HERE... BRRR.
LET'S GET OUR LOVELY YFRIEND AND ET OUT OF HERE...
NO, NOT THIS ONE.
LOKI... WE OWE YOU.
SURE YOU DO.
DO YOU HAVE YOUR WALLET?

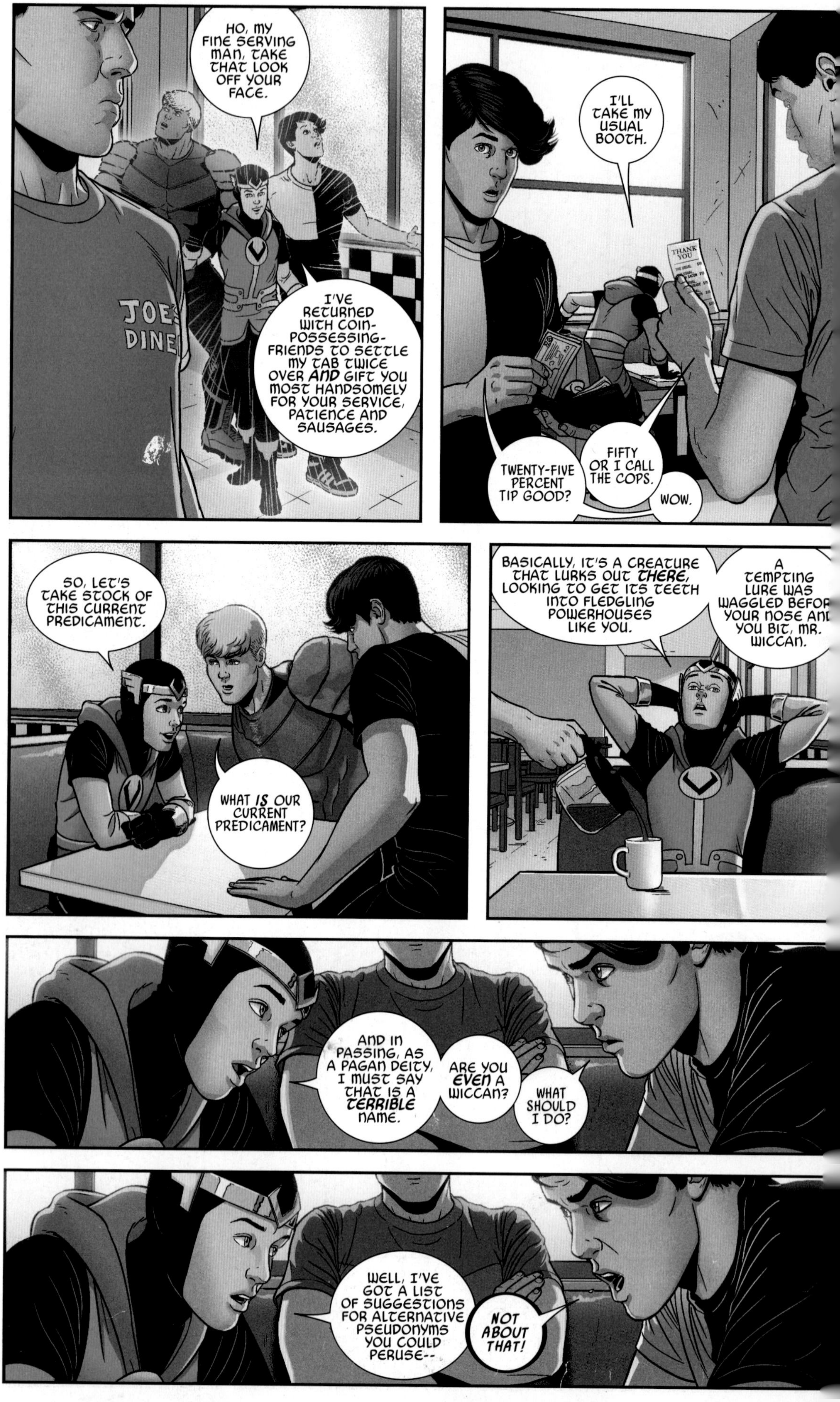
HO, MY FINE SERVING MAN, TAKE THAT LOOK OFF YOUR FACE.
I'VE RETURNED WITH COIN-POSSESSING-FRIENDS TO SETTLE MY TAB TWICE OVER AND GIFT YOU MOST HANDSOMELY FOR YOUR SERVICE, PATIENCE AND SAUSAGES.
JOE'S DINE
I'LL TAKE MY USUAL BOOTH.
THANK YOU
TWENTY-FIVE PERCENT TIP GOOD?
FIFTY OR I CALL THE COPS.
WOW.
SO, LET'S TAKE STOCK OF THIS CURRENT PREDICAMENT.
WHAT IS OUR CURRENT PREDICAMENT?
BASICALLY, IT'S A CREATURE THAT LURKS OUT THERE, LOOKING TO GET ITS TEETH INTO FLEDGLING POWERHOUSES LIKE YOU.
A TEMPTING LURE WAS WAGGLED BEFOR YOUR NOSE AN YOU BIT, MR. WICCAN.
AND IN PASSING, AS A PAGAN DEITY, I MUST SAY THAT IS A TERRIBLE NAME.
ARE YOU EVEN A WICCAN?
WHAT SHOULD I DO?
WELL, I'VE GOT A LIST OF SUGGESTIONS FOR ALTERNATIVE PSEUDONYMS YOU COULD PERUSE--
NOT ABOUT THAT!

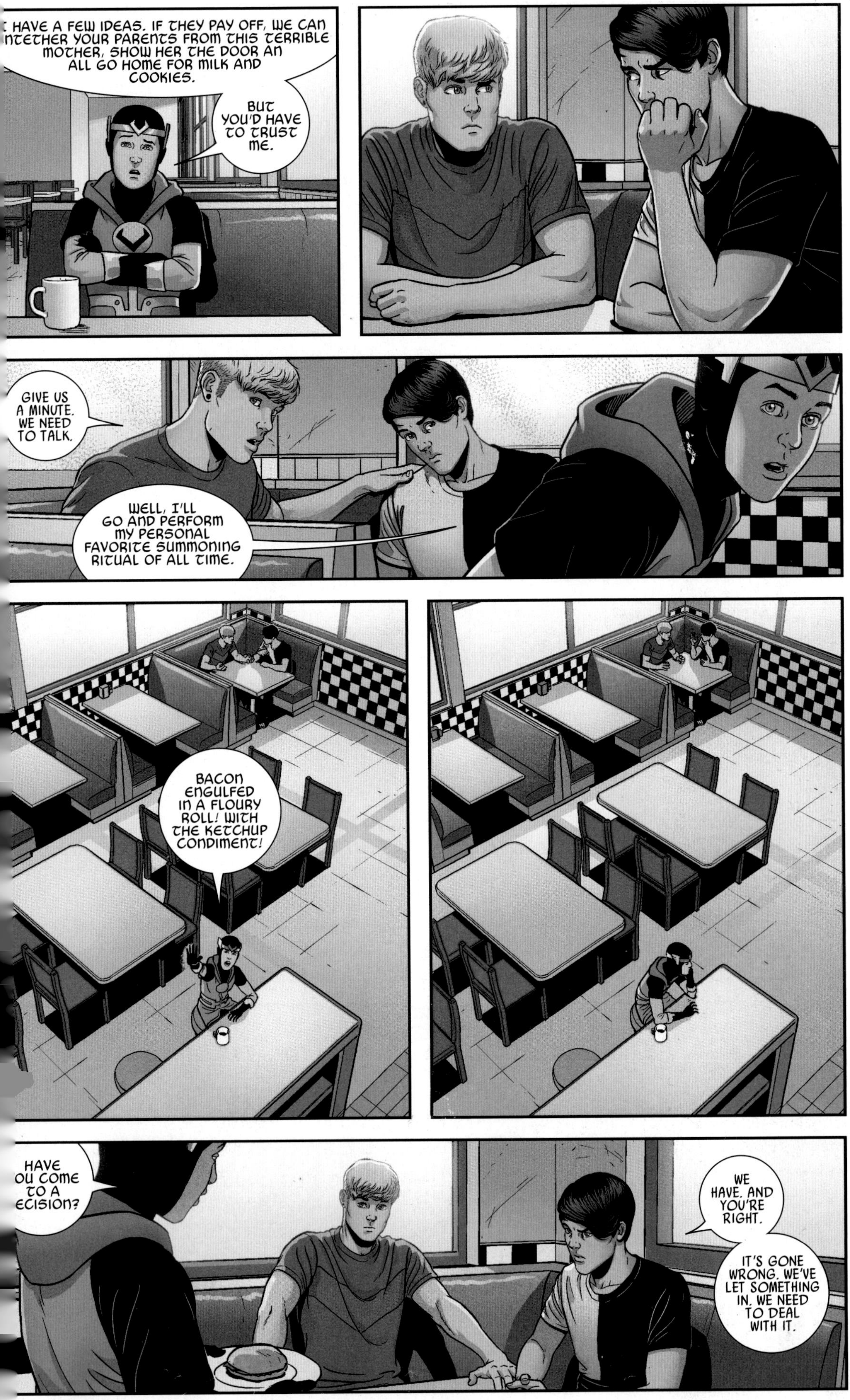
I HAVE A FEW IDEAS. IF THEY PAY OFF, WE CAN NTETHER YOUR PARENTS FROM THIS TERRIBLE MOTHER, SHOW HER THE DOOR AN ALL GO HOME FOR MILK AND COOKIES.
BUT YOU'D HAVE TO TRUST ME.
GIVE US A MINUTE. WE NEED TO TALK.
WELL, I'LL GO AND PERFORM MY PERSONAL FAVORITE SUMMONING RITUAL OF ALL TIME.
BACON ENGULFED IN A FLOURY ROLL! WITH THE KETCHUP CONDIMENT!
HAVE OU COME TO A ECISION?
WE HAVE. AND YOU'RE RIGHT.
IT'S GONE WRONG. WE'VE LET SOMETHING IN. WE NEED TO DEAL WITH IT.

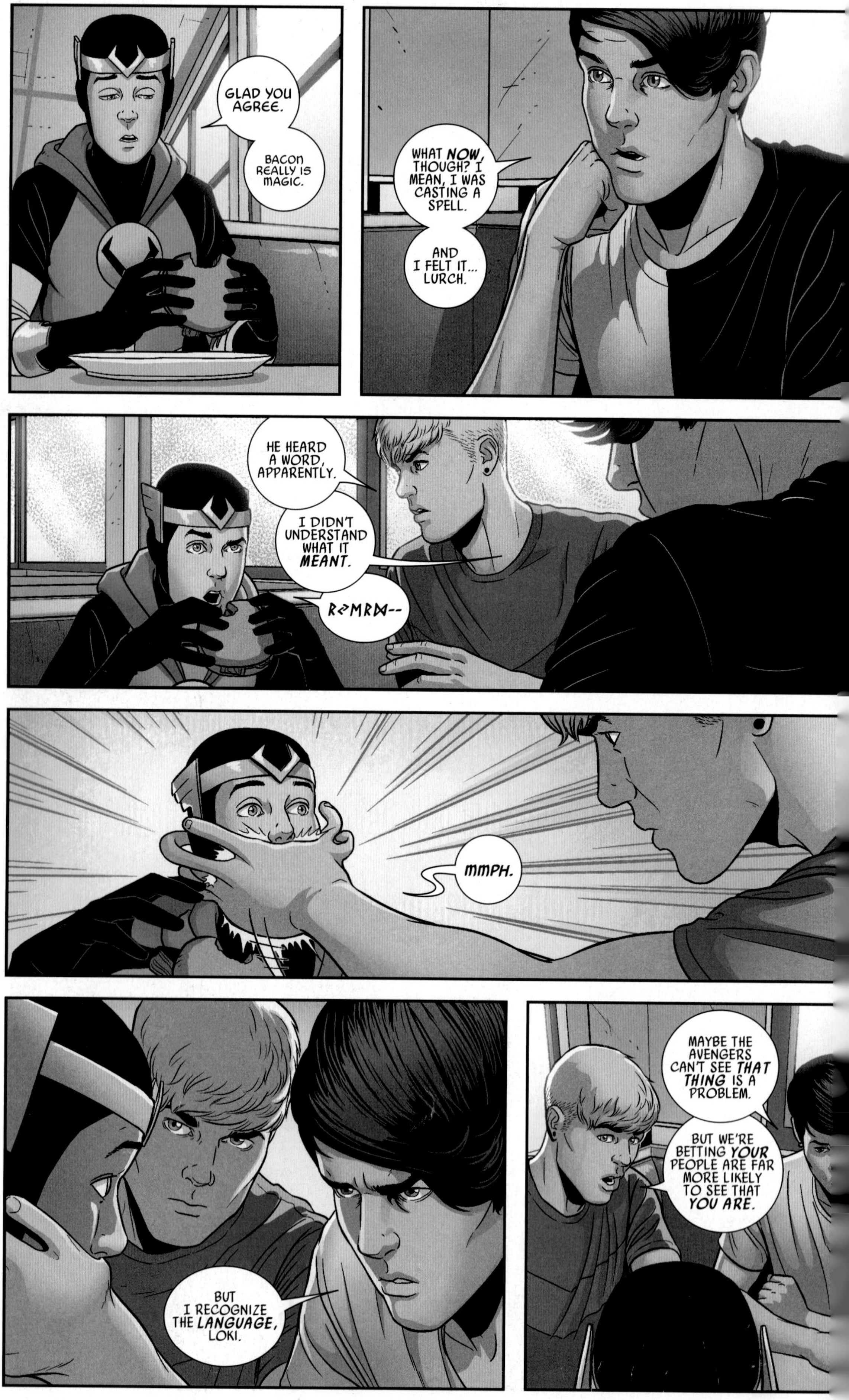
GLAD YOU AGREE.
BACON REALLY IS MAGIC.
WHAT NOW, THOUGH? I MEAN, I WAS CASTING A SPELL.
AND I FELT IT... LURCH.
HE HEARD A WORD, APPARENTLY.
I DIDN'T UNDERSTAND WHAT IT MEANT.
MMPH.
BUT I RECOGNIZE THE LANGUAGE, LOKI.
MAYBE THE AVENGERS CAN'T SEE THAT THING IS A PROBLEM.
BUT WE'RE BETTING YOUR PEOPLE ARE FAR MORE LIKELY TO SEE THAT YOU ARE.

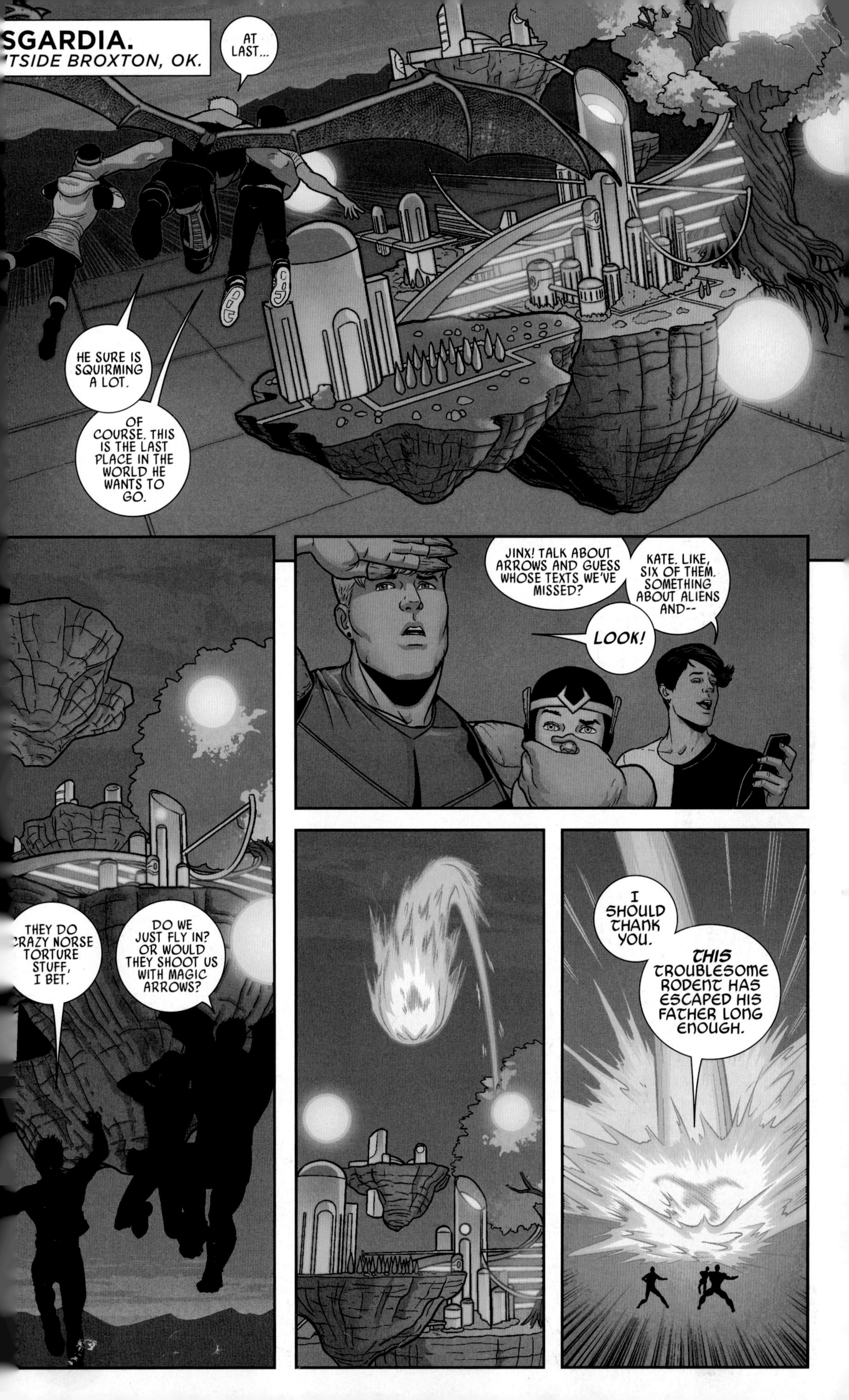
SGARDIA.
TSIDE BROXTON, OK.
AT LAST...
HE SURE IS SQUIRMING A LOT.
OF COURSE. THIS IS THE LAST PLACE IN THE WORLD HE WANTS TO GO.
JINX! TALK ABOUT ARROWS AND GUESS WHOSE TEXTS WE'VE MISSED?
KATE. LIKE, SIX OF THEM. SOMETHING ABOUT ALIENS AND--
LOOK!
THEY DO CRAZY NORSE TORTURE STUFF, I BET.
DO WE JUST FLY IN? OR WOULD THEY SHOOT US WITH MAGIC ARROWS?
I SHOULD THANK YOU.
THIS TROUBLESOME RODENT HAS ESCAPED HIS FATHER LONG ENOUGH.

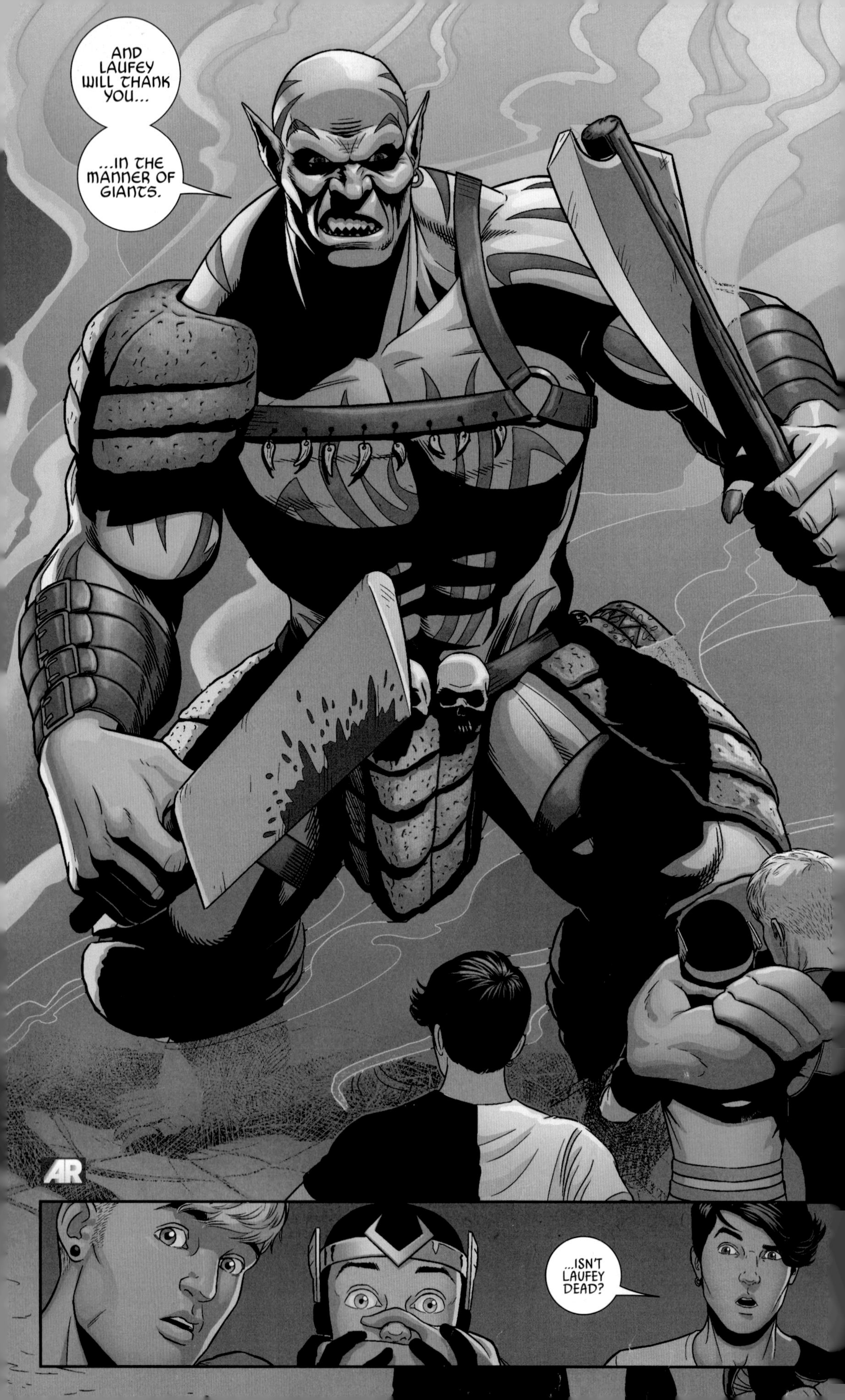
AND LAUFEY WILL THANK YOU...
...IN THE MANNER OF GIANTS.
...ISN'T LAUFEY DEAD?

## #1 VARIANT
BY SKOTTIE YOUNG

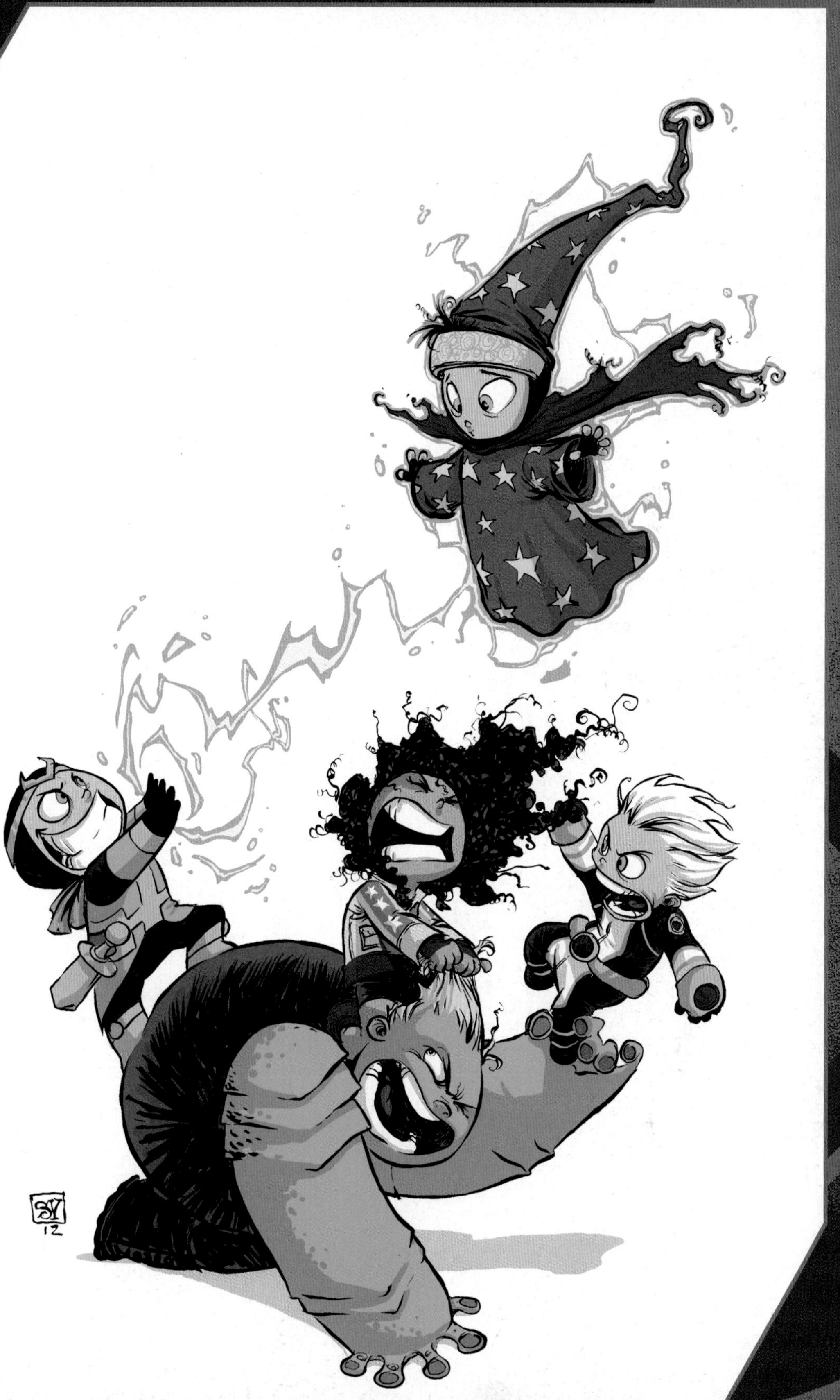
SY
12

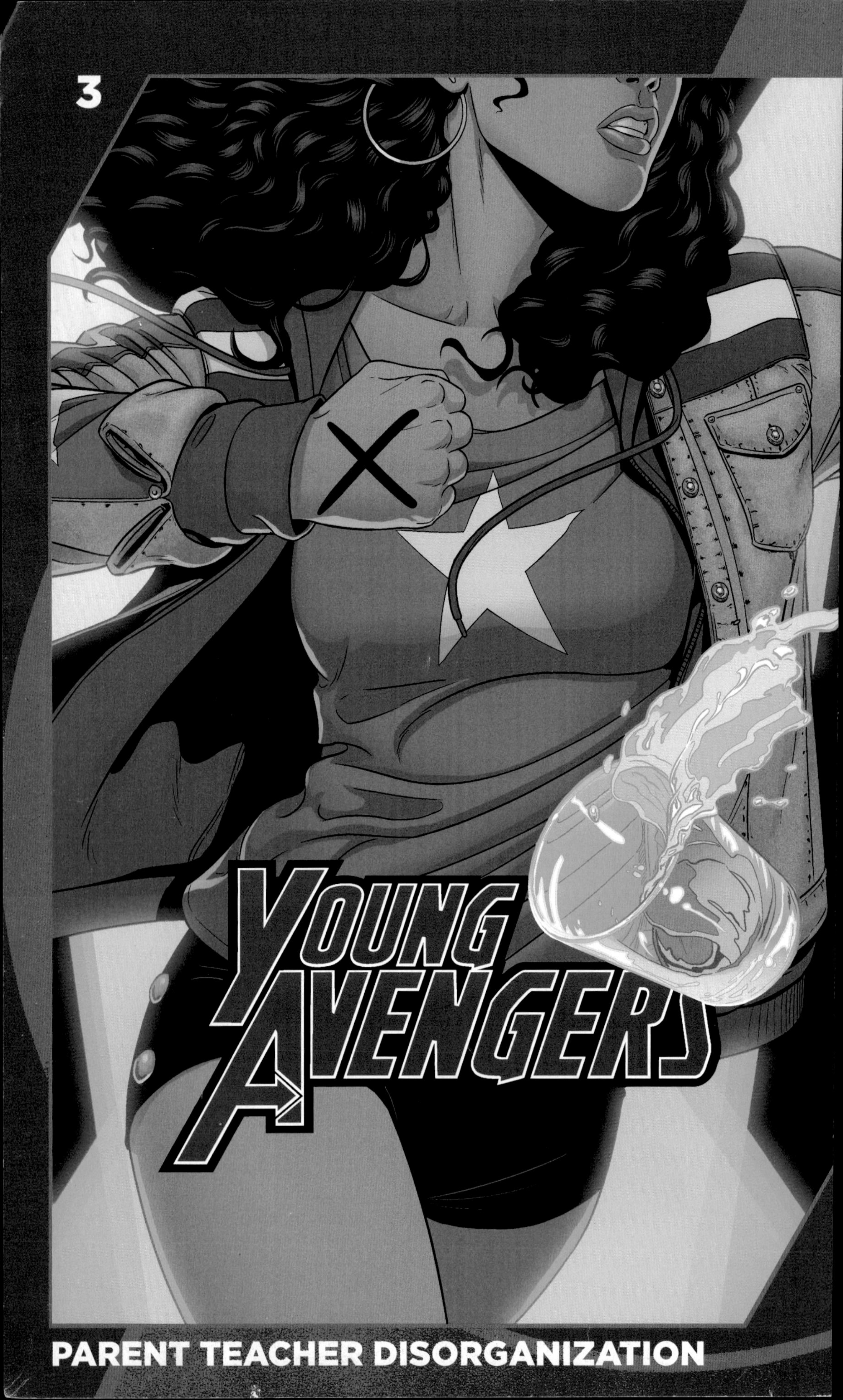
3
YOUNG AVENGERS
PARENT TEACHER DISORGANIZATION

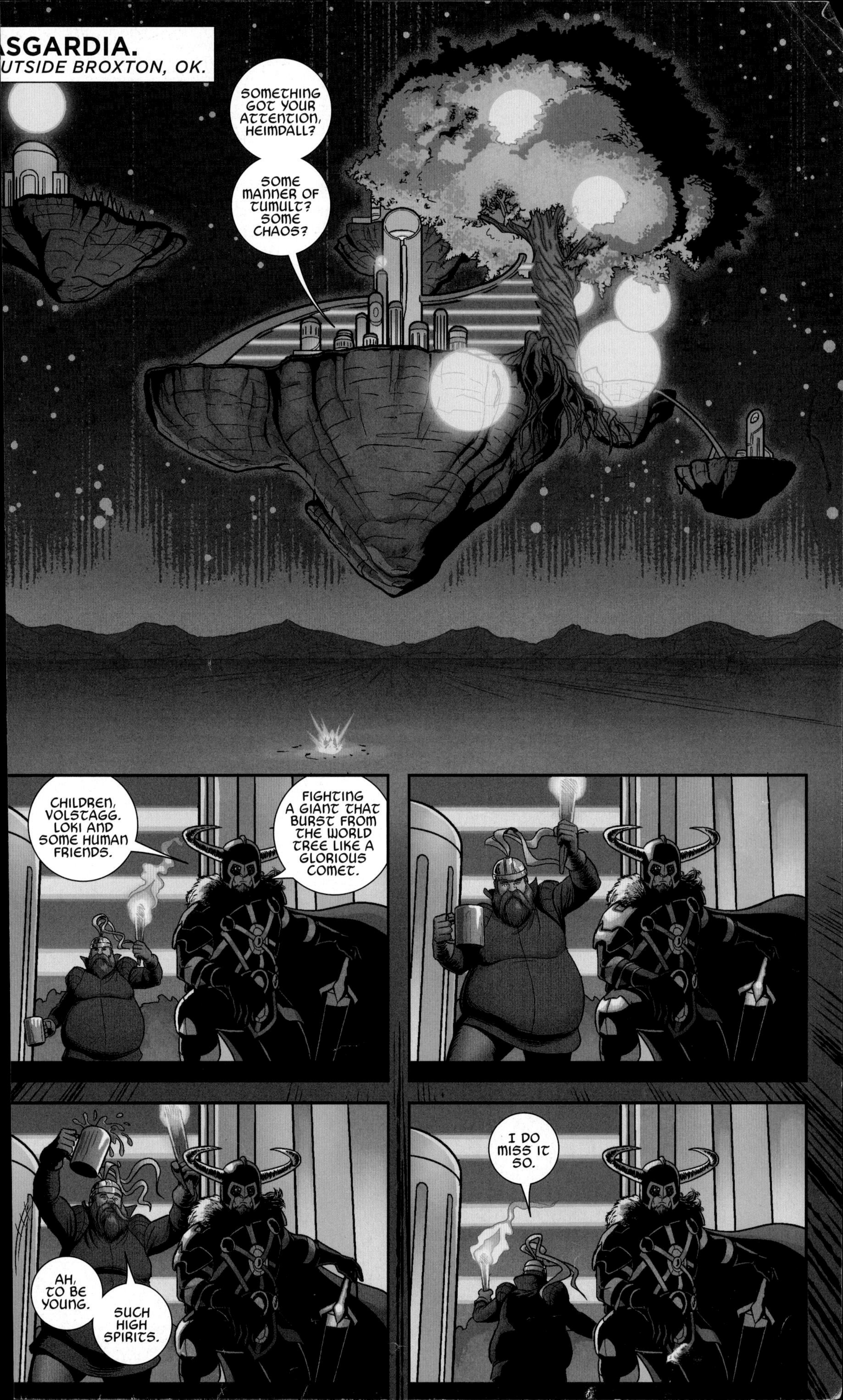
ASGARDIA.
UTSIDE BROXTON, OK.
SOMETHING GOT YOUR ATTENTION, HEIMDALL?
SOME MANNER OF TUMULT? SOME CHAOS?
CHILDREN, VOLSTAGG. LOKI AND SOME HUMAN FRIENDS.
FIGHTING A GIANT THAT BURST FROM THE WORLD TREE LIKE A GLORIOUS COMET.
AH, TO BE YOUNG.
SUCH HIGH SPIRITS.
I DO MISS IT SO.

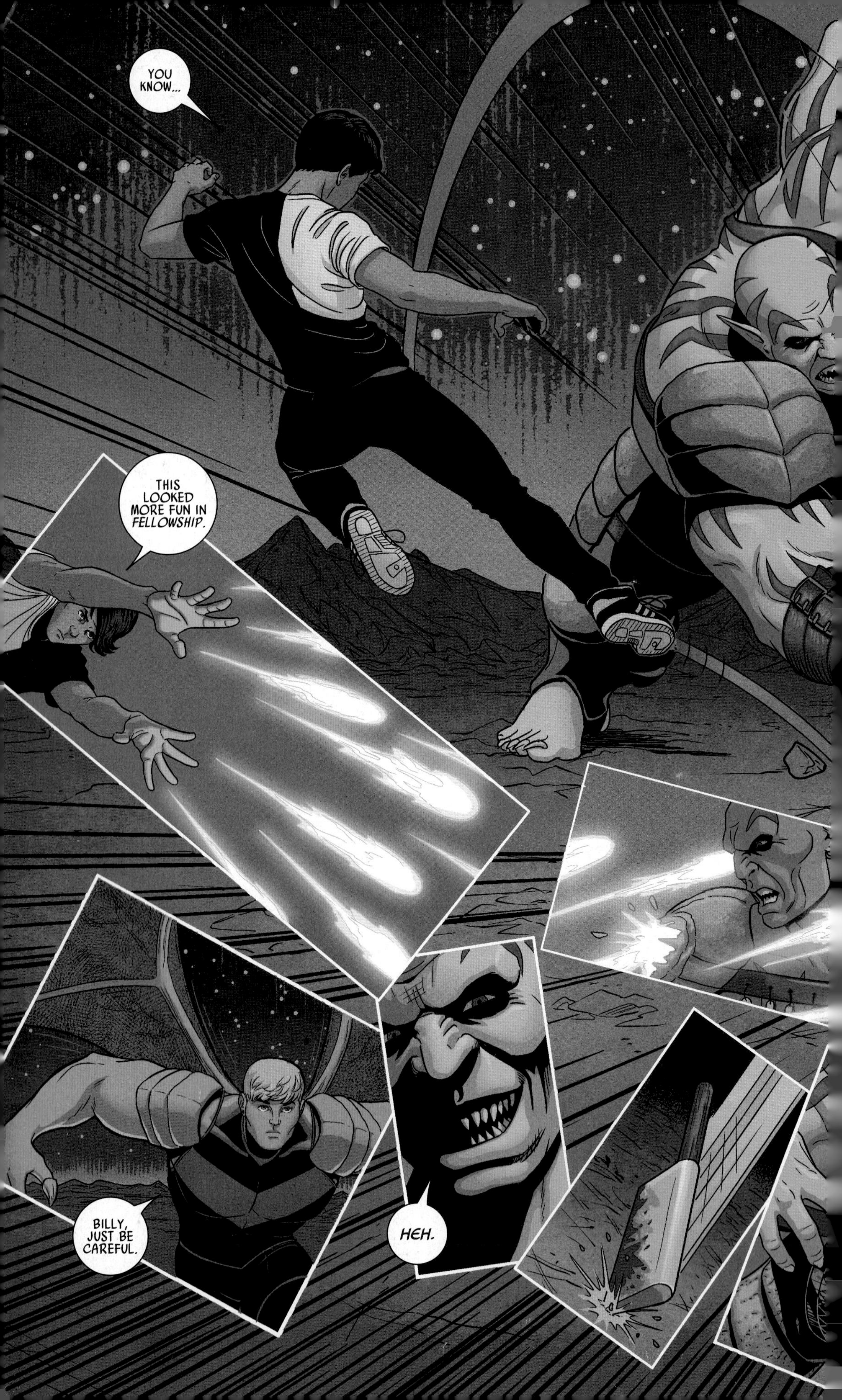
YOU KNOW...
THIS LOOKED MORE FUN IN FELLOWSHIP.
BILLY, JUST BE CAREFUL.
HEH.

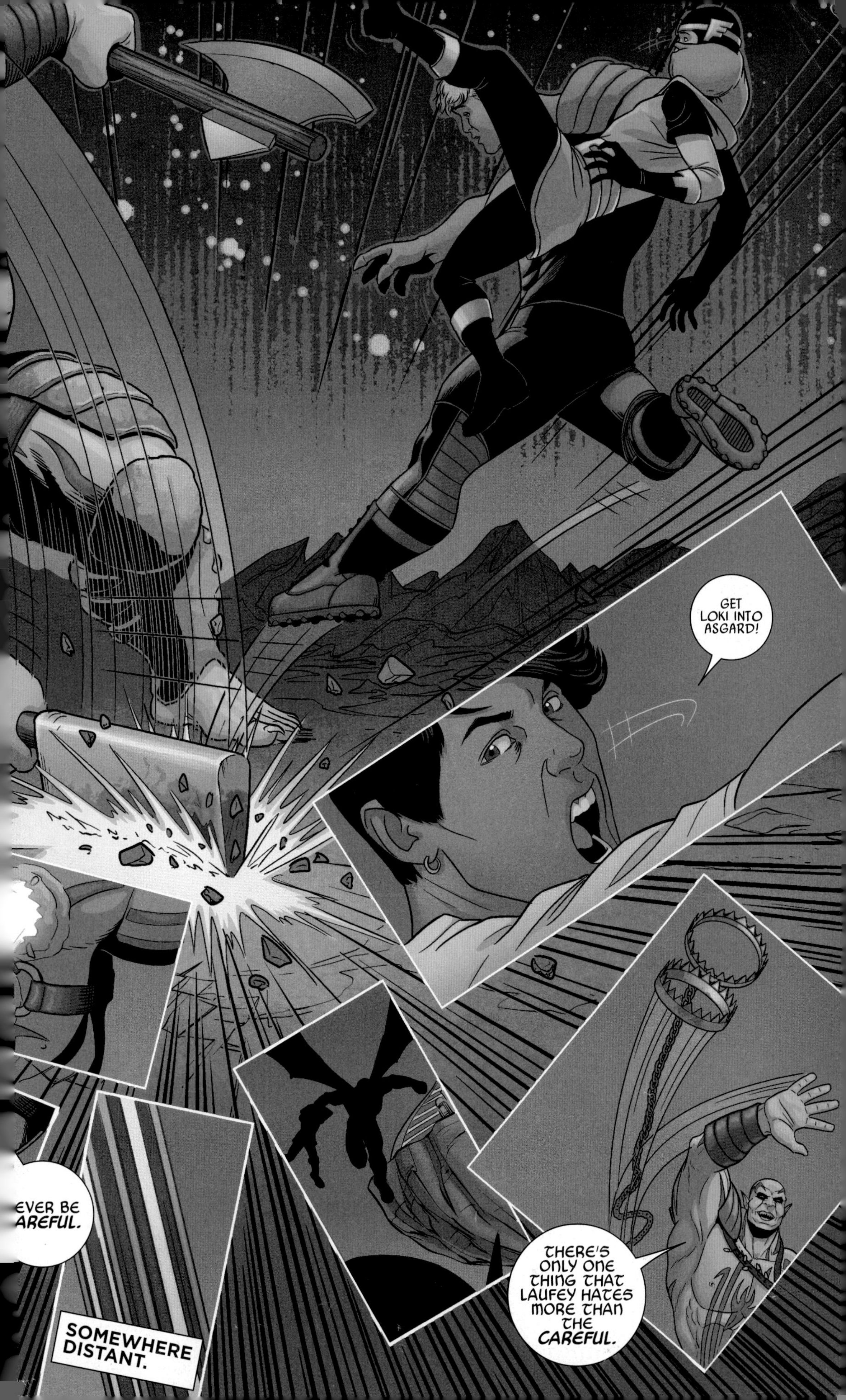
GET LOKI INTO ASGARD!
EVER BE AREFUL.
SOMEWHERE DISTANT.
THERE'S ONLY ONE THING THAT LAUFEY HATES MORE THAN THE CAREFUL.

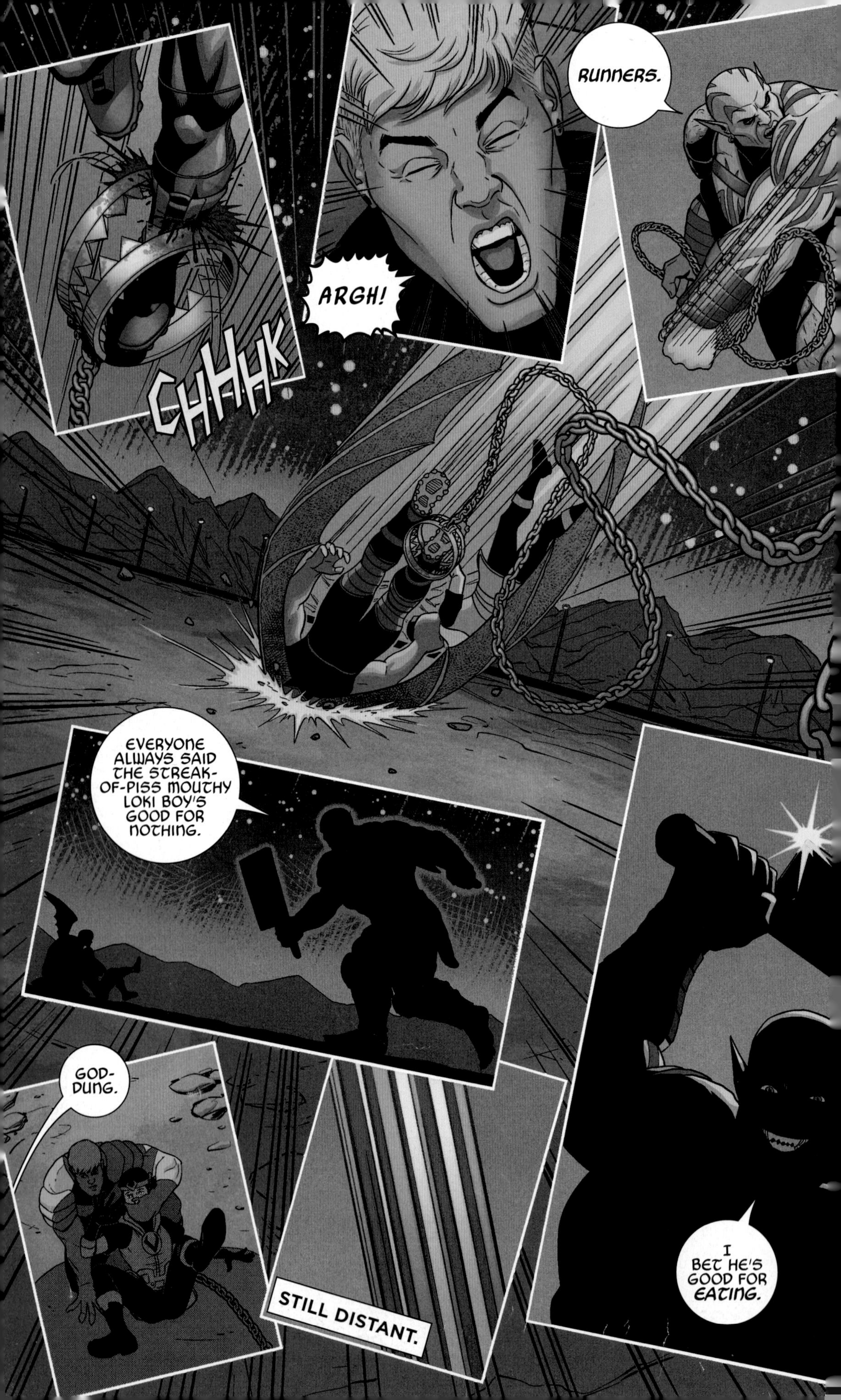
ARGH!
CHHHK
RUNNERS.
EVERYONE ALWAYS SAID THE STREAK-OF-PISS MOUTHY LOKI BOY'S GOOD FOR NOTHING.
I BET HE'S GOOD FOR EATING.
GOD-DUNG.
STILL DISTANT.

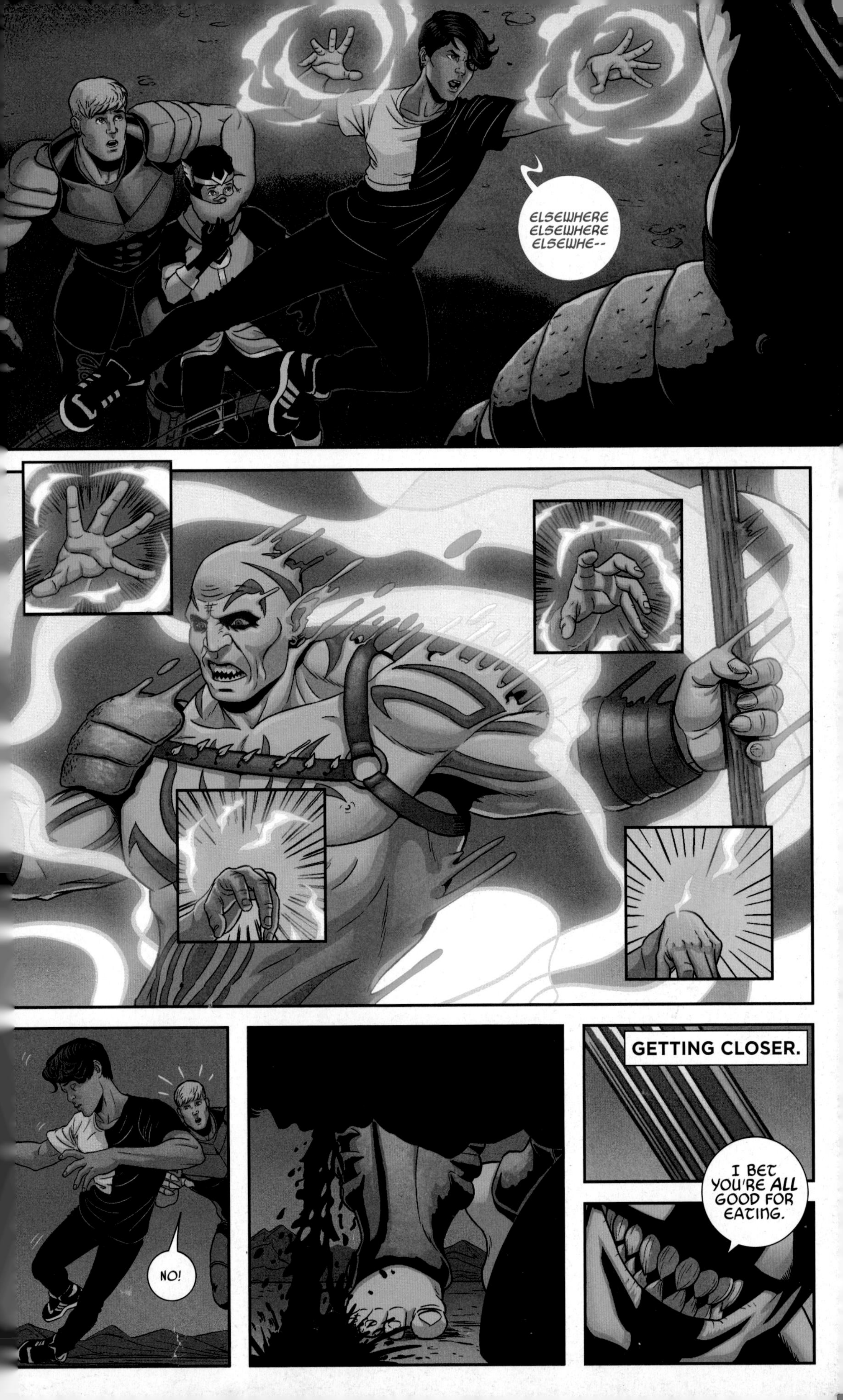
ELSEWHERE ELSEWHERE ELSEWHE--
NO!
GETTING CLOSER.
I BET YOU'RE ALL GOOD FOR EATING.

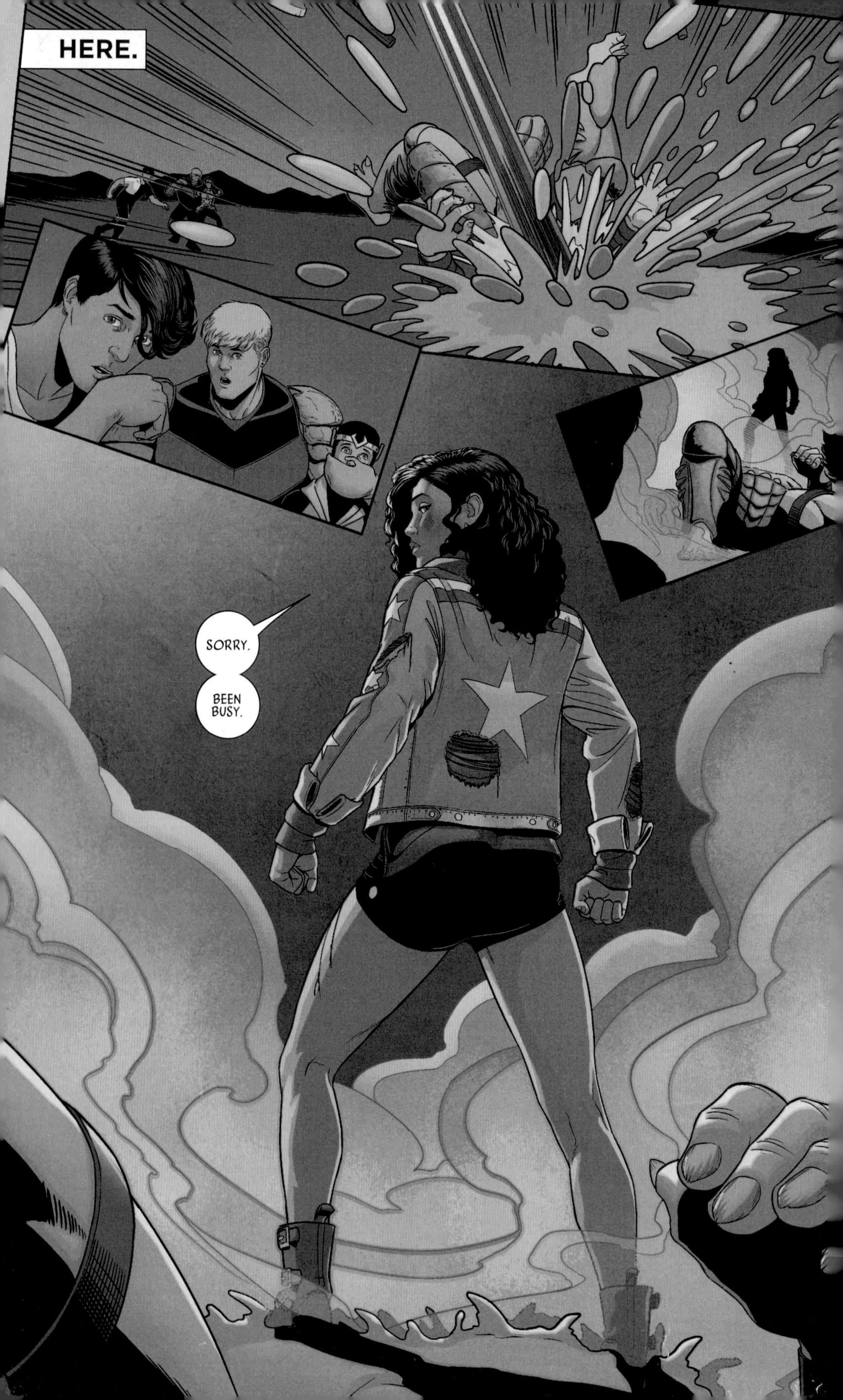
HERE.
SORRY.
BEEN BUSY.

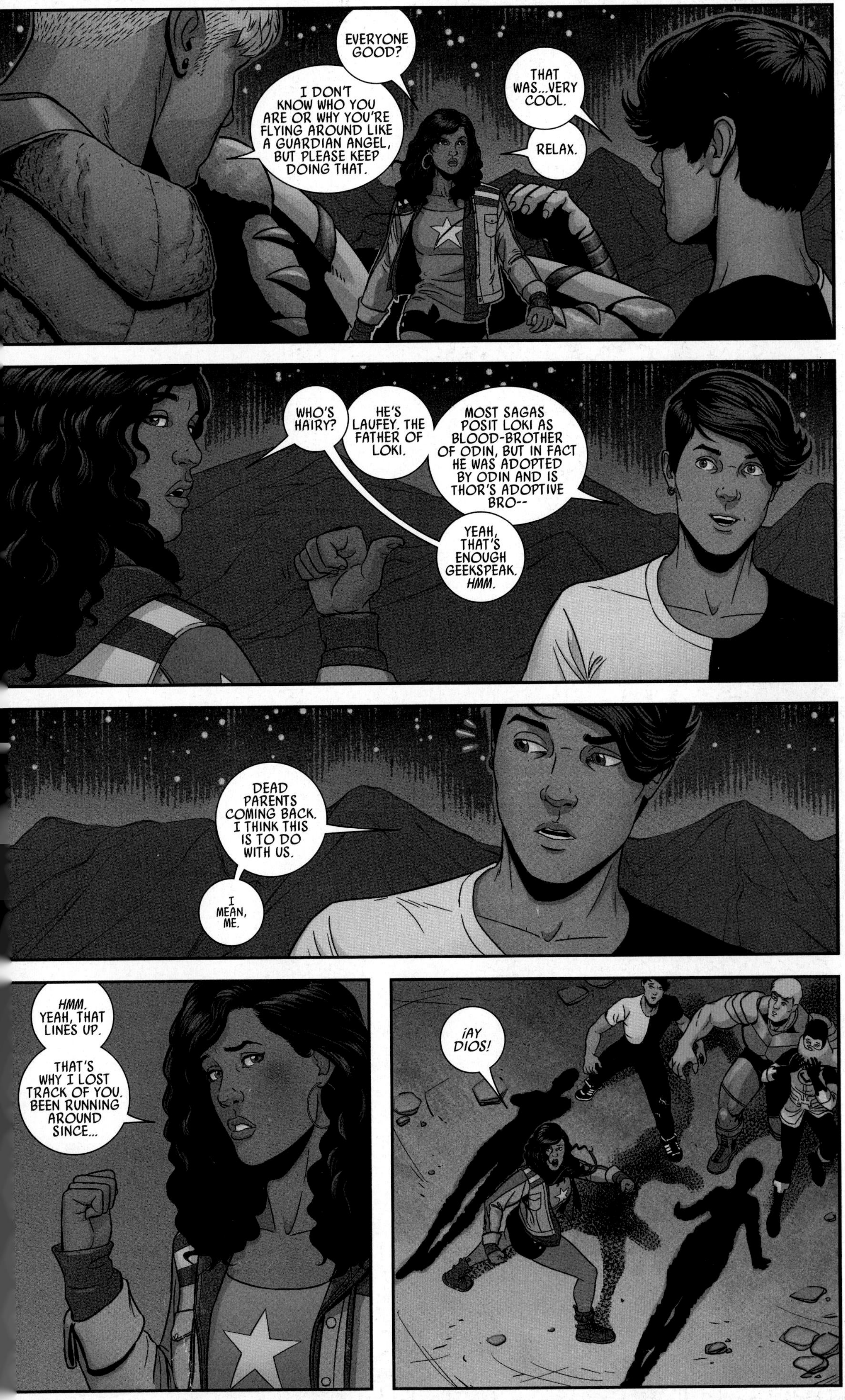
EVERYONE GOOD?
I DON'T KNOW WHO YOU ARE OR WHY YOU'RE FLYING AROUND LIKE A GUARDIAN ANGEL, BUT PLEASE KEEP DOING THAT.
THAT WAS...VERY COOL.
RELAX.
WHO'S HAIRY?
HE'S LAUFEY. THE FATHER OF LOKI.
MOST SAGAS POSIT LOKI AS BLOOD-BROTHER OF ODIN, BUT IN FACT HE WAS ADOPTED BY ODIN AND IS THOR'S ADOPTIVE BRO--
YEAH, THAT'S ENOUGH GEEKSPEAK. HMM.
DEAD PARENTS COMING BACK. I THINK THIS IS TO DO WITH US.
I MEAN, ME.
HMM. YEAH, THAT LINES UP.
THAT'S WHY I LOST TRACK OF YOU. BEEN RUNNING AROUND SINCE...
¡AY DIOS!

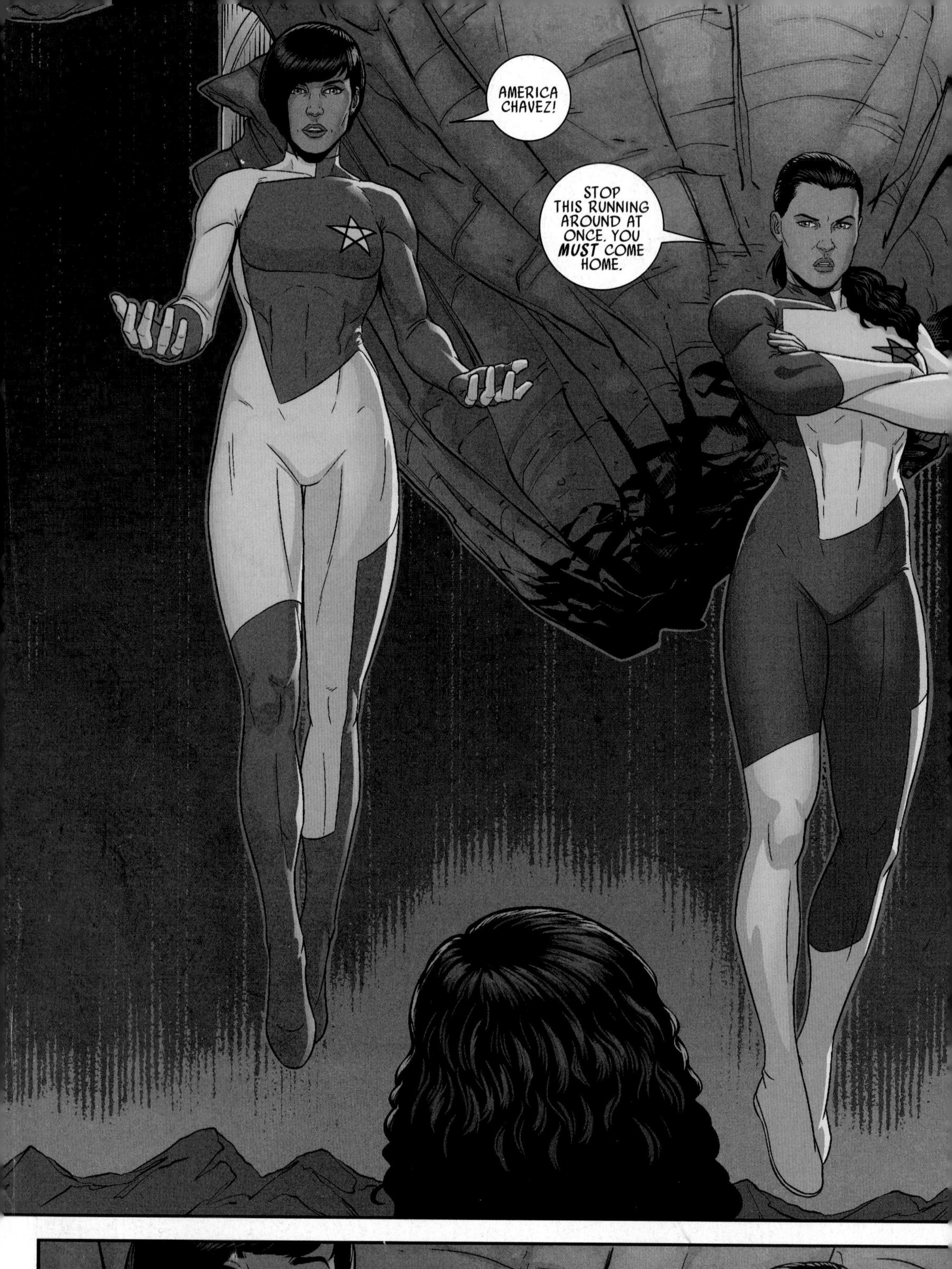
AMERICA CHAVEZ!
STOP THIS RUNNING AROUND AT ONCE. YOU MUST COME HOME.

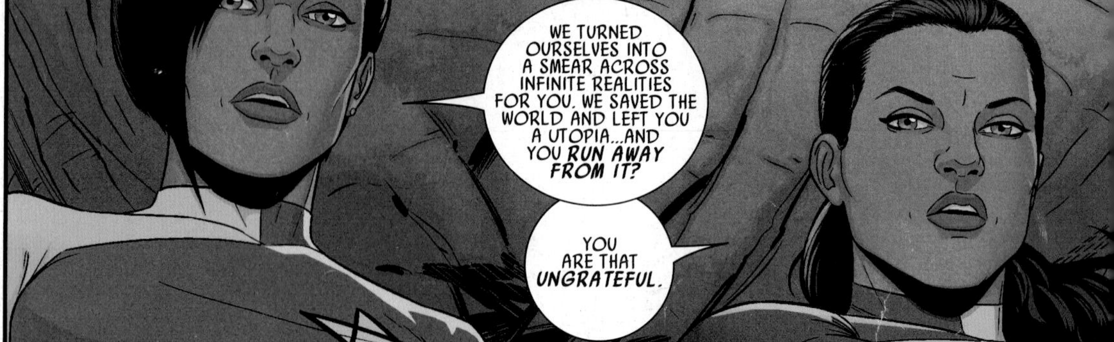
WE TURNED OURSELVES INTO A SMEAR ACROSS INFINITE REALITIES FOR YOU. WE SAVED THE WORLD AND LEFT YOU A UTOPIA...AND YOU RUN AWAY FROM IT?
YOU ARE THAT UNGRATEFUL.

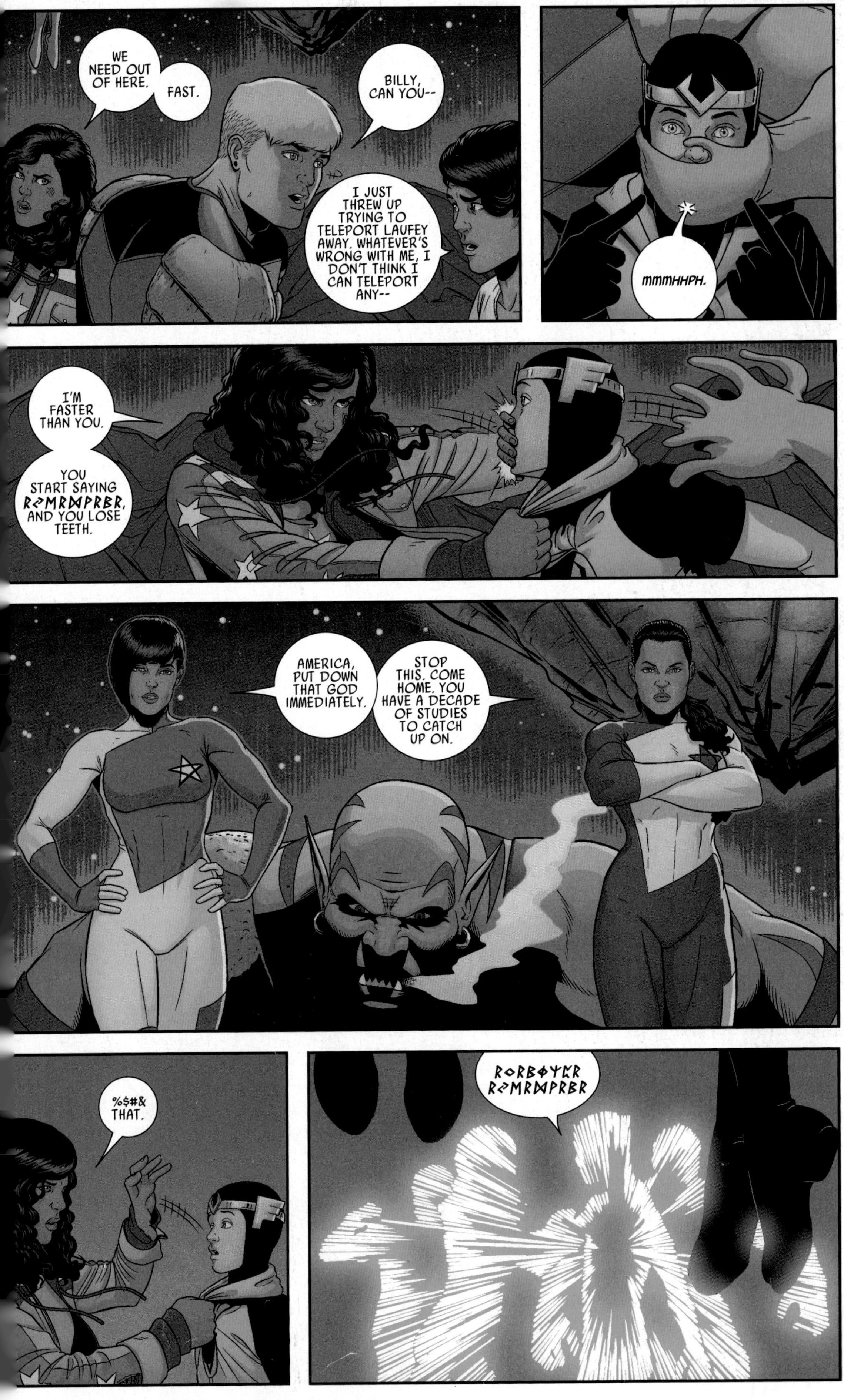
WE NEED OUT OF HERE.
FAST.
BILLY, CAN YOU--
I JUST THREW UP TRYING TO TELEPORT LAUFEY AWAY. WHATEVER'S WRONG WITH ME, I DON'T THINK I CAN TELEPORT ANY--
MMMHHPH.
I'M FASTER THAN YOU.
YOU START SAYING, AND YOU LOSE TEETH.
AMERICA, PUT DOWN THAT GOD IMMEDIATELY.
STOP THIS. COME HOME. YOU HAVE A DECADE OF STUDIES TO CATCH UP ON.
%$#& THAT.

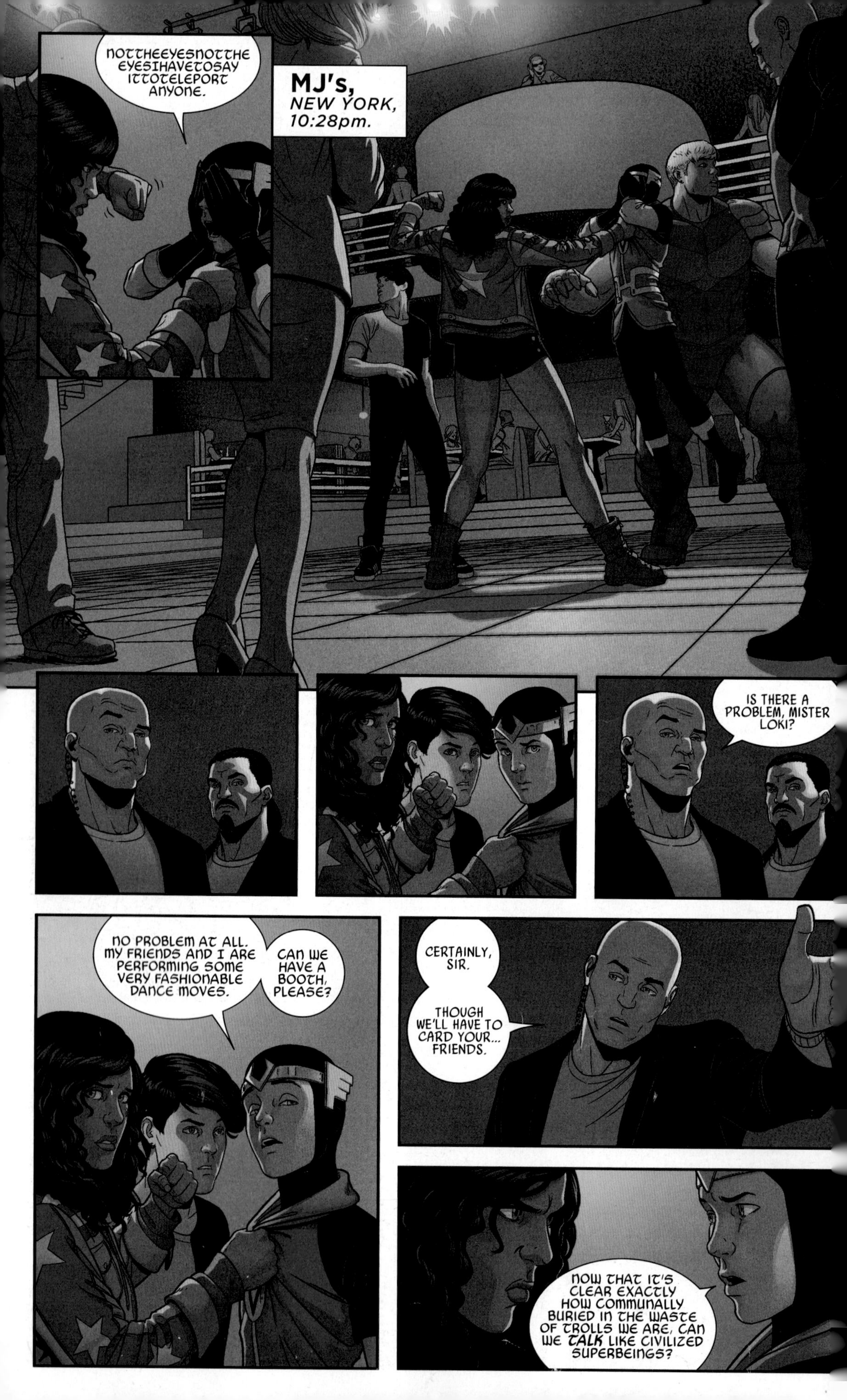
NOTTHEEYESNOTTHE EYESIHAVETOSAY ITTOTELEPORT ANYONE.
MJ's, NEW YORK, 10:28pm.
IS THERE A PROBLEM, MISTER LOKI?
NO PROBLEM AT ALL. MY FRIENDS AND I ARE PERFORMING SOME VERY FASHIONABLE DANCE MOVES.
CAN WE HAVE A BOOTH, PLEASE?
CERTAINLY, SIR.
THOUGH WE'LL HAVE TO CARD YOUR... FRIENDS.
NOW THAT IT'S CLEAR EXACTLY HOW COMMUNALLY BURIED IN THE WASTE OF TROLLS WE ARE, CAN WE TALK LIKE CIVILIZED SUPERBEINGS?

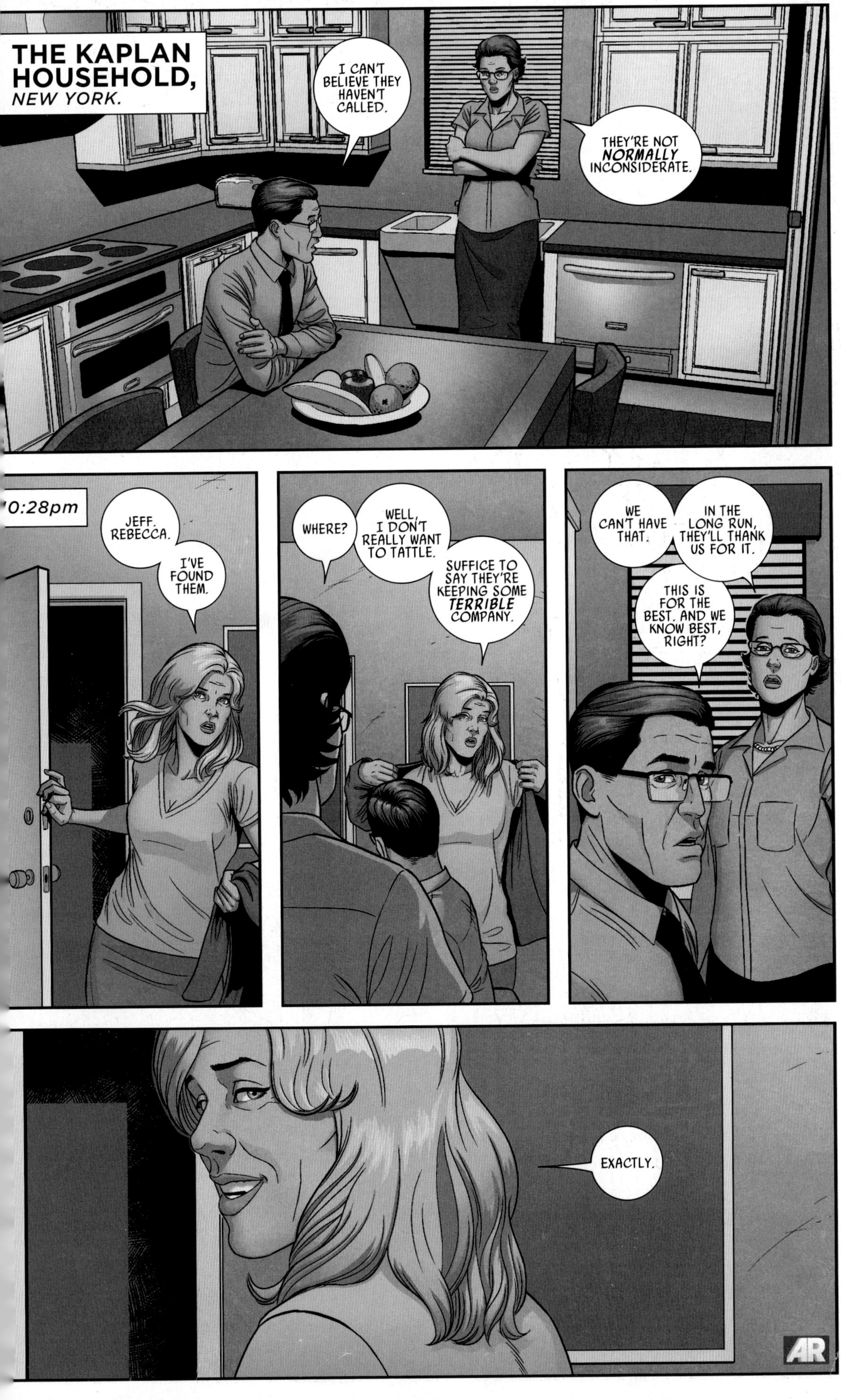
THE KAPLAN HOUSEHOLD, NEW YORK.
I CAN'T BELIEVE THEY HAVEN'T CALLED.
THEY'RE NOT NORMALLY INCONSIDERATE.
10:28pm
JEFF. REBECCA.
I'VE FOUND THEM.
WHERE?
WELL, I DON'T REALLY WANT TO TATTLE.
SUFFICE TO SAY THEY'RE KEEPING SOME TERRIBLE COMPANY.
WE CAN'T HAVE THAT.
IN THE LONG RUN, THEY'LL THANK US FOR IT.
THIS IS FOR THE BEST. AND WE KNOW BEST, RIGHT?
EXACTLY.

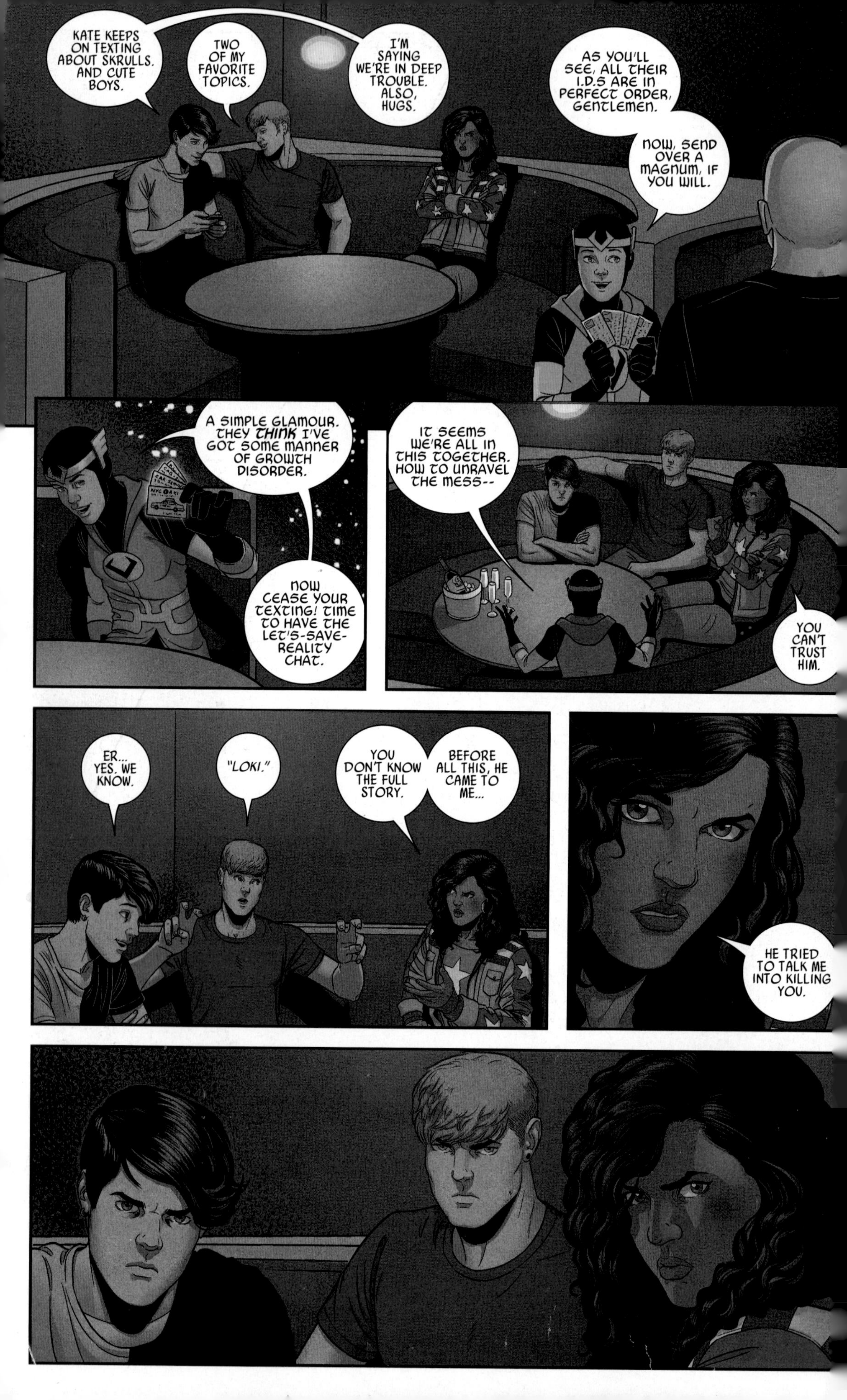
KATE KEEPS ON TEXTING ABOUT SKRULLS. AND CUTE BOYS.
TWO OF MY FAVORITE TOPICS.
I'M SAYING WE'RE IN DEEP TROUBLE. ALSO, HUGS.
AS YOU'LL SEE, ALL THEIR I.D.S ARE IN PERFECT ORDER, GENTLEMEN.
NOW, SEND OVER A MAGNUM, IF YOU WILL.
A SIMPLE GLAMOUR. THEY THINK I'VE GOT SOME MANNER OF GROWTH DISORDER.
NOW CEASE YOUR TEXTING! TIME TO HAVE THE LET'S-SAVE-REALITY CHAT.
IT SEEMS WE'RE ALL IN THIS TOGETHER. HOW TO UNRAVEL THE MESS--
YOU CAN'T TRUST HIM.
ER... YES. WE KNOW.
"LOKI."
YOU DON'T KNOW THE FULL STORY.
BEFORE ALL THIS, HE CAME TO ME...
HE TRIED TO TALK ME INTO KILLING YOU.

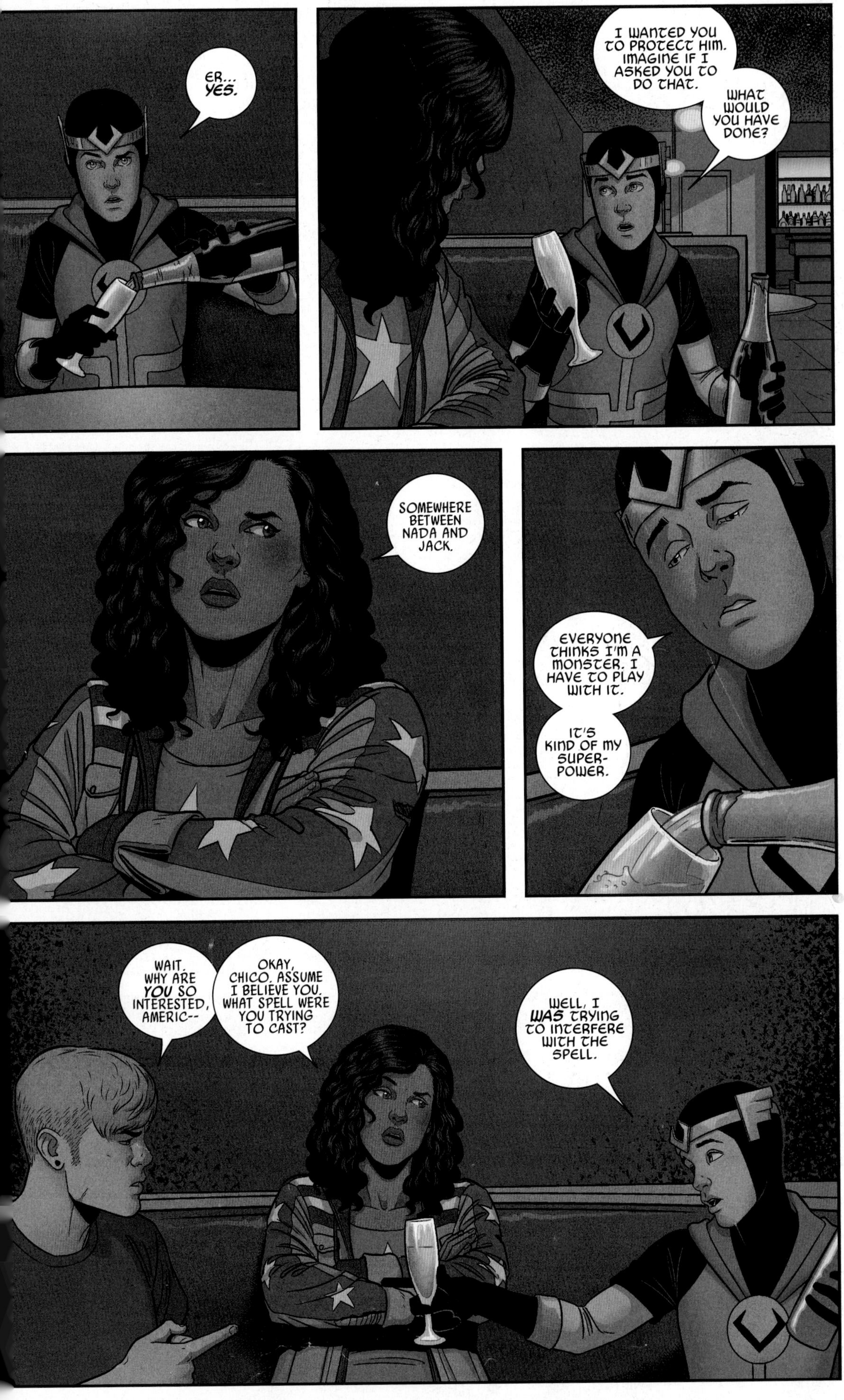
ER... YES.
I WANTED YOU TO PROTECT HIM. IMAGINE IF I ASKED YOU TO DO THAT.
WHAT WOULD YOU HAVE DONE?
SOMEWHERE BETWEEN NADA AND JACK.
EVERYONE THINKS I'M A MONSTER. I HAVE TO PLAY WITH IT.
IT'S KIND OF MY SUPER-POWER.
WAIT. WHY ARE YOU SO INTERESTED, AMERIC--
OKAY, CHICO. ASSUME I BELIEVE YOU. WHAT SPELL WERE YOU TRYING TO CAST?
WELL, I WAS TRYING TO INTERFERE WITH THE SPELL.

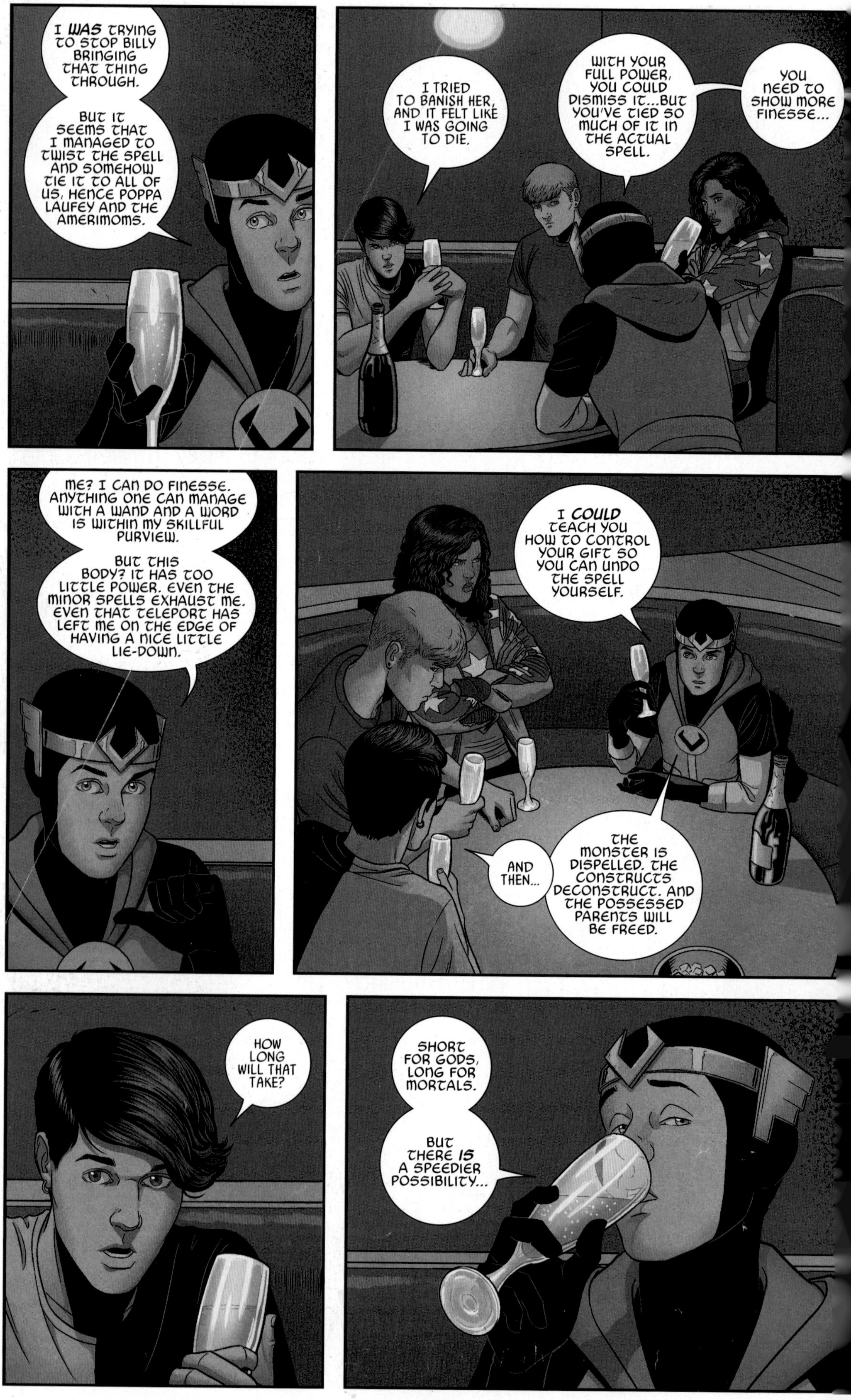
I WAS TRYING TO STOP BILLY BRINGING THAT THING THROUGH.
BUT IT SEEMS THAT I MANAGED TO TWIST THE SPELL AND SOMEHOW TIE IT TO ALL OF US, HENCE POPPA LAUFEY AND THE AMERIMOMS.
I TRIED TO BANISH HER, AND IT FELT LIKE I WAS GOING TO DIE.
WITH YOUR FULL POWER, YOU COULD DISMISS IT...BUT YOU'VE TIED SO MUCH OF IT IN THE ACTUAL SPELL.
YOU NEED TO SHOW MORE FINESSE...
ME? I CAN DO FINESSE. ANYTHING ONE CAN MANAGE WITH A WAND AND A WORD IS WITHIN MY SKILLFUL PURVIEW.
BUT THIS BODY? IT HAS TOO LITTLE POWER. EVEN THE MINOR SPELLS EXHAUST ME. EVEN THAT TELEPORT HAS LEFT ME ON THE EDGE OF HAVING A NICE LITTLE LIE-DOWN.
I COULD TEACH YOU HOW TO CONTROL YOUR GIFT SO YOU CAN UNDO THE SPELL YOURSELF.
AND THEN...
THE MONSTER IS DISPELLED. THE CONSTRUCTS DECONSTRUCT. AND THE POSSESSED PARENTS WILL BE FREED.
HOW LONG WILL THAT TAKE?
SHORT FOR GODS, LONG FOR MORTALS.
BUT THERE IS A SPEEDIER POSSIBILITY...

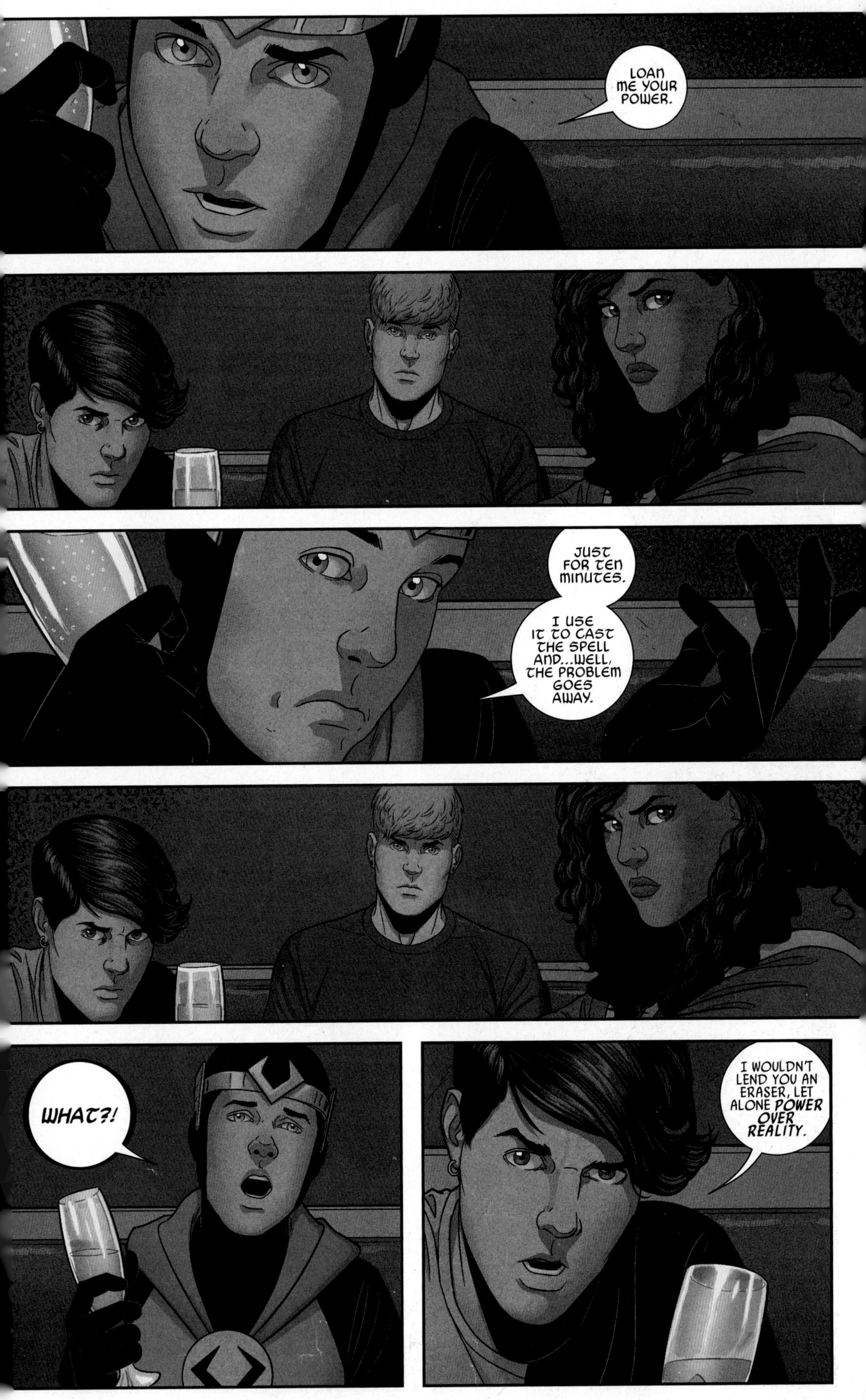
LOAN ME YOUR POWER.
JUST FOR TEN MINUTES.
I USE IT TO CAST THE SPELL AND...WELL, THE PROBLEM GOES AWAY.
WHAT?!
I WOULDN'T LEND YOU AN ERASER, LET ALONE POWER OVER REALITY.

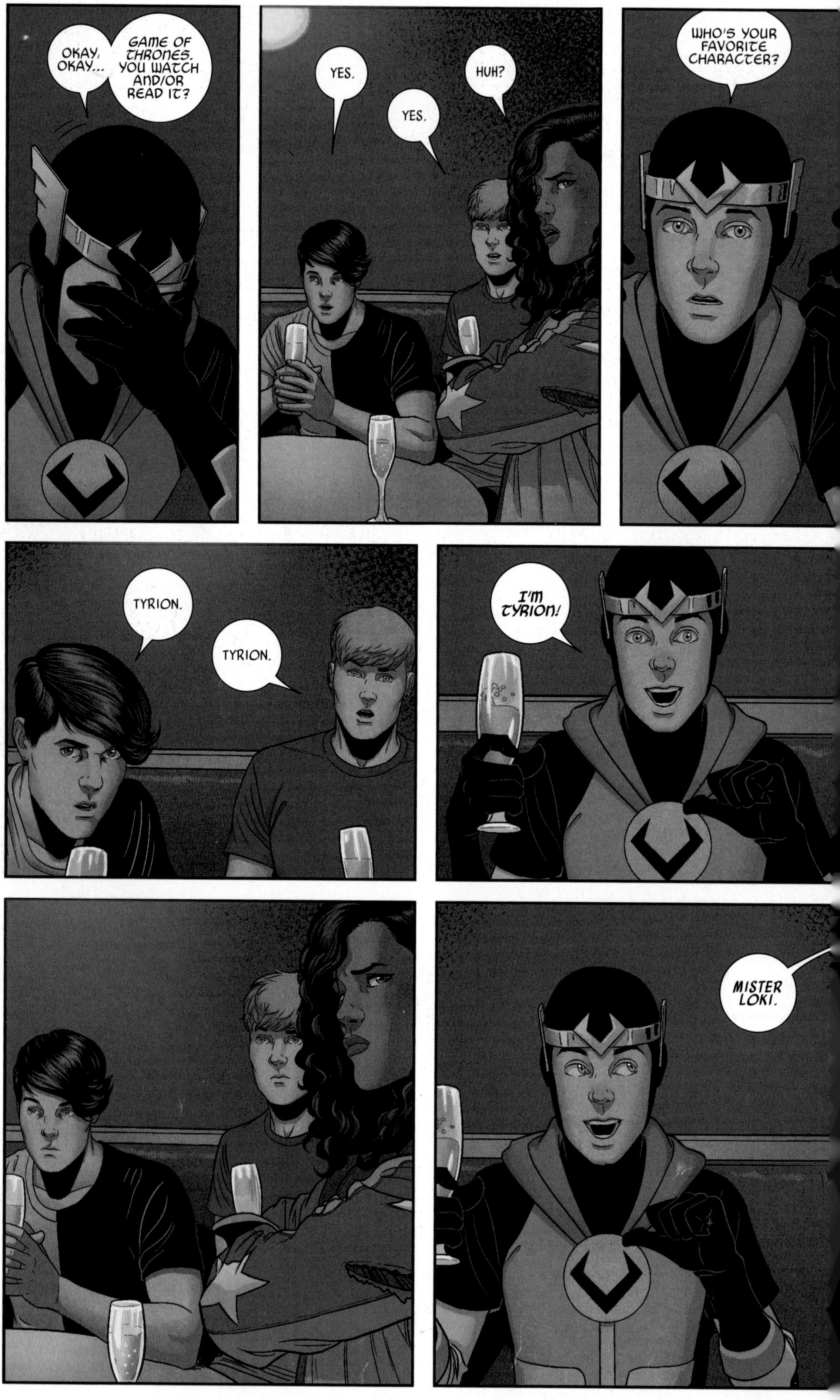

OKAY, OKAY...
GAME OF THRONES. YOU WATCH AND/OR READ IT?
YES.
YES.
HUH?
WHO'S YOUR FAVORITE CHARACTER?
TYRION.
TYRION.
I'M TYRION!
MISTER LOKI.

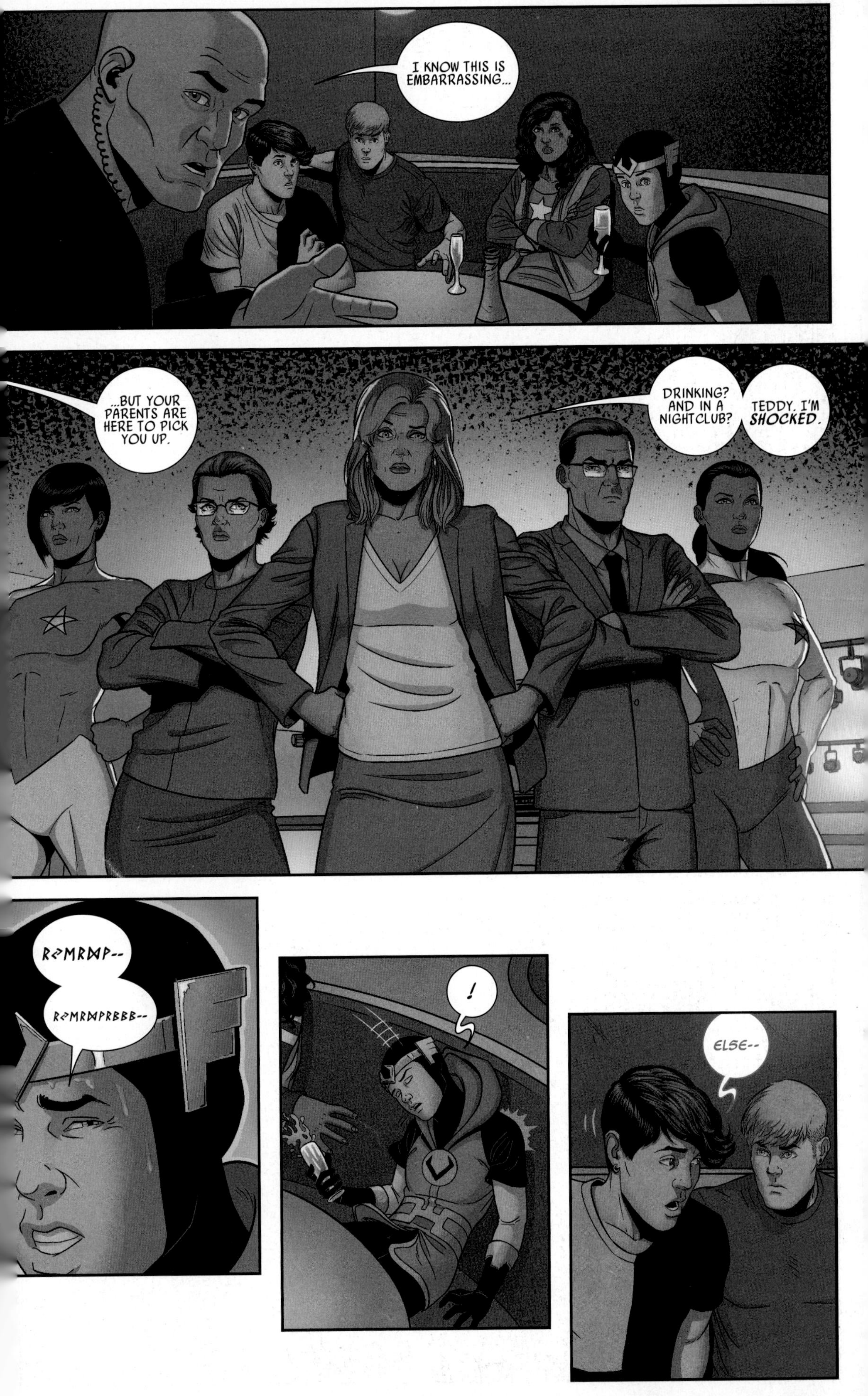
I KNOW THIS IS EMBARRASSING...
...BUT YOUR PARENTS ARE HERE TO PICK YOU UP.
DRINKING? AND IN A NIGHTCLUB?
TEDDY. I'M SHOCKED.
!
ELSE--

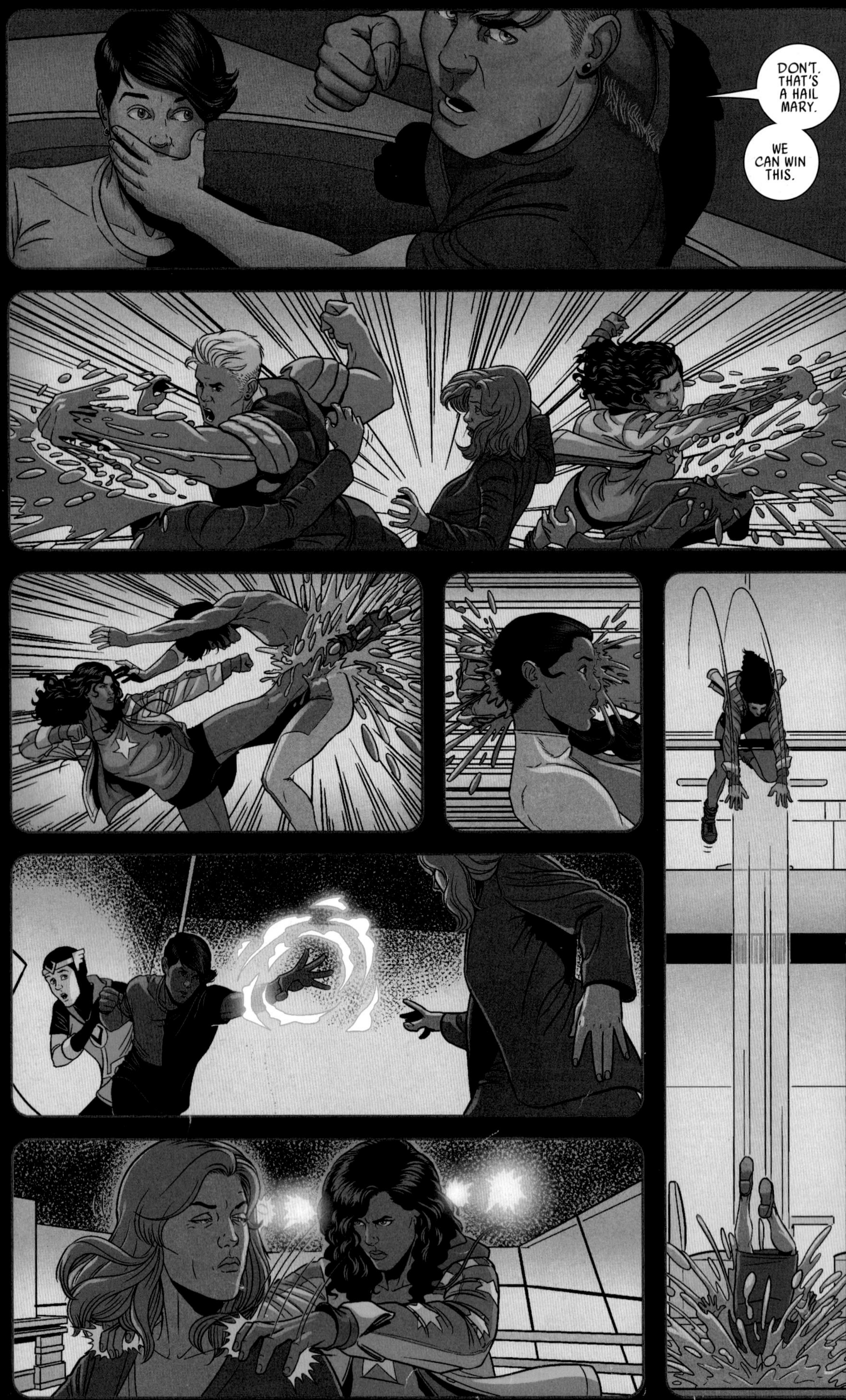
DON'T. THAT'S A HAIL MARY.
WE CAN WIN THIS.

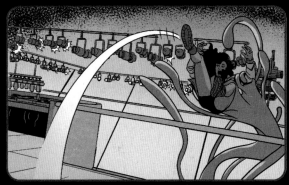

BILLY.
WAKE UP,
BILLY.

FIGHT'S
OVER.

WE ASKED
THE PARENTS
TO STAY AND
EVERYONE ELSE
TO LEAVE.

THEY ALL
DID. THEY ALL
UNDERSTOOD.

GROWN-UPS
ALWAYS
DO.

AND THEN
WE HAD A
LITTLE CHAT
ABOUT YOUR
FUTURE.

AND
WONDERFUL
NEWS!

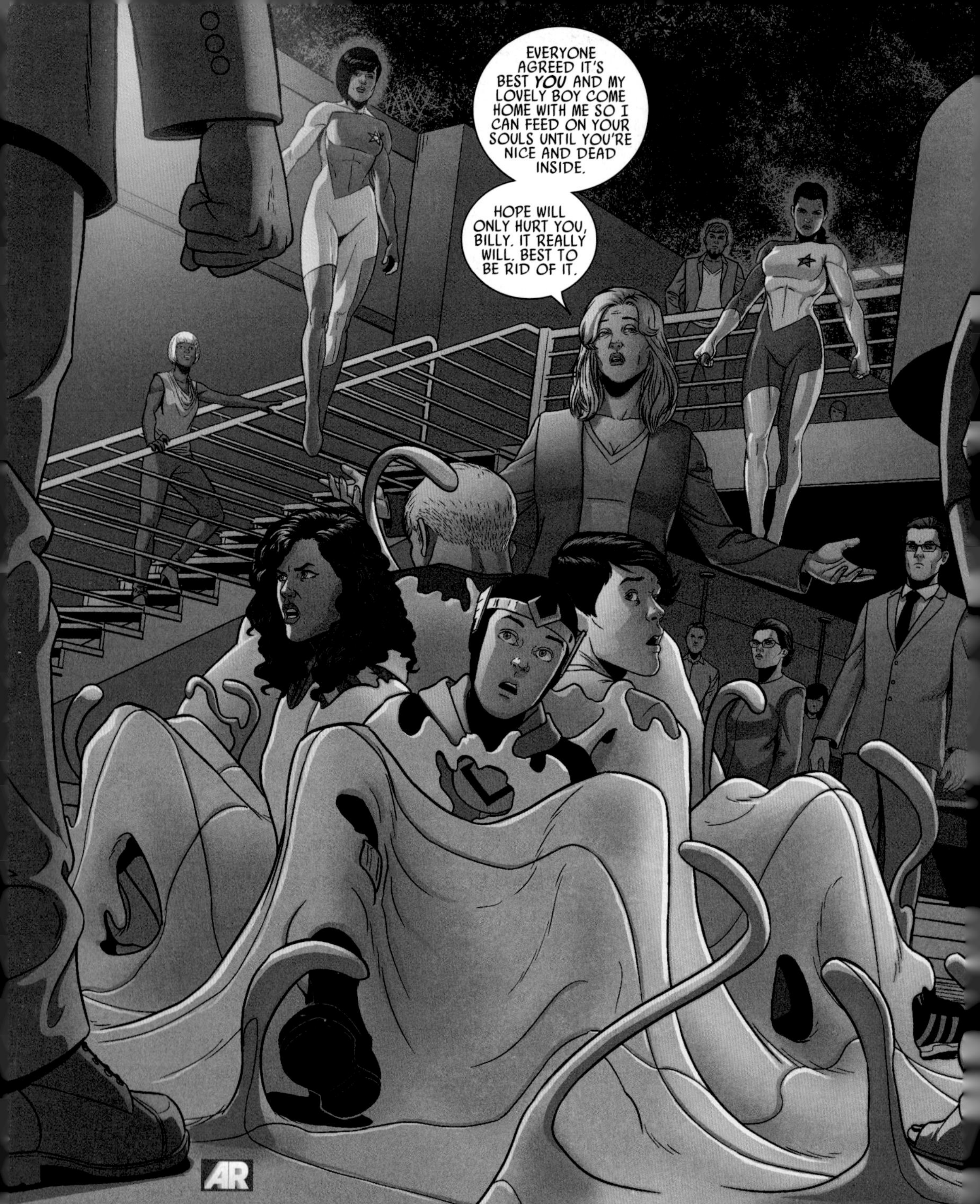
EVERYONE AGREED IT'S BEST *YOU* AND MY LOVELY BOY COME HOME WITH ME SO I CAN FEED ON YOUR SOULS UNTIL YOU'RE NICE AND DEAD INSIDE.
HOPE WILL ONLY HURT YOU, BILLY. IT REALLY WILL. BEST TO BE RID OF IT.

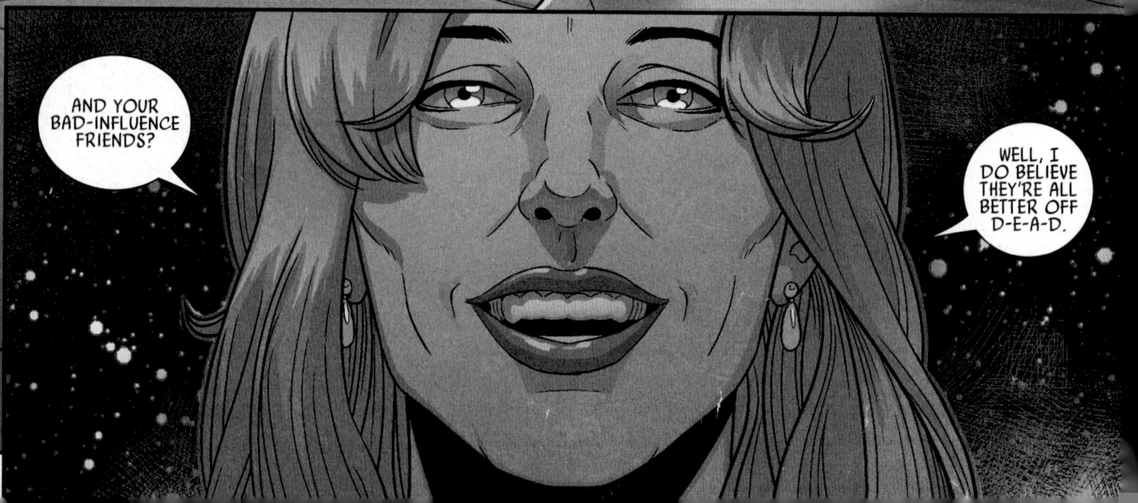
AND YOUR BAD-INFLUENCE FRIENDS?
WELL, I DO BELIEVE THEY'RE ALL BETTER OFF D-E-A-D.

**#2 VARIANT**
BY STEPHANIE HANS

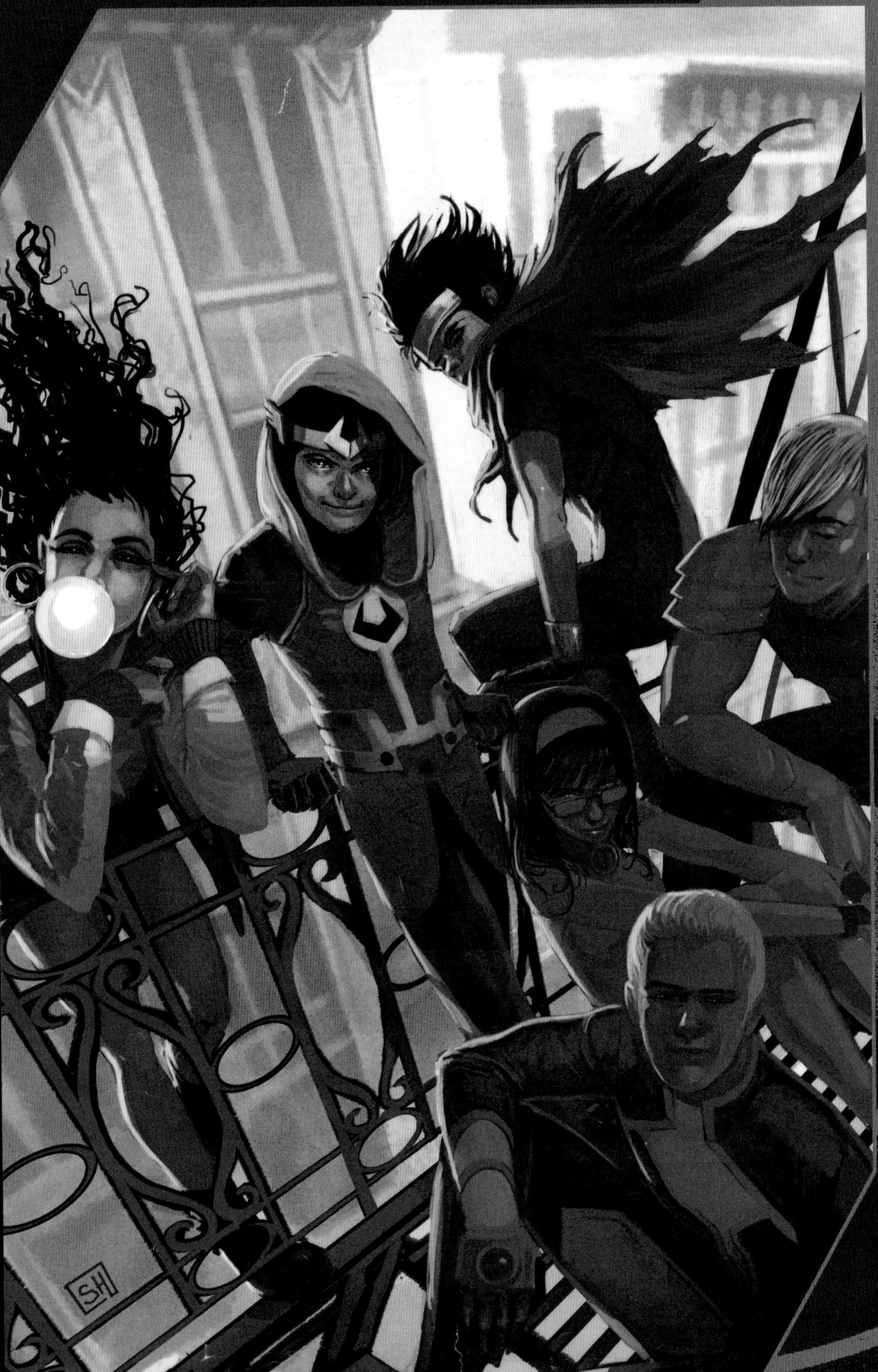
SH

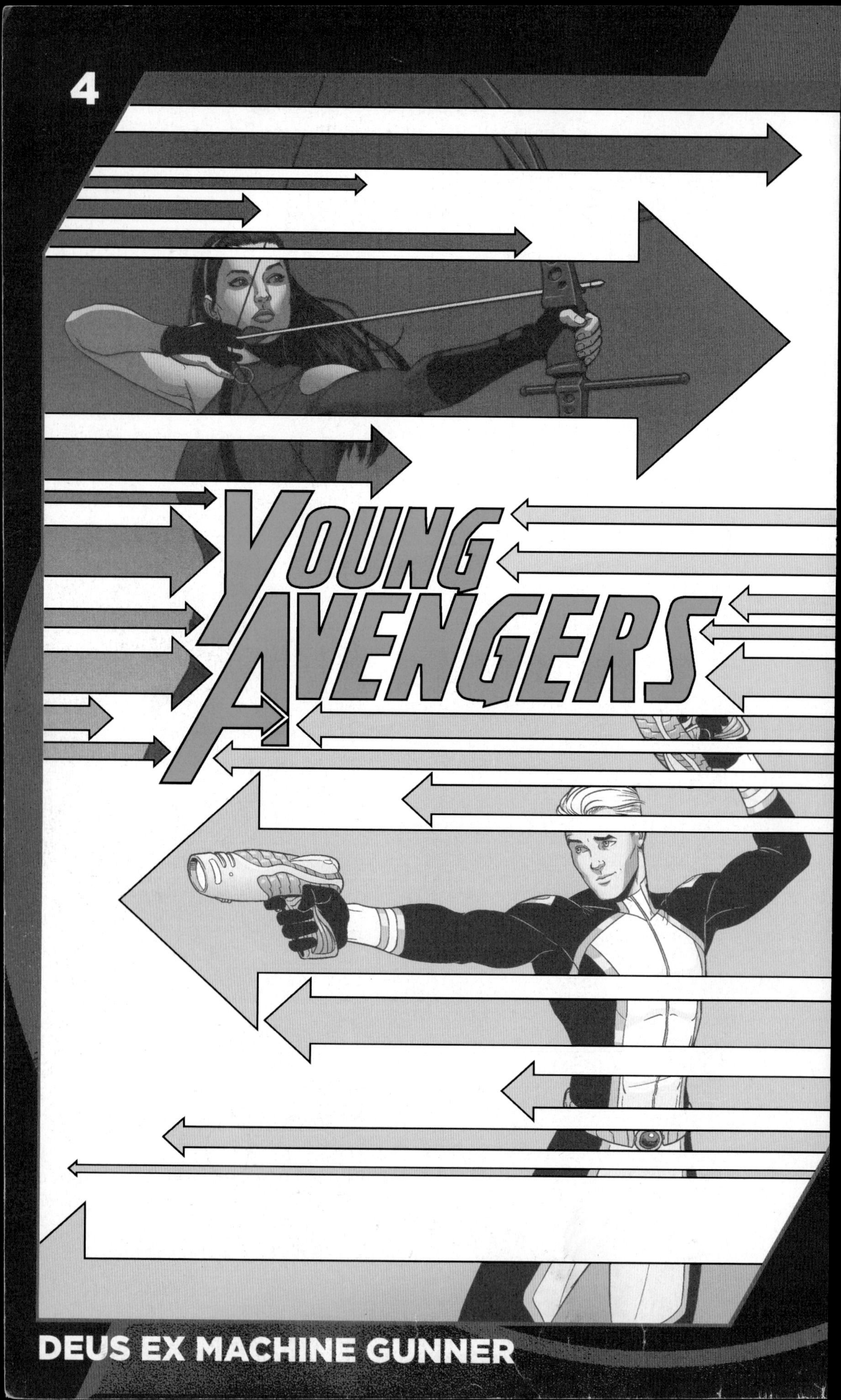
4
YOUNG AVENGERS
DEUS EX MACHINE GUNNER

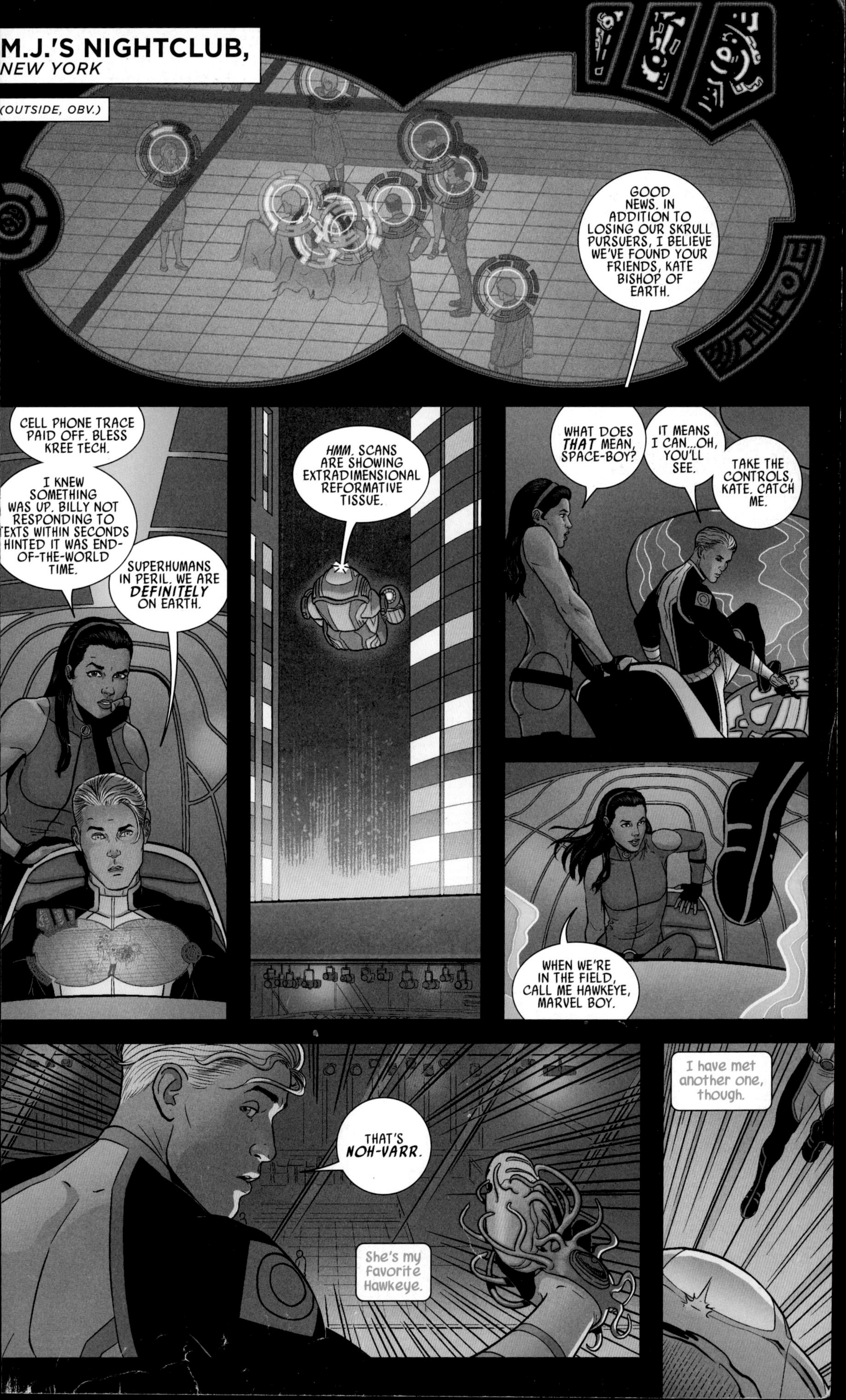
M.J.'S NIGHTCLUB,
NEW YORK
(OUTSIDE, OBV.)
GOOD NEWS. IN ADDITION TO LOSING OUR SKRULL PURSUERS, I BELIEVE WE'VE FOUND YOUR FRIENDS, KATE BISHOP OF EARTH.
CELL PHONE TRACE PAID OFF. BLESS KREE TECH.
I KNEW SOMETHING WAS UP. BILLY NOT RESPONDING TO TEXTS WITHIN SECONDS HINTED IT WAS END-OF-THE-WORLD TIME.
SUPERHUMANS IN PERIL. WE ARE DEFINITELY ON EARTH.
HMM. SCANS ARE SHOWING EXTRADIMENSIONAL REFORMATIVE TISSUE.
WHAT DOES THAT MEAN, SPACE-BOY?
IT MEANS I CAN...OH, YOU'LL SEE.
TAKE THE CONTROLS, KATE. CATCH ME.
WHEN WE'RE IN THE FIELD, CALL ME HAWKEYE, MARVEL BOY.
THAT'S NOH-VARR.
She's my favorite Hawkeye.
I have met another one, though.

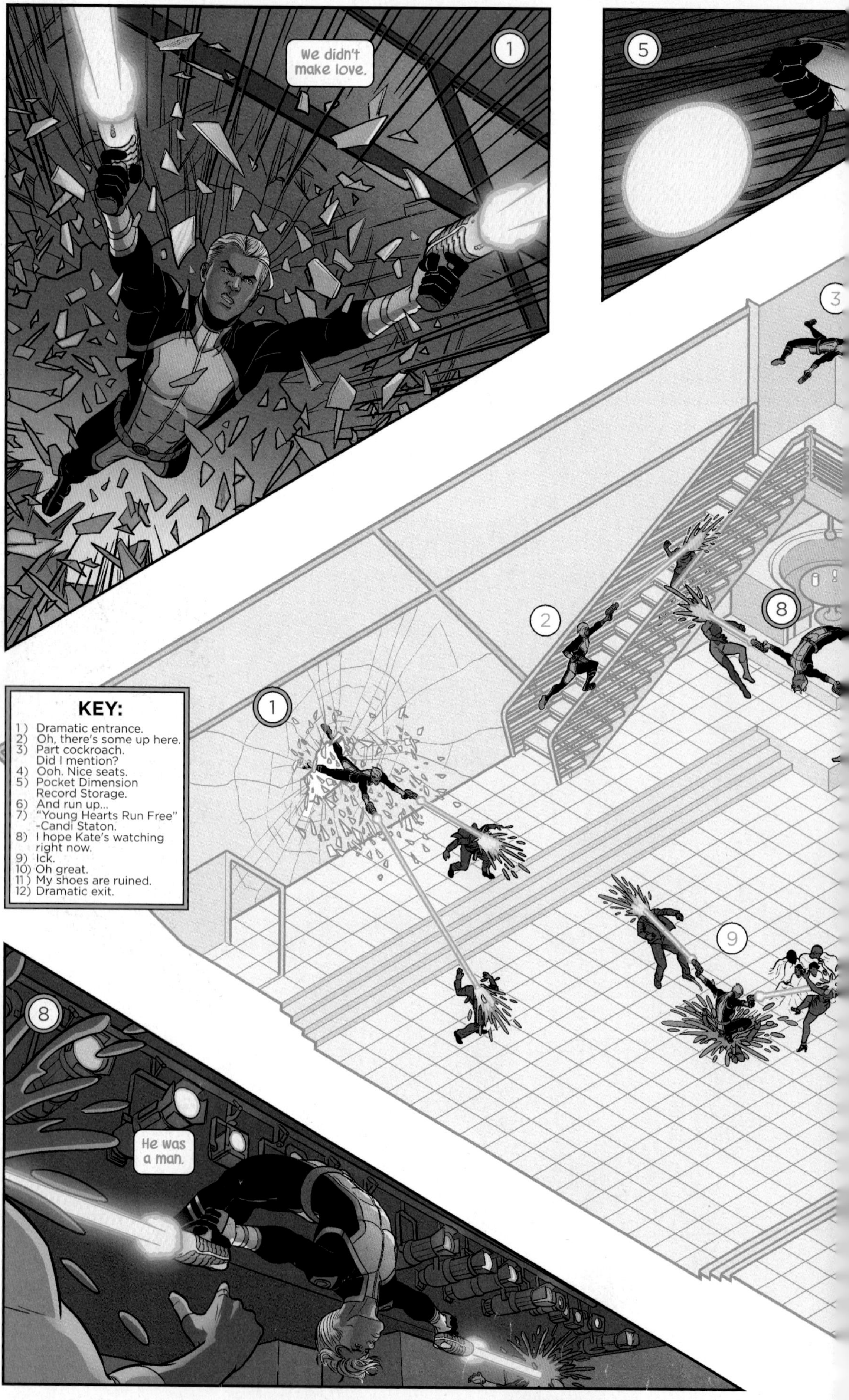

1
We didn't make love.
5
3
2
8
KEY:
1) Dramatic entrance.
2) Oh, there's some up here.
3) Part cockroach. Did I mention?
4) Ooh. Nice seats.
5) Pocket Dimension Record Storage.
6) And run up...
7) "Young Hearts Run Free" -Candi Staton.
8) I hope Kate's watching right now.
9) Ick.
10) Oh great.
11) My shoes are ruined.
12) Dramatic exit.
1
9
8
He was a man.

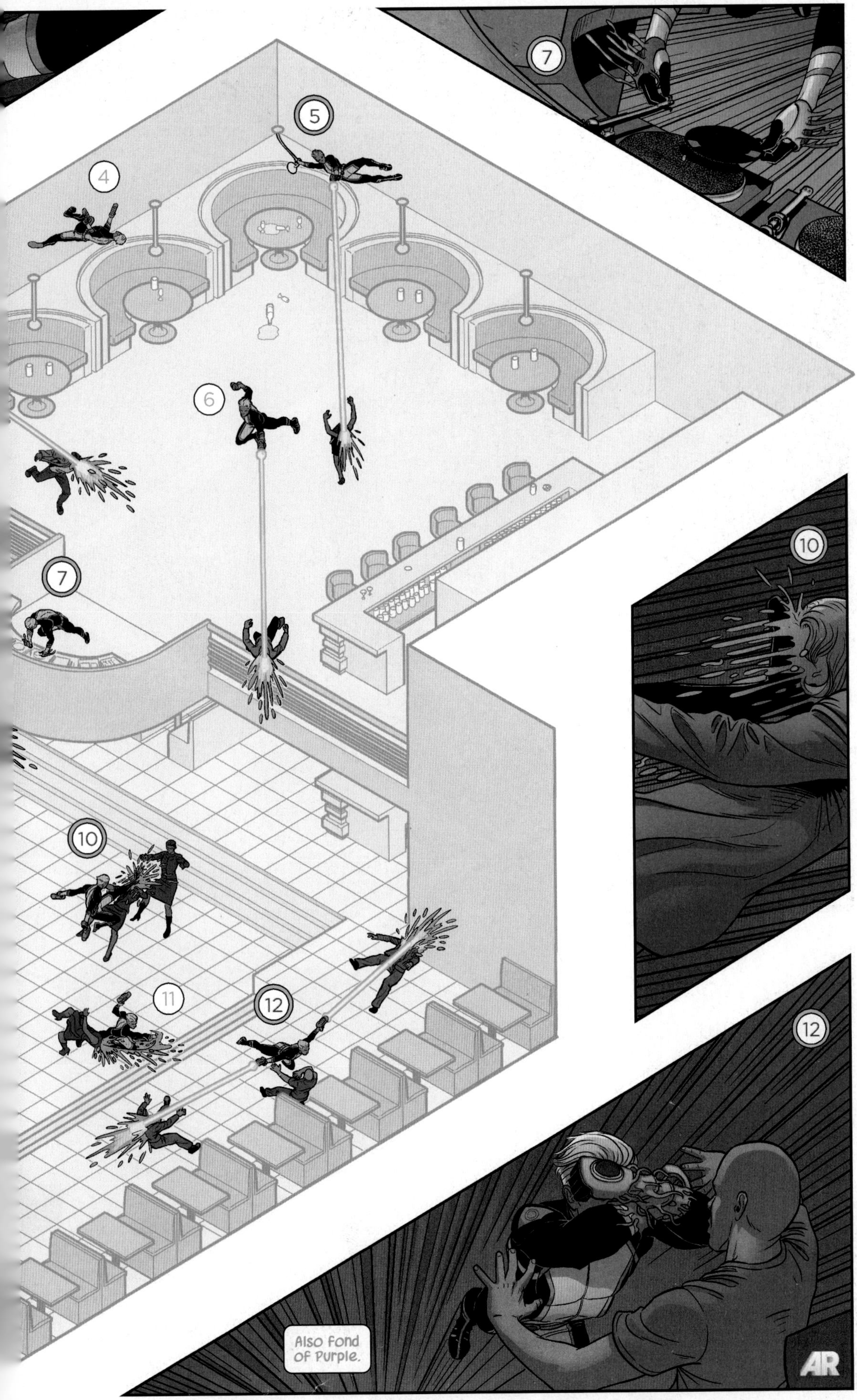

7
5
4
6
7
10
10
11
12
12
Also fond
of purple.
AR

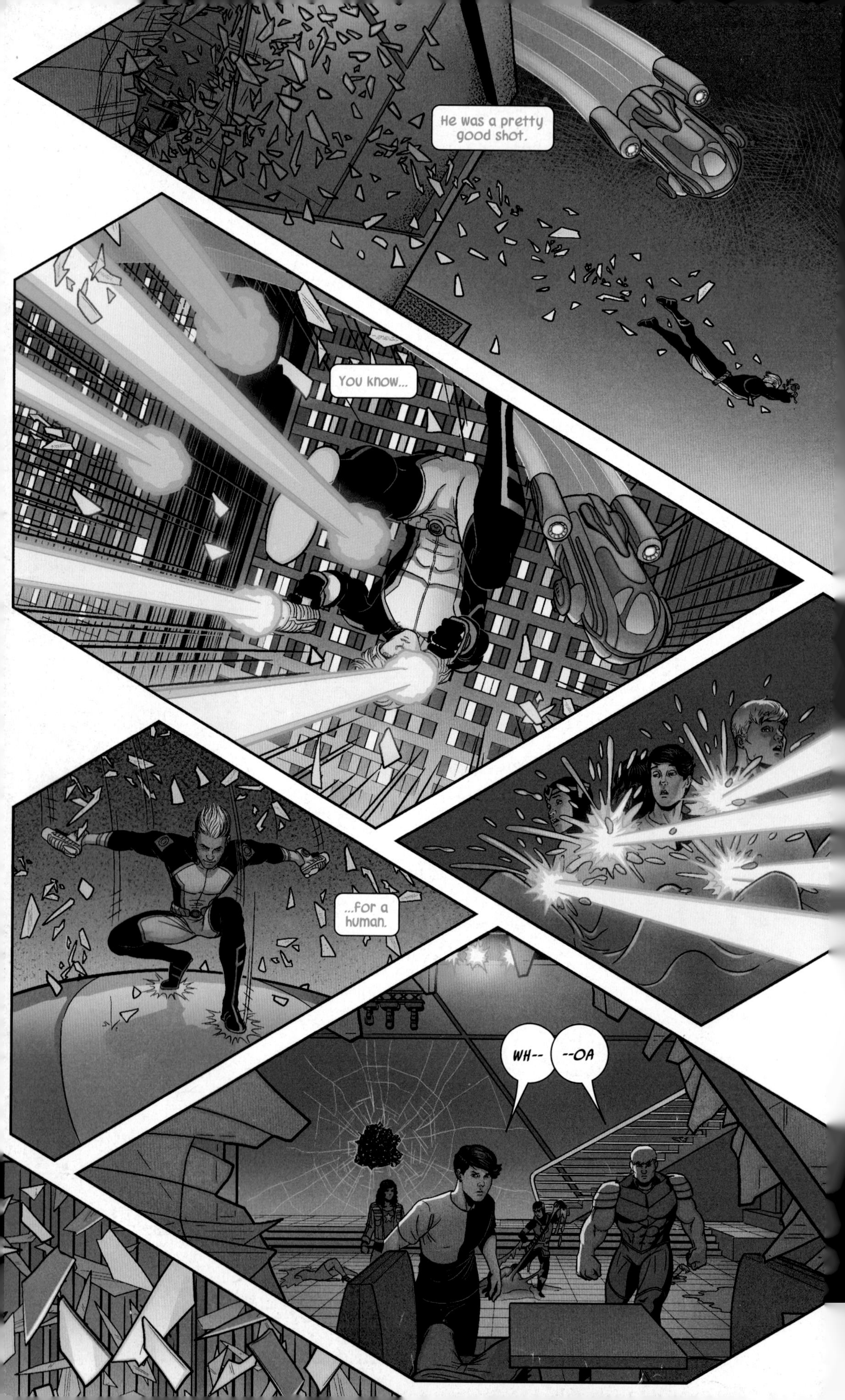
He was a pretty good shot.
You know...
...for a human.
WH--
--OA

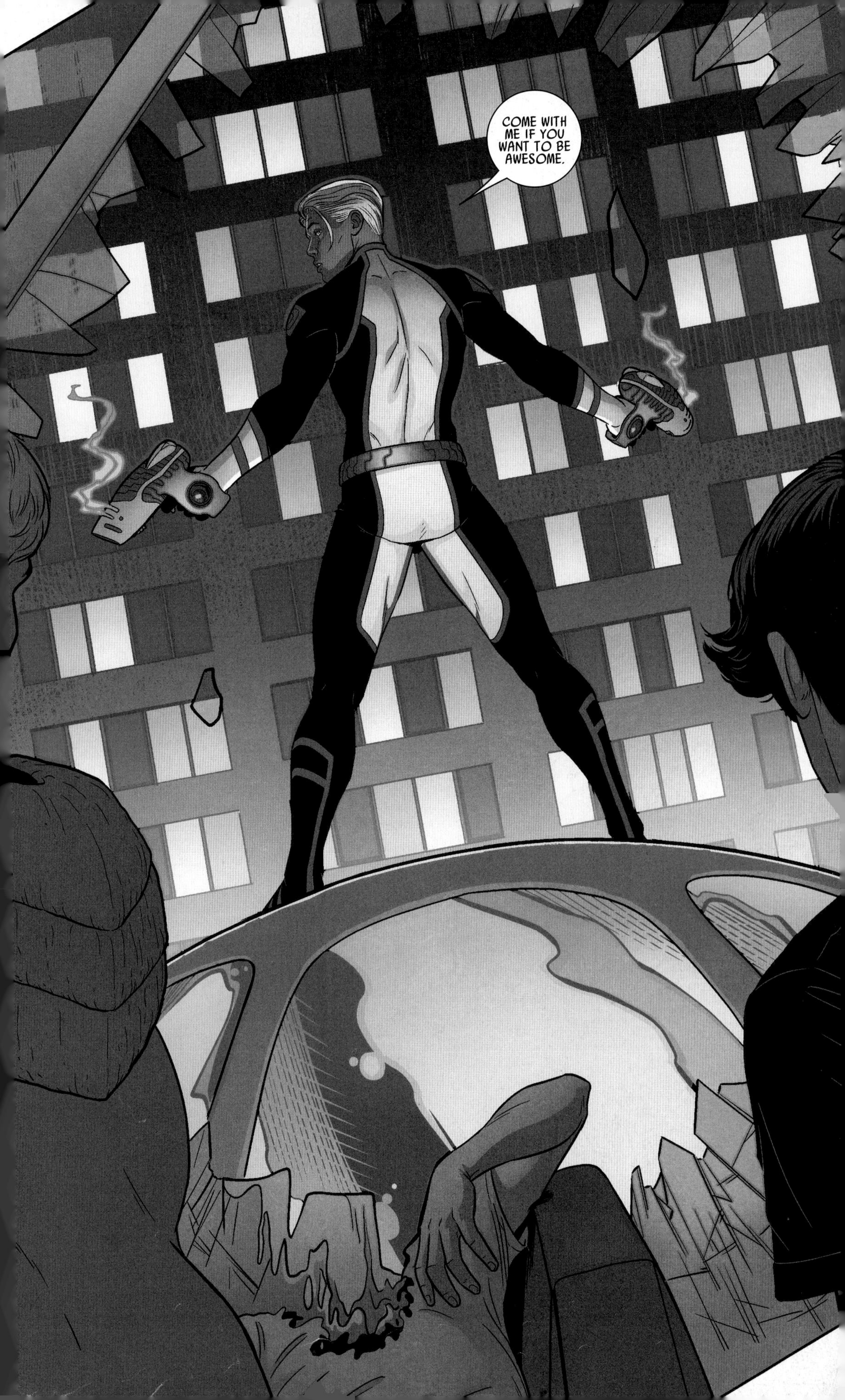
COME WITH ME IF YOU WANT TO BE AWESOME.

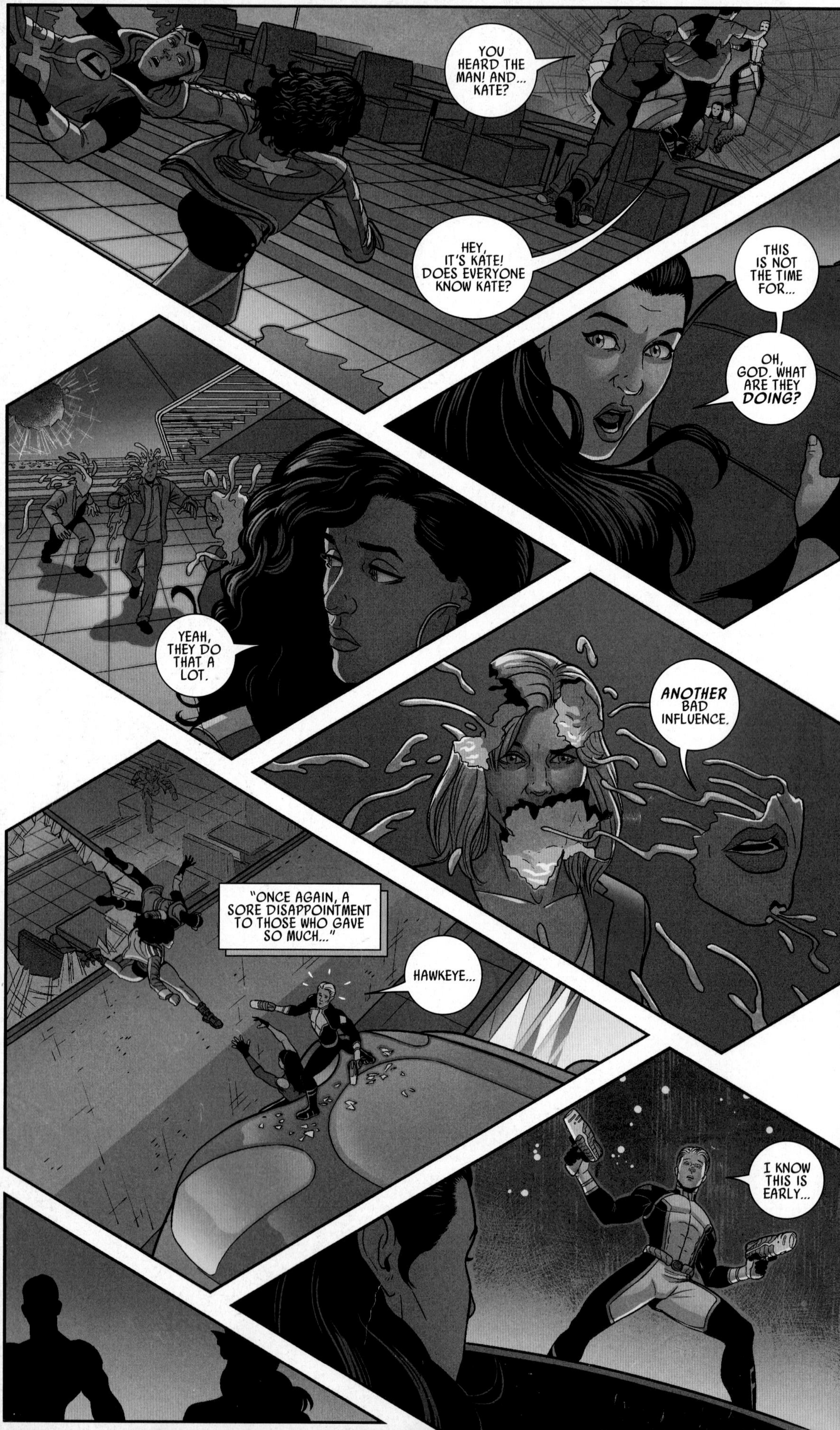
YOU HEARD THE MAN! AND... KATE?
HEY, IT'S KATE! DOES EVERYONE KNOW KATE?
THIS IS NOT THE TIME FOR...
OH, GOD. WHAT ARE THEY DOING?
YEAH, THEY DO THAT A LOT.
ANOTHER BAD INFLUENCE.
"ONCE AGAIN, A SORE DISAPPOINTMENT TO THOSE WHO GAVE SO MUCH..."
HAWKEYE...
I KNOW THIS IS EARLY...

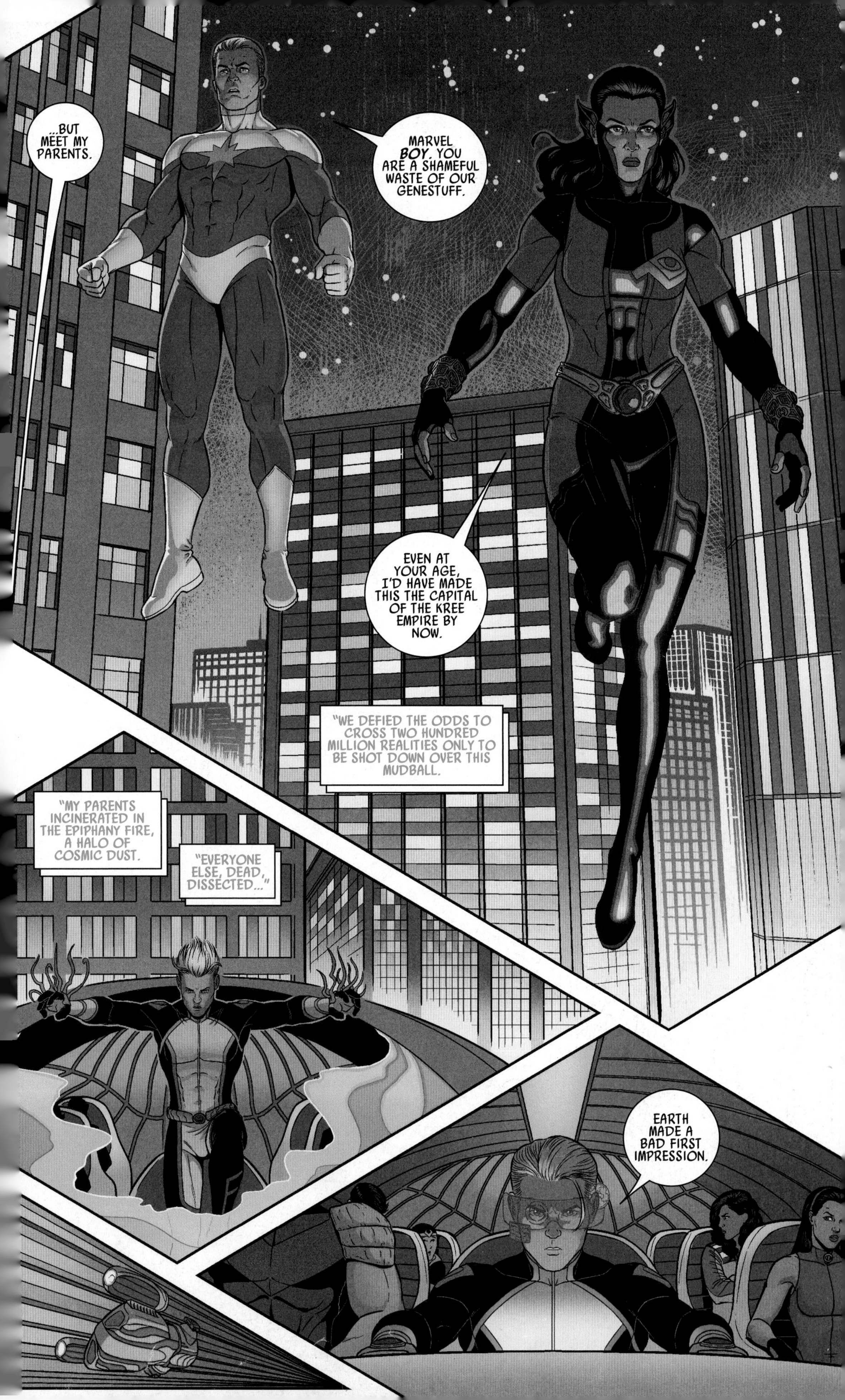

...BUT MEET MY PARENTS.
MARVEL BOY. YOU ARE A SHAMEFUL WASTE OF OUR GENESTUFF.
EVEN AT YOUR AGE, I'D HAVE MADE THIS THE CAPITAL OF THE KREE EMPIRE BY NOW.
"WE DEFIED THE ODDS TO CROSS TWO HUNDRED MILLION REALITIES ONLY TO BE SHOT DOWN OVER THIS MUDBALL.
"MY PARENTS INCINERATED IN THE EPIPHANY FIRE, A HALO OF COSMIC DUST.
"EVERYONE ELSE, DEAD, DISSECTED..."
EARTH MADE A BAD FIRST IMPRESSION.

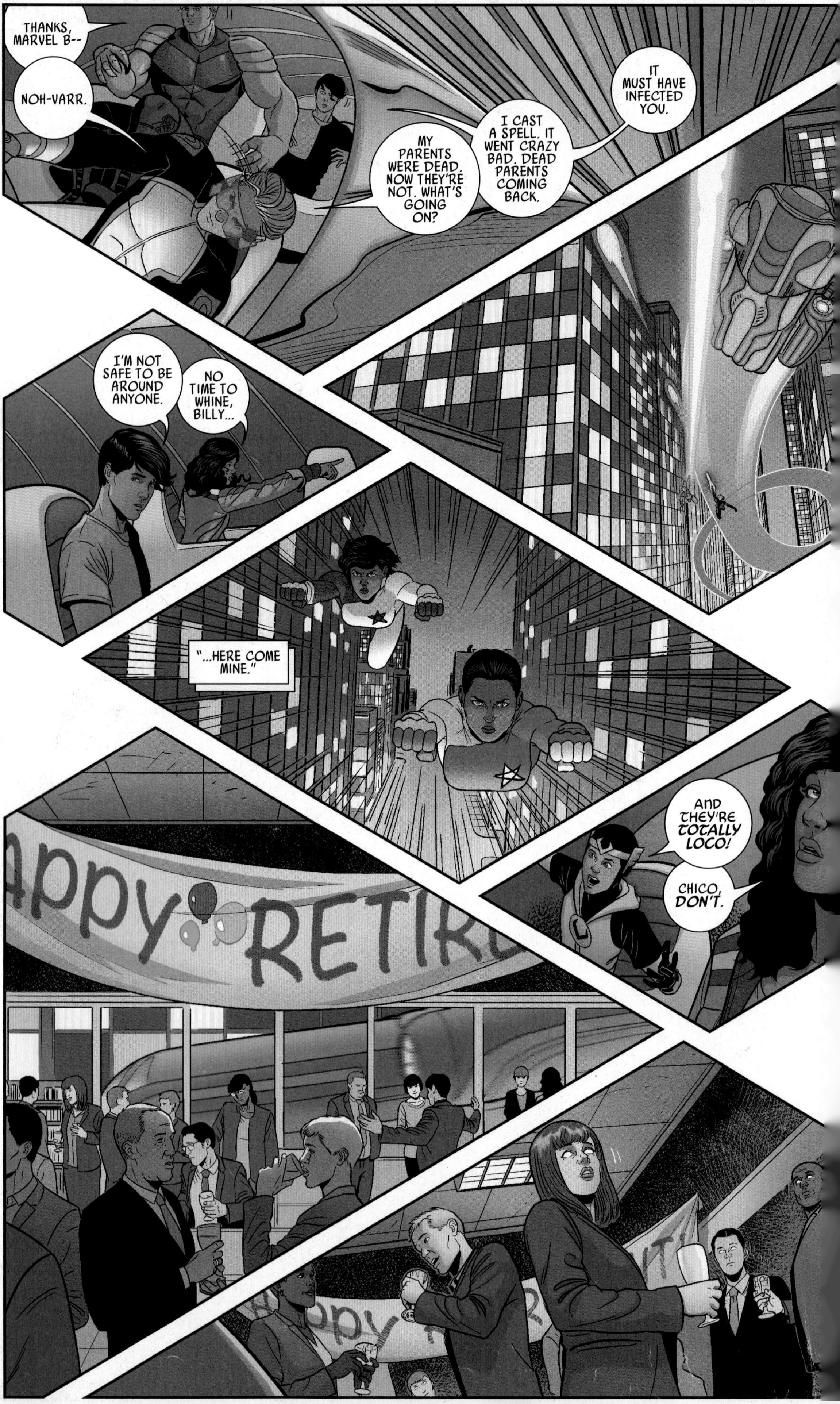
THANKS, MARVEL B--
NOH-VARR.
MY PARENTS WERE DEAD. NOW THEY'RE NOT. WHAT'S GOING ON?
I CAST A SPELL. IT WENT CRAZY BAD. DEAD PARENTS COMING BACK.
IT MUST HAVE INFECTED YOU.
I'M NOT SAFE TO BE AROUND ANYONE.
NO TIME TO WHINE, BILLY...
"...HERE COME MINE."
AND THEY'RE *TOTALLY LOCO!*
CHICO, **DON'T.**
appy RETIR

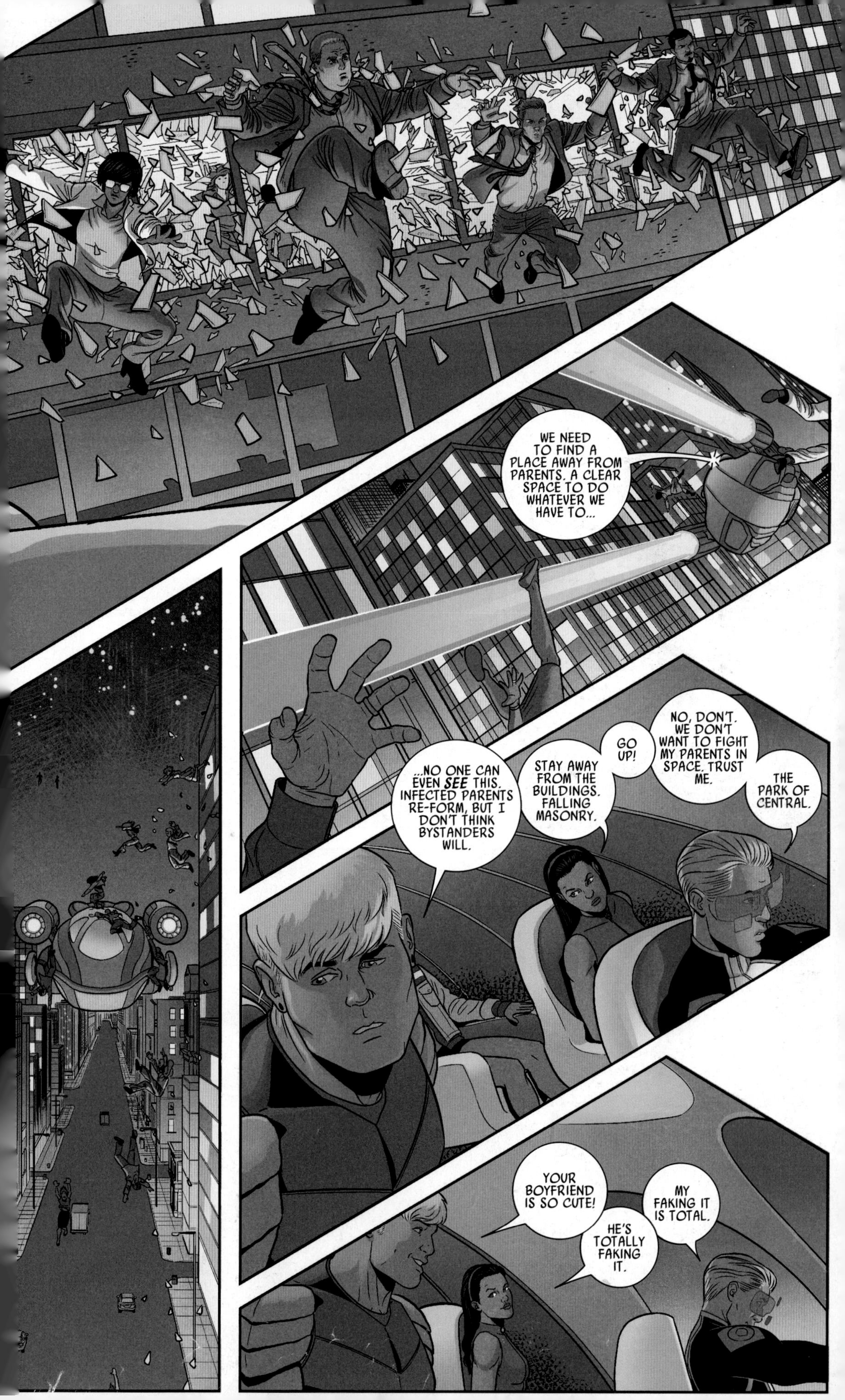
WE NEED TO FIND A PLACE AWAY FROM PARENTS. A CLEAR SPACE TO DO WHATEVER WE HAVE TO...
...NO ONE CAN EVEN SEE THIS. INFECTED PARENTS RE-FORM, BUT I DON'T THINK BYSTANDERS WILL.
STAY AWAY FROM THE BUILDINGS. FALLING MASONRY.
GO UP!
NO, DON'T. WE DON'T WANT TO FIGHT MY PARENTS IN SPACE. TRUST ME.
THE PARK OF CENTRAL.
YOUR BOYFRIEND IS SO CUTE!
HE'S TOTALLY FAKING IT.
MY FAKING IT IS TOTAL.

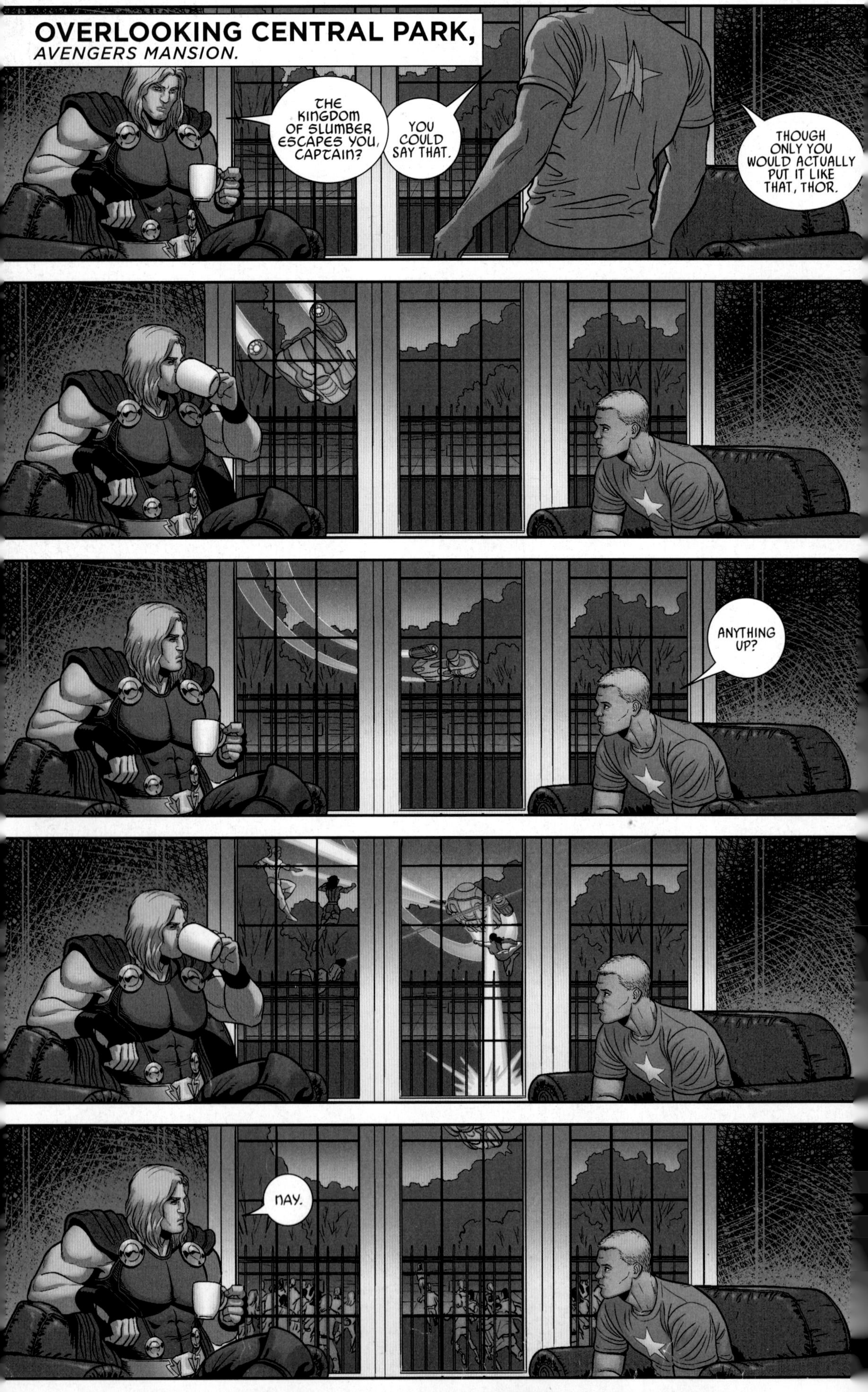
OVERLOOKING CENTRAL PARK,
AVENGERS MANSION.
THE KINGDOM OF SLUMBER ESCAPES YOU, CAPTAIN?
YOU COULD SAY THAT.
THOUGH ONLY YOU WOULD ACTUALLY PUT IT LIKE THAT, THOR.
ANYTHING UP?
NAY.

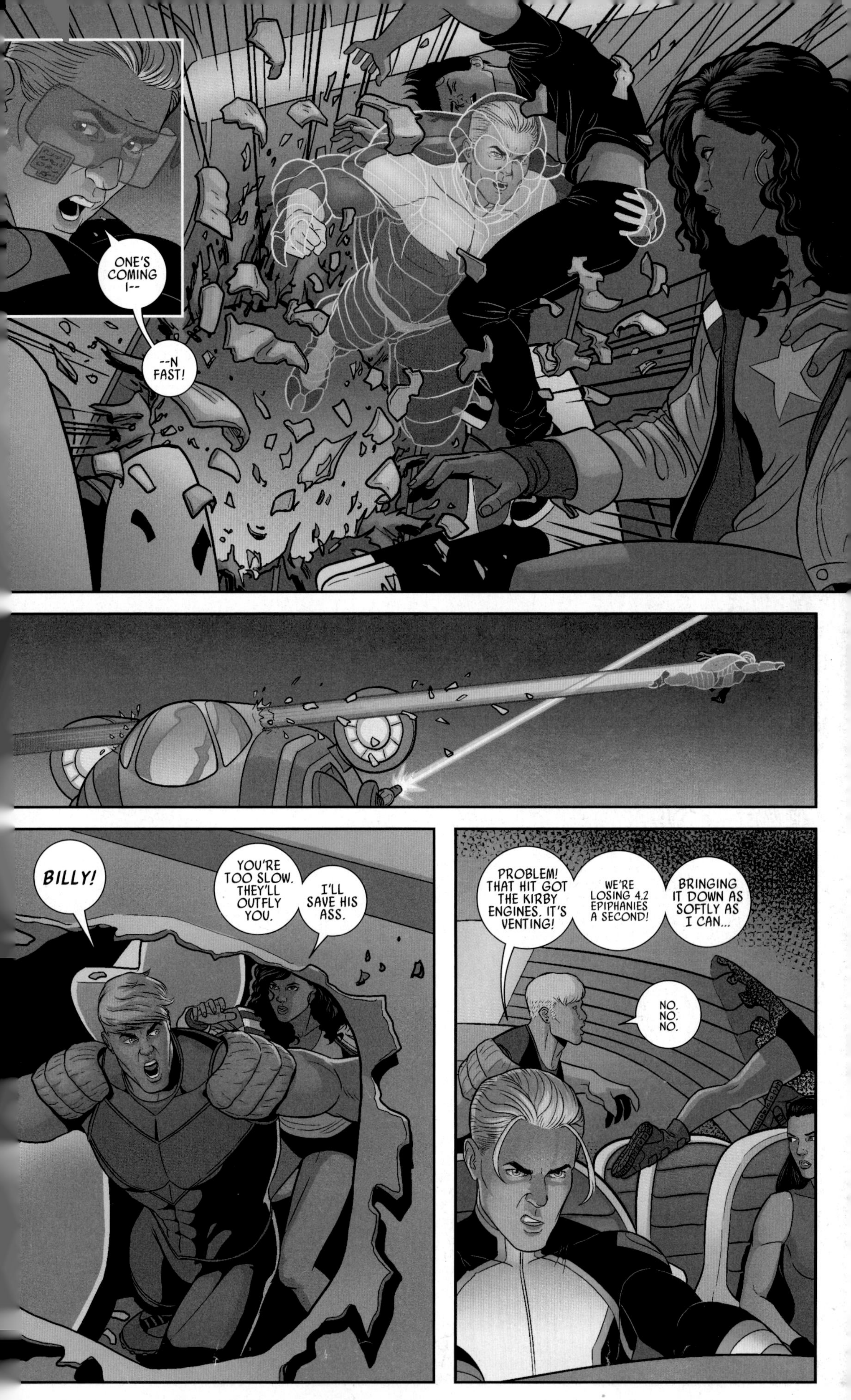
ONE'S COMING I--
--N FAST!
BILLY!
YOU'RE TOO SLOW. THEY'LL OUTFLY YOU.
I'LL SAVE HIS ASS.
PROBLEM! THAT HIT GOT THE KIRBY ENGINES. IT'S VENTING!
WE'RE LOSING 4.2 EPIPHANIES A SECOND!
BRINGING IT DOWN AS SOFTLY AS I CAN...
NO. NO. NO.

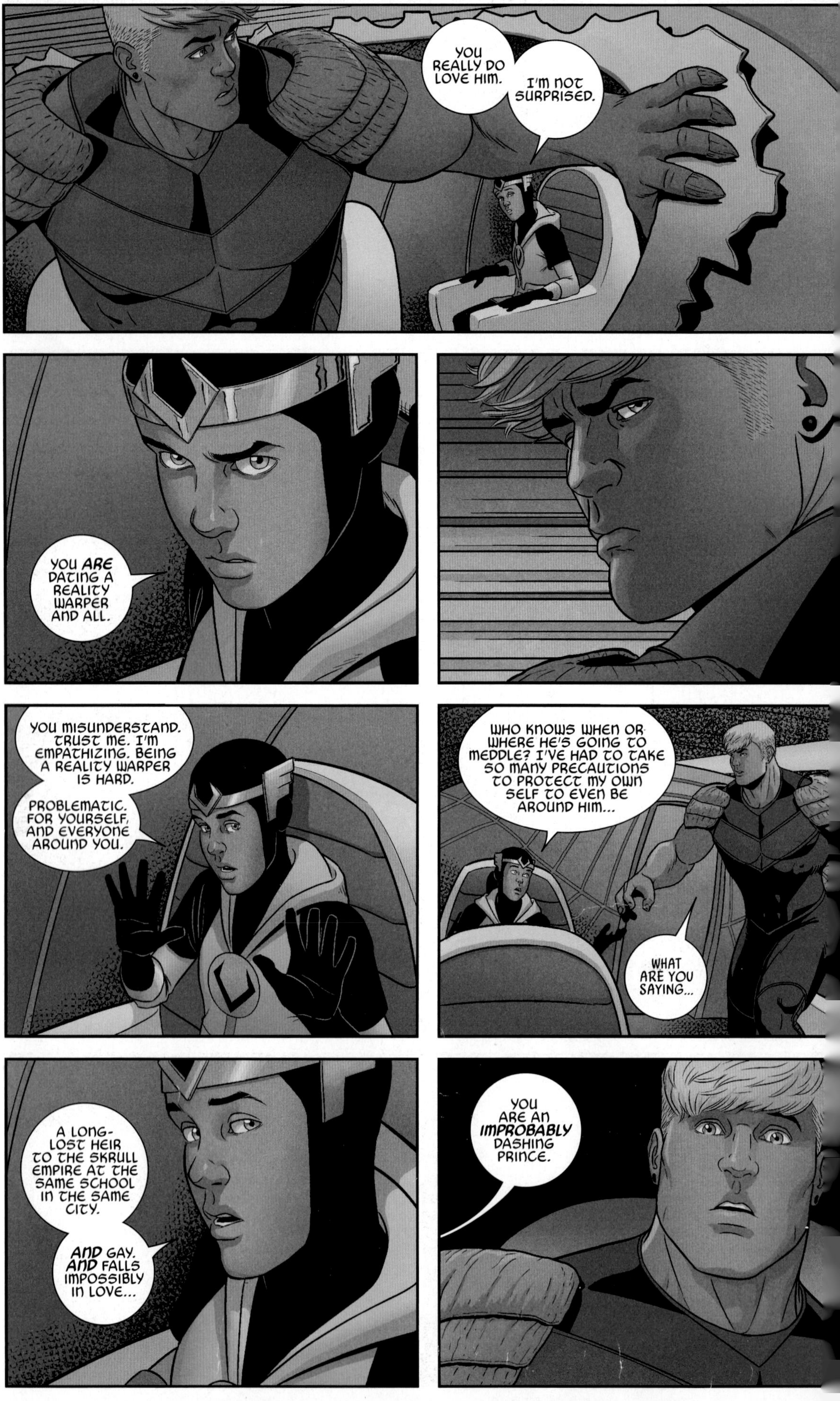
YOU REALLY DO LOVE HIM.
I'M NOT SURPRISED.
YOU *ARE* DATING A REALITY WARPER AND ALL.
YOU MISUNDERSTAND. TRUST ME. I'M EMPATHIZING. BEING A REALITY WARPER IS HARD.
PROBLEMATIC. FOR YOURSELF, AND EVERYONE AROUND YOU.
WHO KNOWS WHEN OR WHERE HE'S GOING TO MEDDLE? I'VE HAD TO TAKE SO MANY PRECAUTIONS TO PROTECT MY OWN SELF TO EVEN BE AROUND HIM...
WHAT ARE YOU SAYING...
A LONG-LOST HEIR TO THE SKRULL EMPIRE AT THE SAME SCHOOL IN THE SAME CITY.
*AND* GAY. *AND* FALLS IMPOSSIBLY IN LOVE...
YOU ARE AN *IMPROBABLY* DASHING PRINCE.

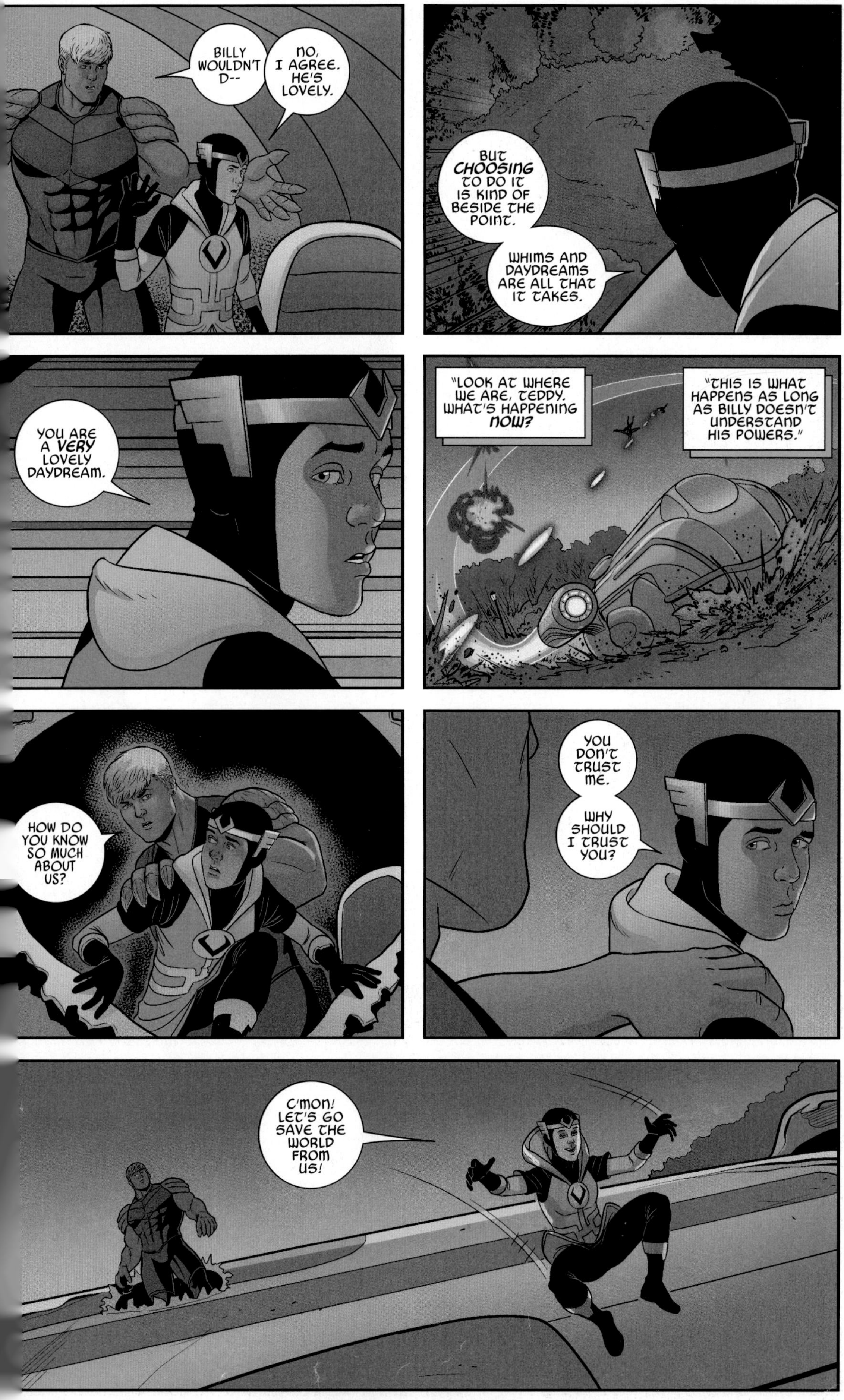
BILLY WOULDN'T D--
NO, I AGREE. HE'S LOVELY.
BUT CHOOSING TO DO IT IS KIND OF BESIDE THE POINT.
WHIMS AND DAYDREAMS ARE ALL THAT IT TAKES.
YOU ARE A VERY LOVELY DAYDREAM.
"LOOK AT WHERE WE ARE, TEDDY. WHAT'S HAPPENING NOW?
"THIS IS WHAT HAPPENS AS LONG AS BILLY DOESN'T UNDERSTAND HIS POWERS."
HOW DO YOU KNOW SO MUCH ABOUT US?
YOU DON'T TRUST ME.
WHY SHOULD I TRUST YOU?
C'MON! LET'S GO SAVE THE WORLD FROM US!

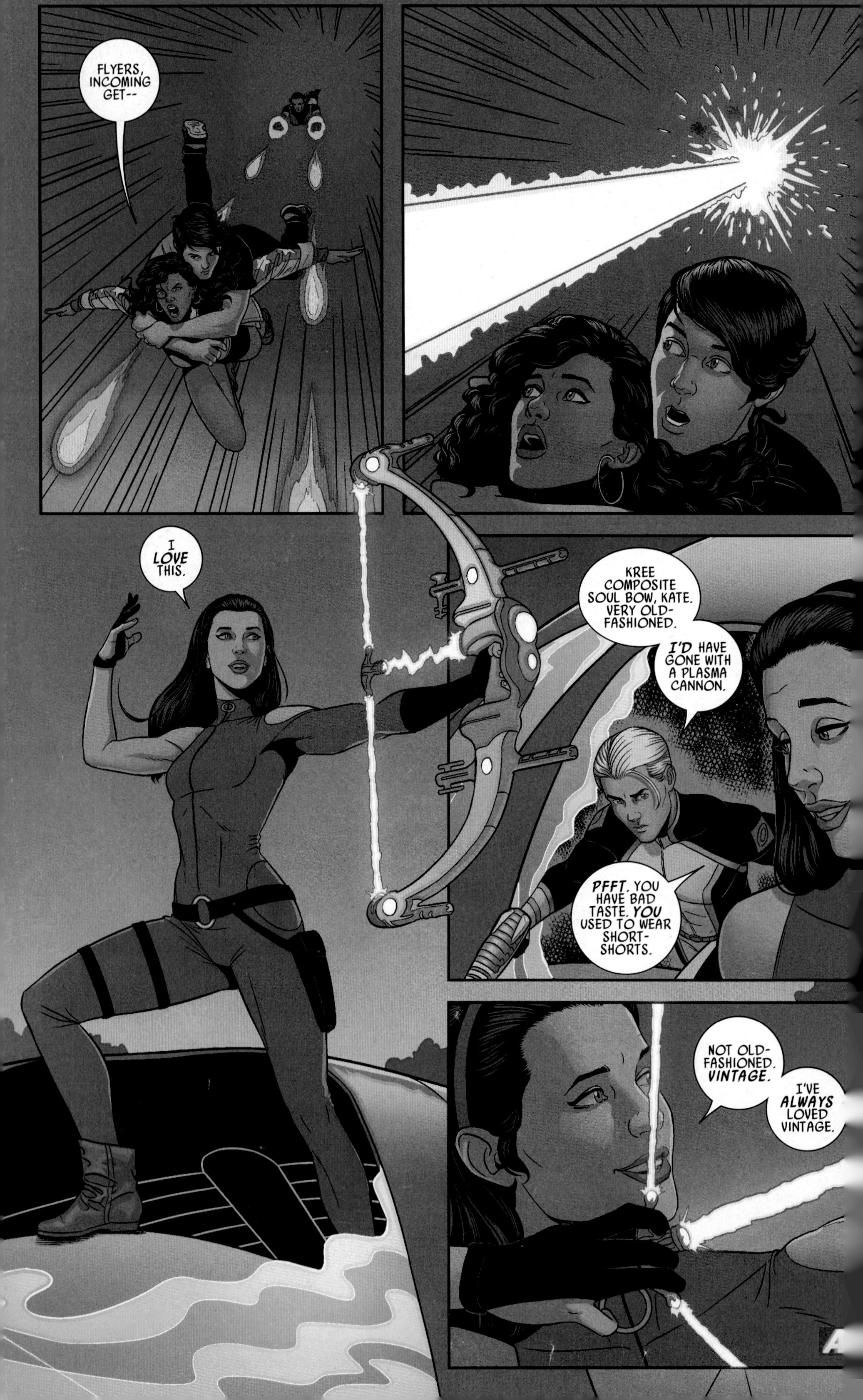
FLYERS, INCOMING GET--
I LOVE THIS.
KREE COMPOSITE SOUL BOW, KATE. VERY OLD-FASHIONED.
I'D HAVE GONE WITH A PLASMA CANNON.
PFFT. YOU HAVE BAD TASTE. YOU USED TO WEAR SHORT-SHORTS.
NOT OLD-FASHIONED. VINTAGE.
I'VE ALWAYS LOVED VINTAGE.

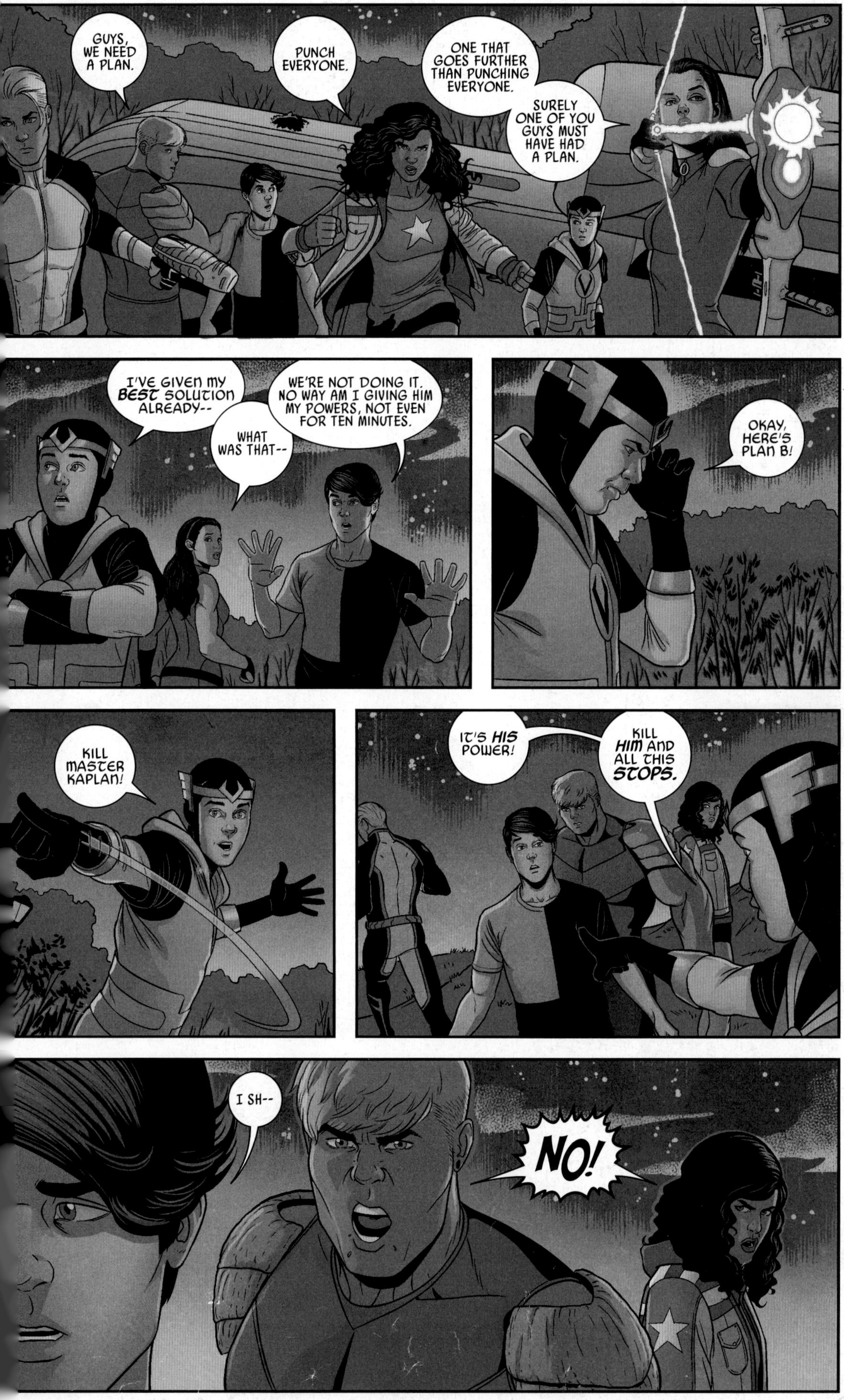
GUYS, WE NEED A PLAN.
PUNCH EVERYONE.
ONE THAT GOES FURTHER THAN PUNCHING EVERYONE.
SURELY ONE OF YOU GUYS MUST HAVE HAD A PLAN.
I'VE GIVEN MY BEST SOLUTION ALREADY--
WHAT WAS THAT--
WE'RE NOT DOING IT. NO WAY AM I GIVING HIM MY POWERS, NOT EVEN FOR TEN MINUTES.
OKAY, HERE'S PLAN B!
KILL MASTER KAPLAN!
IT'S HIS POWER!
KILL HIM AND ALL THIS STOPS.
I SH--
NO!

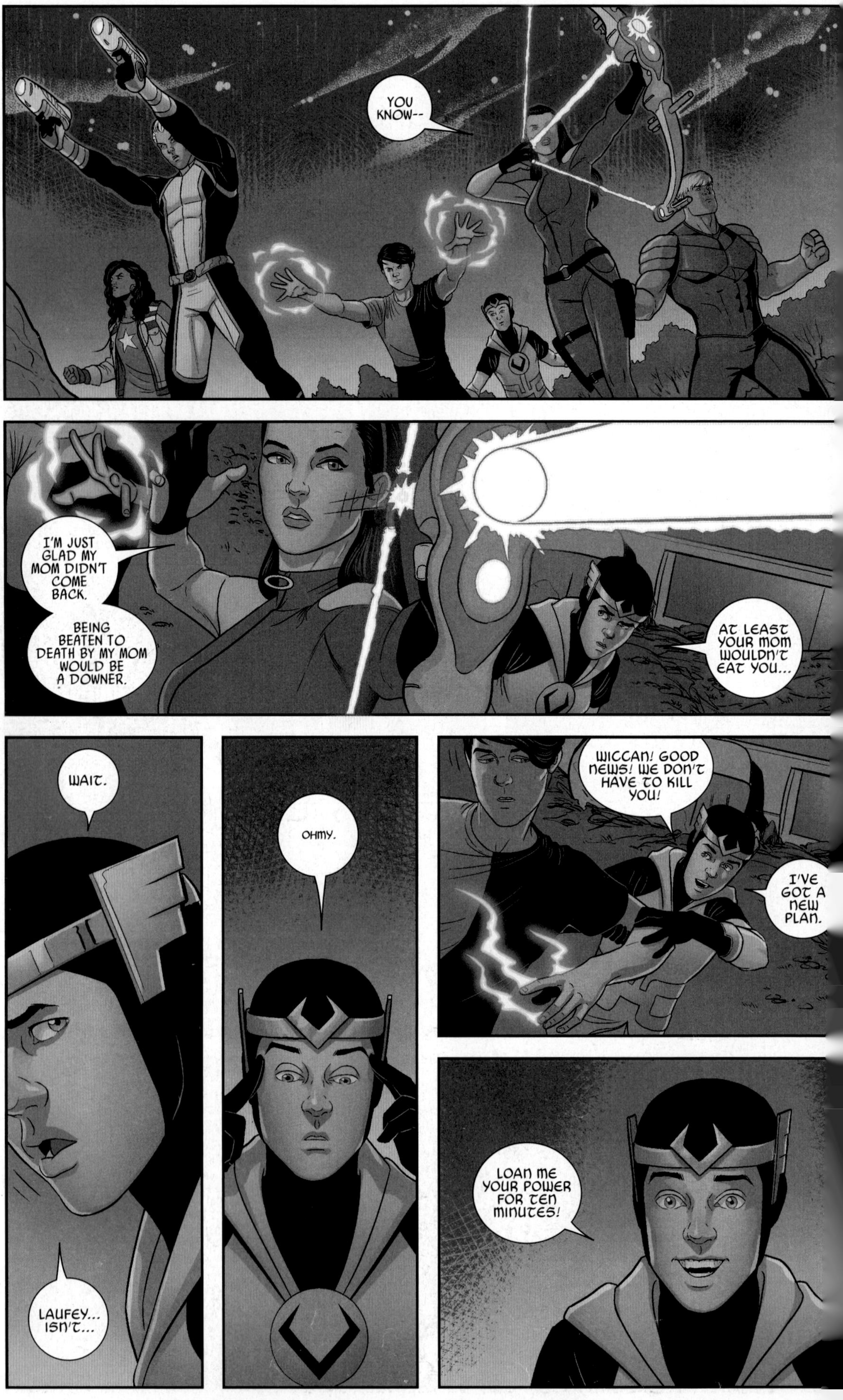
YOU KNOW--
I'M JUST GLAD MY MOM DIDN'T COME BACK.
BEING BEATEN TO DEATH BY MY MOM WOULD BE A DOWNER.
AT LEAST YOUR MOM WOULDN'T EAT YOU...
WAIT.
LAUFEY... ISN'T...
OHMY.
WICCAN! GOOD NEWS! WE DON'T HAVE TO KILL YOU!
I'VE GOT A NEW PLAN.
LOAN ME YOUR POWER FOR TEN MINUTES!

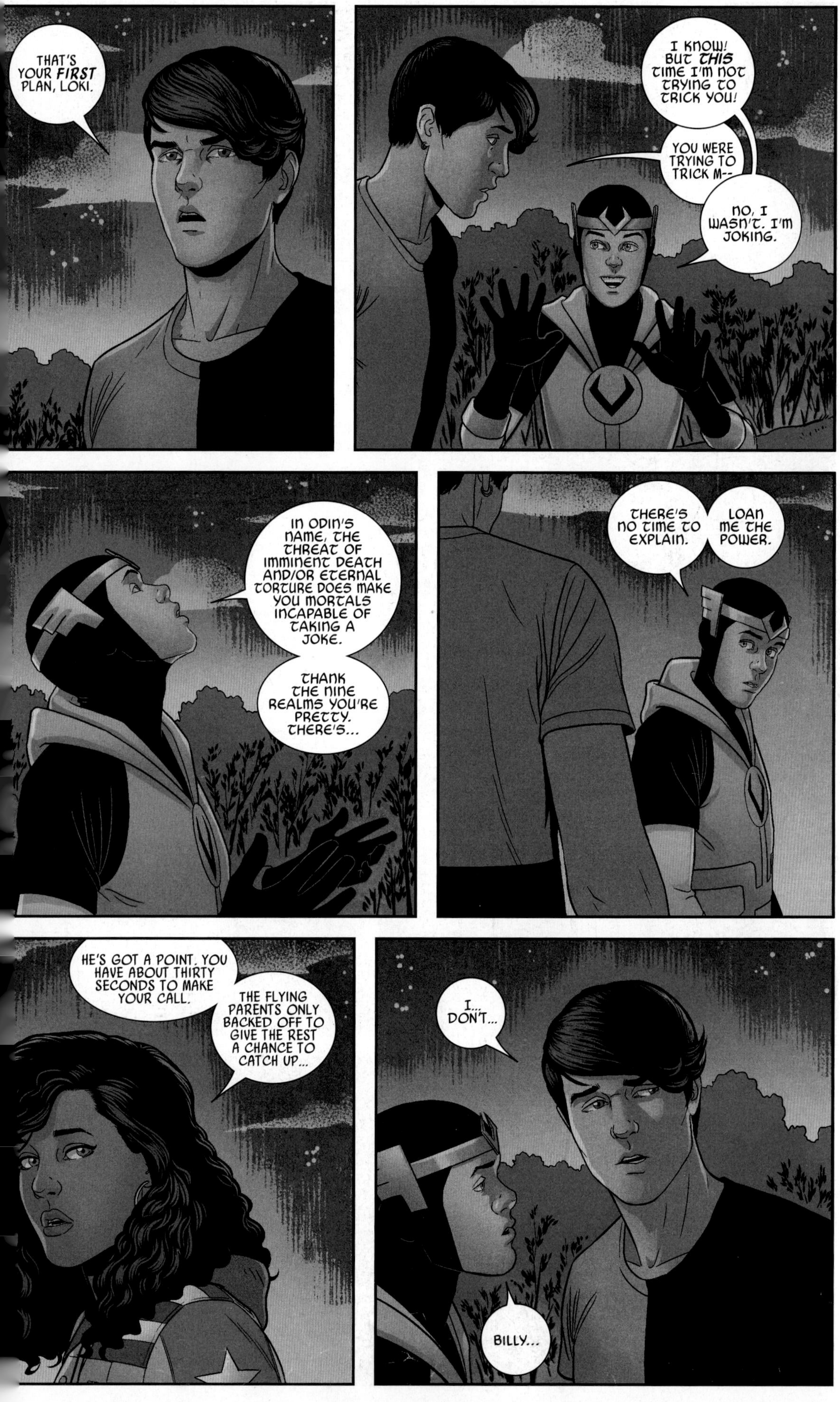
THAT'S YOUR FIRST PLAN, LOKI.
I KNOW! BUT THIS TIME I'M NOT TRYING TO TRICK YOU!
YOU WERE TRYING TO TRICK M--
NO, I WASN'T. I'M JOKING.
IN ODIN'S NAME, THE THREAT OF IMMINENT DEATH AND/OR ETERNAL TORTURE DOES MAKE YOU MORTALS INCAPABLE OF TAKING A JOKE.
THANK THE NINE REALMS YOU'RE PRETTY. THERE'S...
THERE'S NO TIME TO EXPLAIN.
LOAN ME THE POWER.
HE'S GOT A POINT. YOU HAVE ABOUT THIRTY SECONDS TO MAKE YOUR CALL.
THE FLYING PARENTS ONLY BACKED OFF TO GIVE THE REST A CHANCE TO CATCH UP...
I... DON'T...
BILLY...

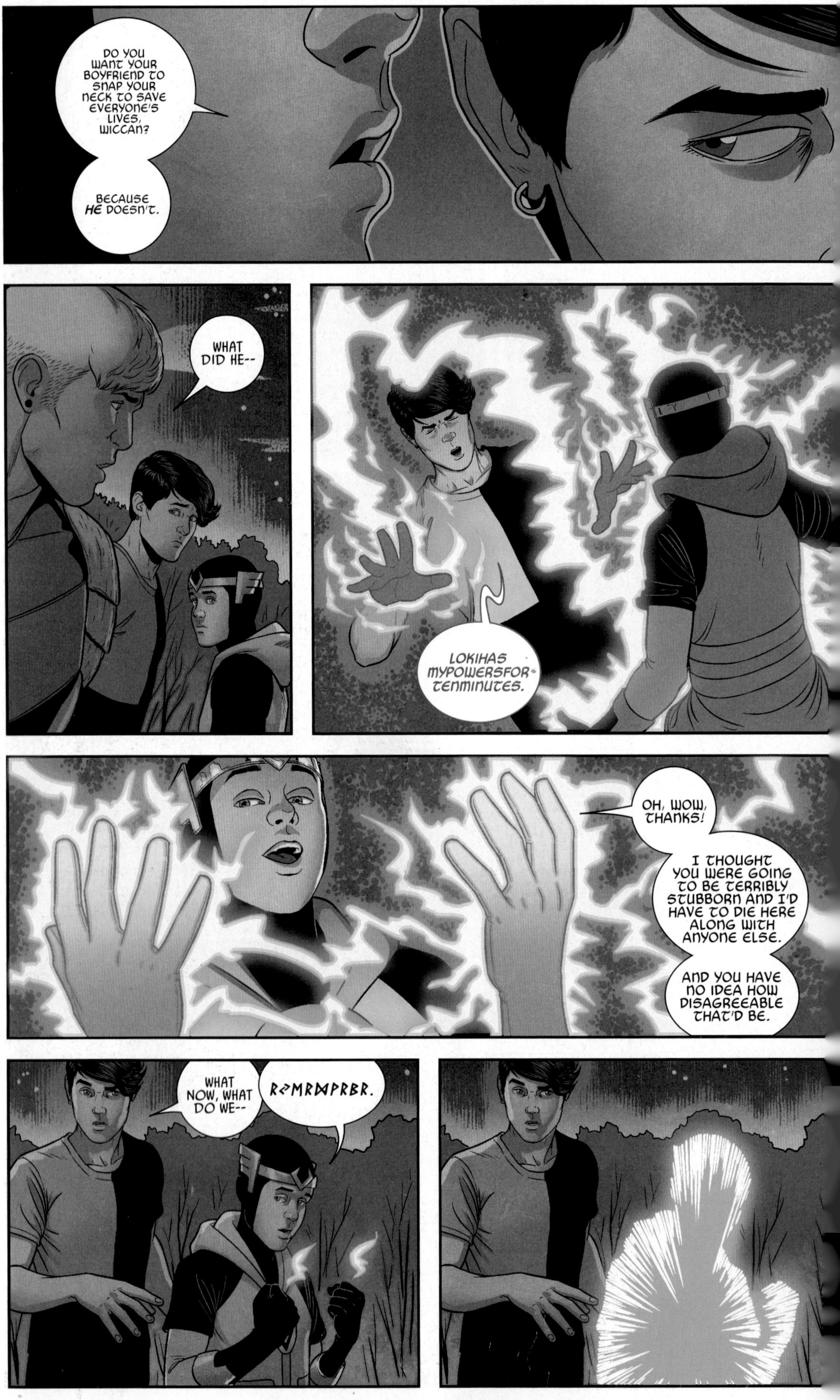

DO YOU WANT YOUR BOYFRIEND TO SNAP YOUR NECK TO SAVE EVERYONE'S LIVES, WICCAN?
BECAUSE *HE* DOESN'T.
WHAT DID HE--
LOKIHAS MYPOWERSFOR TENMINUTES.
OH, WOW, THANKS!
I THOUGHT YOU WERE GOING TO BE TERRIBLY STUBBORN AND I'D HAVE TO DIE HERE ALONG WITH ANYONE ELSE.
AND YOU HAVE NO IDEA HOW DISAGREEABLE THAT'D BE.
WHAT NOW, WHAT DO WE--

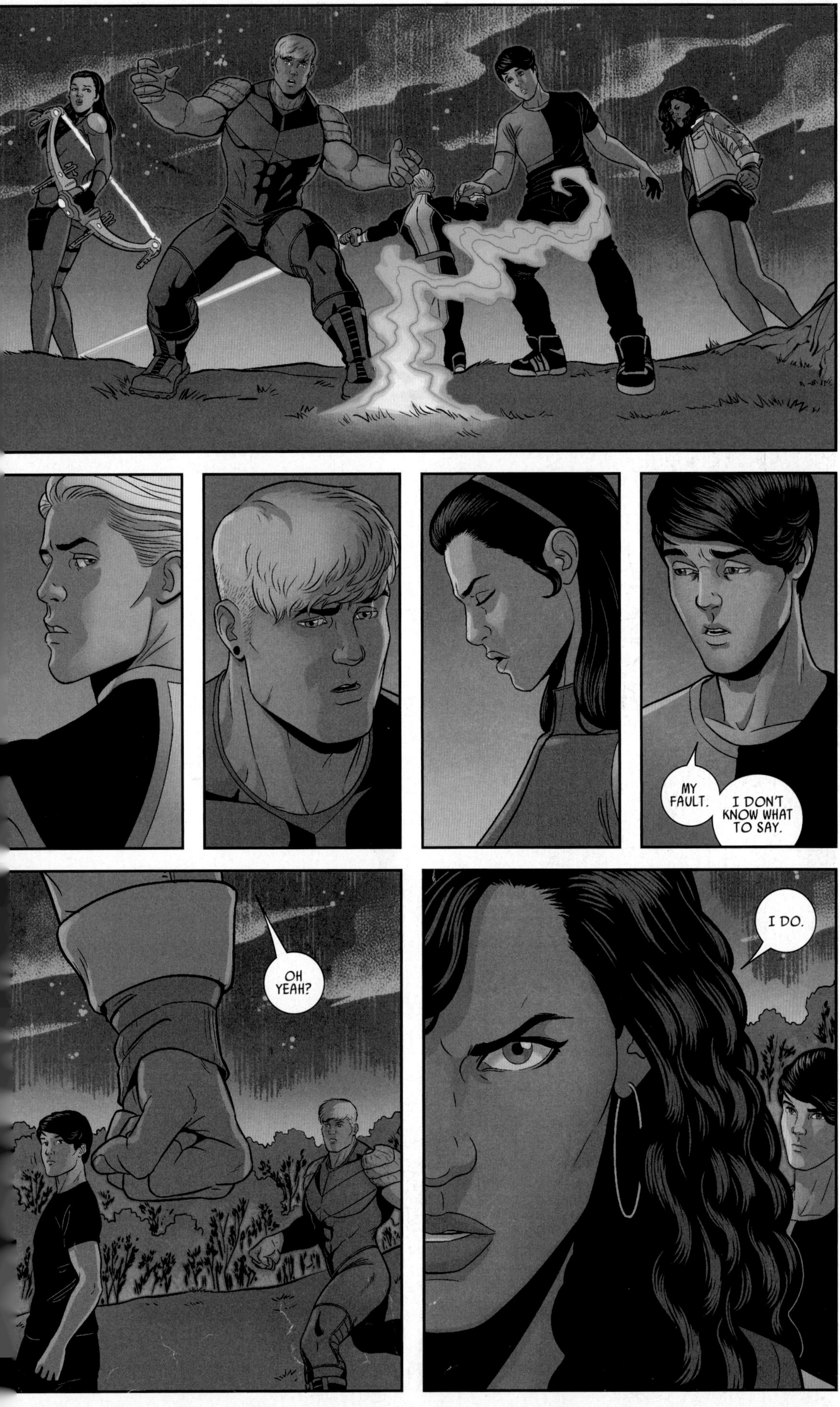
MY FAULT.
I DON'T KNOW WHAT TO SAY.
OH YEAH?
I DO.

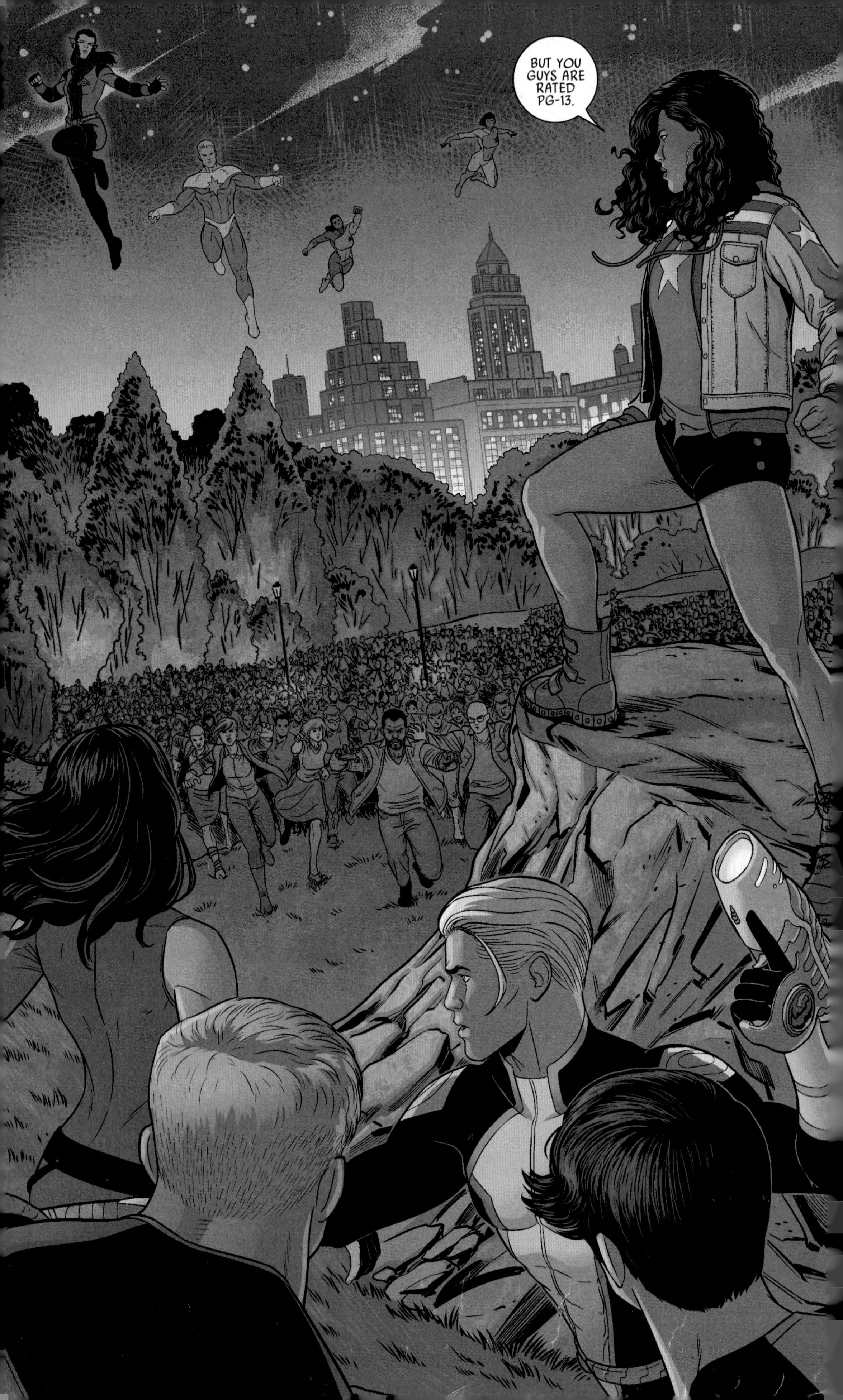
BUT YOU GUYS ARE RATED PG-13.

## #3 VARIANT
BY TRADD MOORE & MATTHEW WILSON

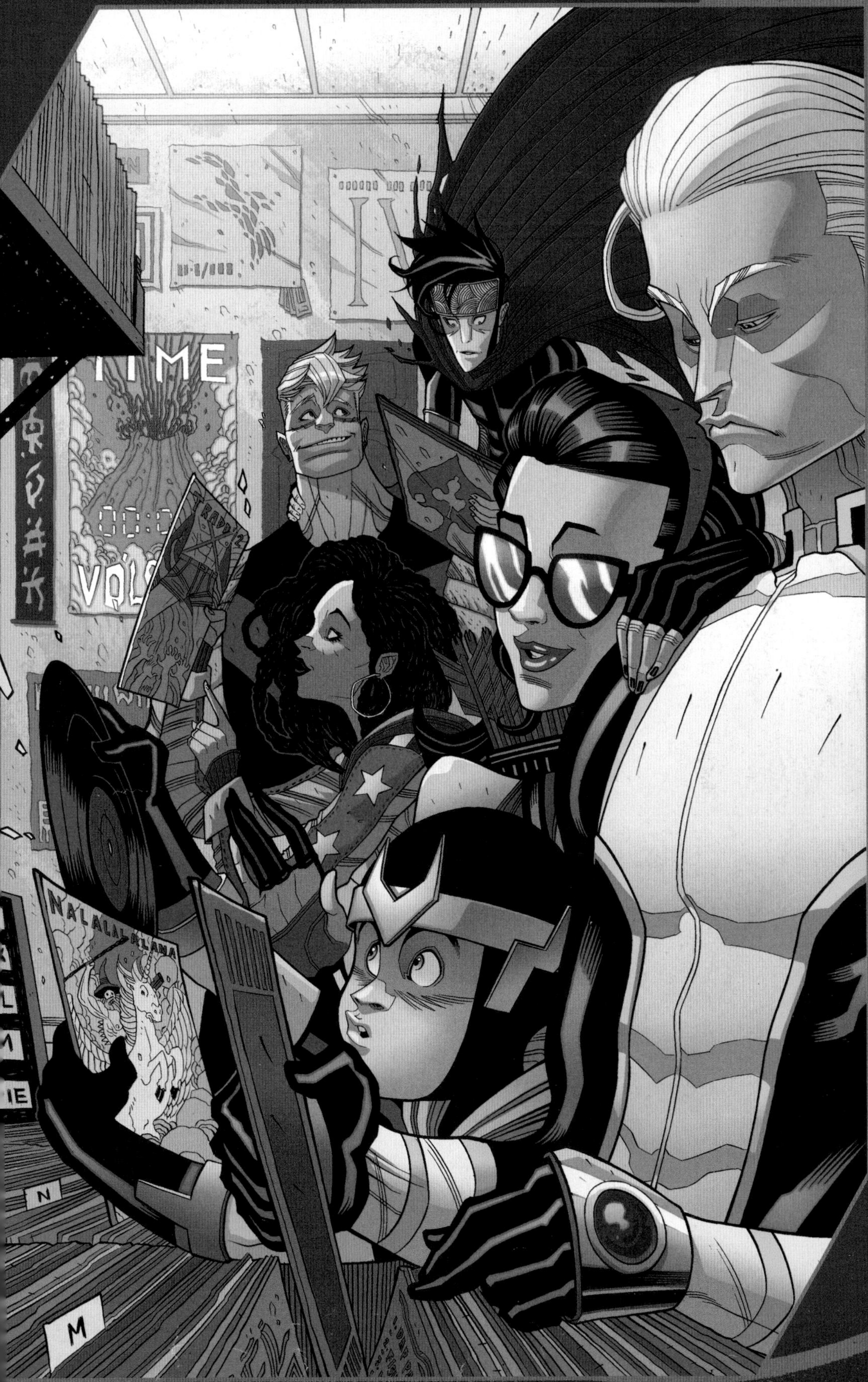

TIME

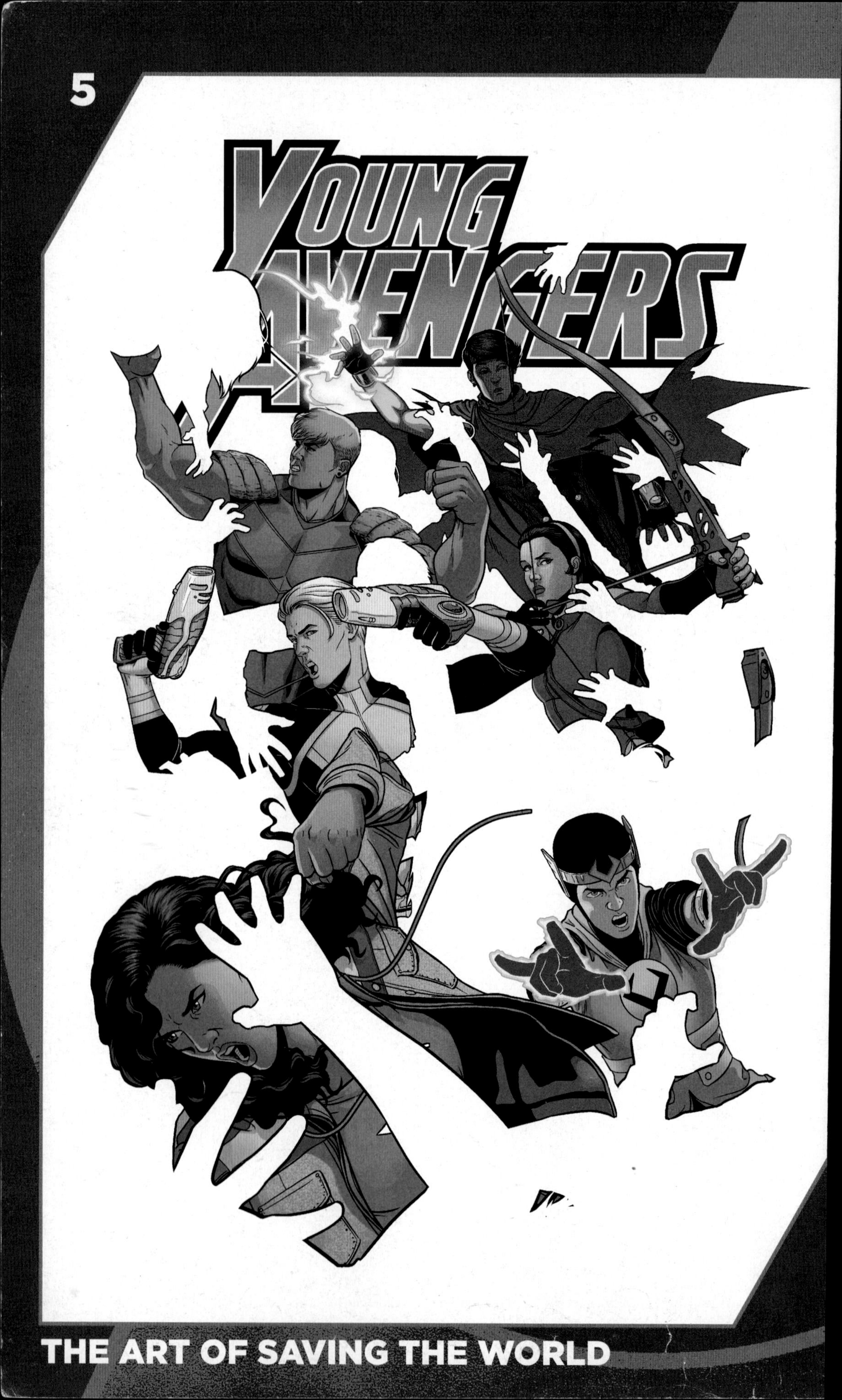
5
YOUNG AVENGERS
THE ART OF SAVING THE WORLD

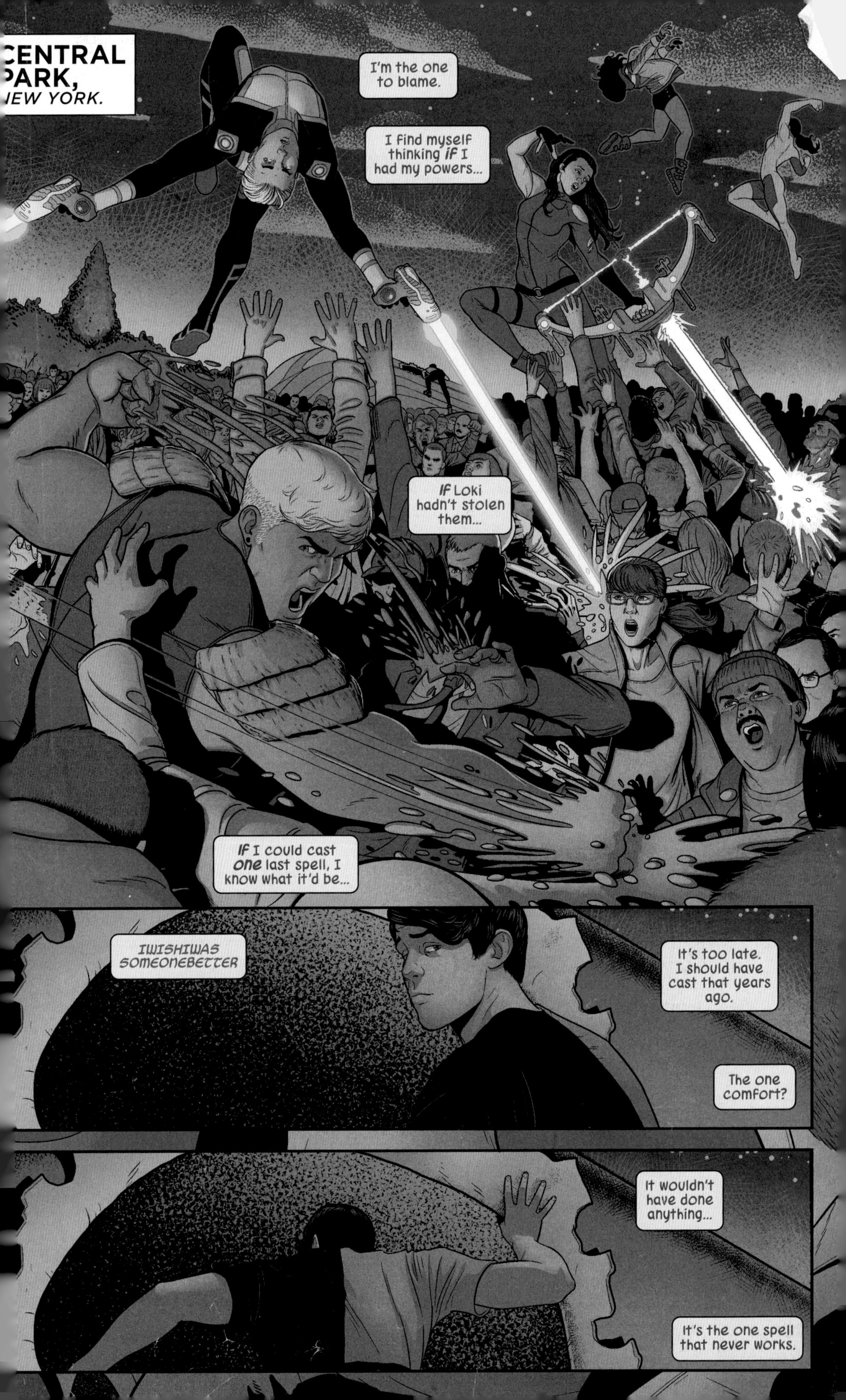
CENTRAL PARK, NEW YORK.
I'm the one to blame.
I find myself thinking IF I had my powers...
IF Loki hadn't stolen them...
IF I could cast ONE last spell, I know what it'd be...
IWISHIWAS SOMEONEBETTER
It's too late. I should have cast that years ago.
The one comfort?
It wouldn't have done anything...
It's the one spell that never works.

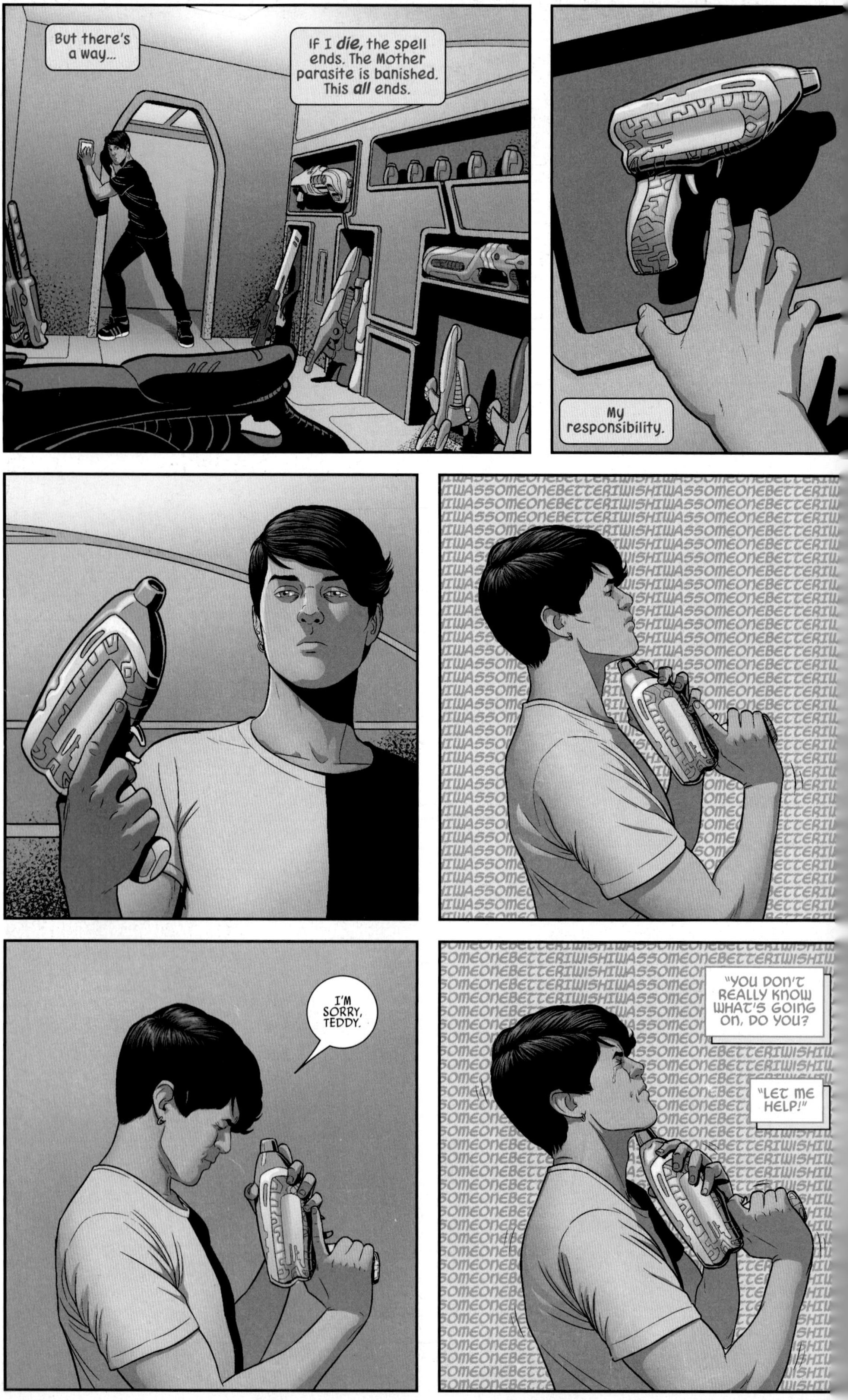
But there's a way...
If I *die,* the spell ends. The Mother parasite is banished. This *all* ends.
My responsibility.
I'M SORRY, TEDDY.
"YOU DON'T REALLY KNOW WHAT'S GOING ON, DO YOU?
"LET ME HELP!"

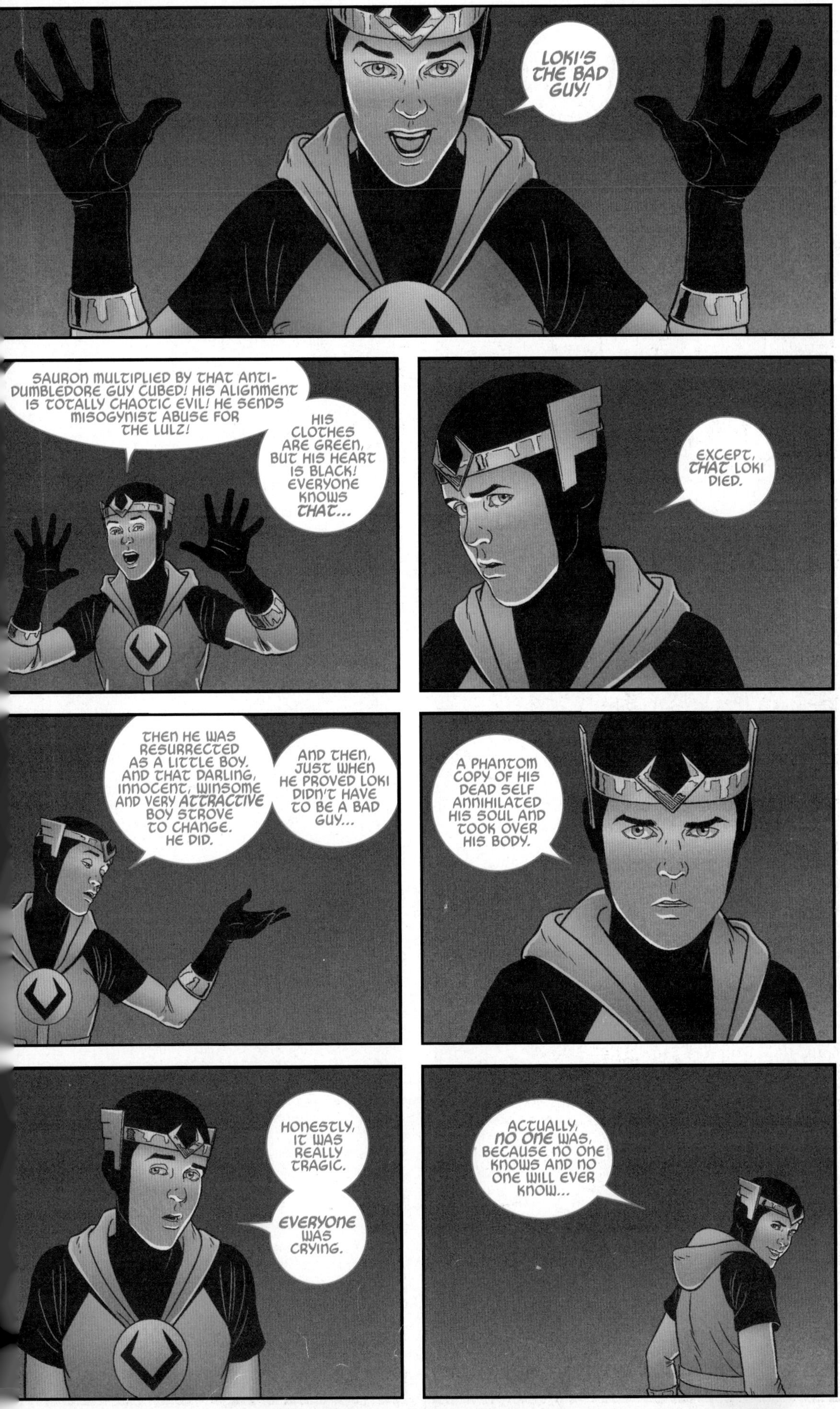

LOKI'S THE BAD GUY!
SAURON MULTIPLIED BY THAT ANTI-DUMBLEDORE GUY CUBED! HIS ALIGNMENT IS TOTALLY CHAOTIC EVIL! HE SENDS MISOGYNIST ABUSE FOR THE LULZ!
HIS CLOTHES ARE GREEN, BUT HIS HEART IS BLACK! EVERYONE KNOWS THAT...
EXCEPT, THAT LOKI DIED.
THEN HE WAS RESURRECTED AS A LITTLE BOY. AND THAT DARLING, INNOCENT, WINSOME AND VERY ATTRACTIVE BOY STROVE TO CHANGE. HE DID.
AND THEN, JUST WHEN HE PROVED LOKI DIDN'T HAVE TO BE A BAD GUY...
A PHANTOM COPY OF HIS DEAD SELF ANNIHILATED HIS SOUL AND TOOK OVER HIS BODY.
HONESTLY, IT WAS REALLY TRAGIC.
EVERYONE WAS CRYING.
ACTUALLY, NO ONE WAS, BECAUSE NO ONE KNOWS AND NO ONE WILL EVER KNOW...

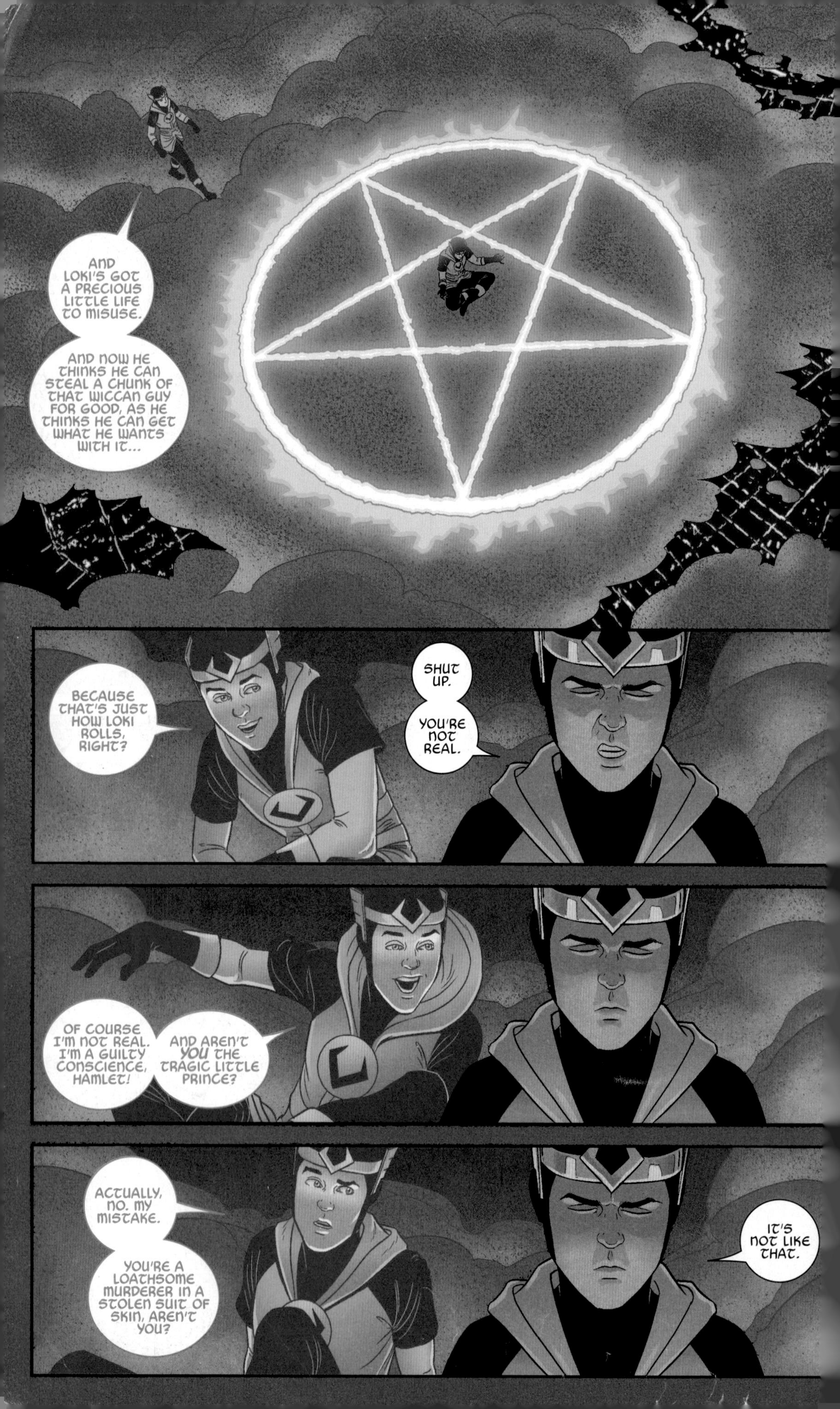
AND LOKI'S GOT A PRECIOUS LITTLE LIFE TO MISUSE.
AND NOW HE THINKS HE CAN STEAL A CHUNK OF THAT WICCAN GUY FOR GOOD, AS HE THINKS HE CAN GET WHAT HE WANTS WITH IT...
BECAUSE THAT'S JUST HOW LOKI ROLLS, RIGHT?
SHUT UP.
YOU'RE NOT REAL.
OF COURSE I'M NOT REAL. I'M A GUILTY CONSCIENCE, HAMLET!
AND AREN'T *YOU* THE TRAGIC LITTLE PRINCE?
ACTUALLY, NO. MY MISTAKE.
YOU'RE A LOATHSOME MURDERER IN A STOLEN SUIT OF SKIN, AREN'T YOU?
IT'S NOT LIKE THAT.

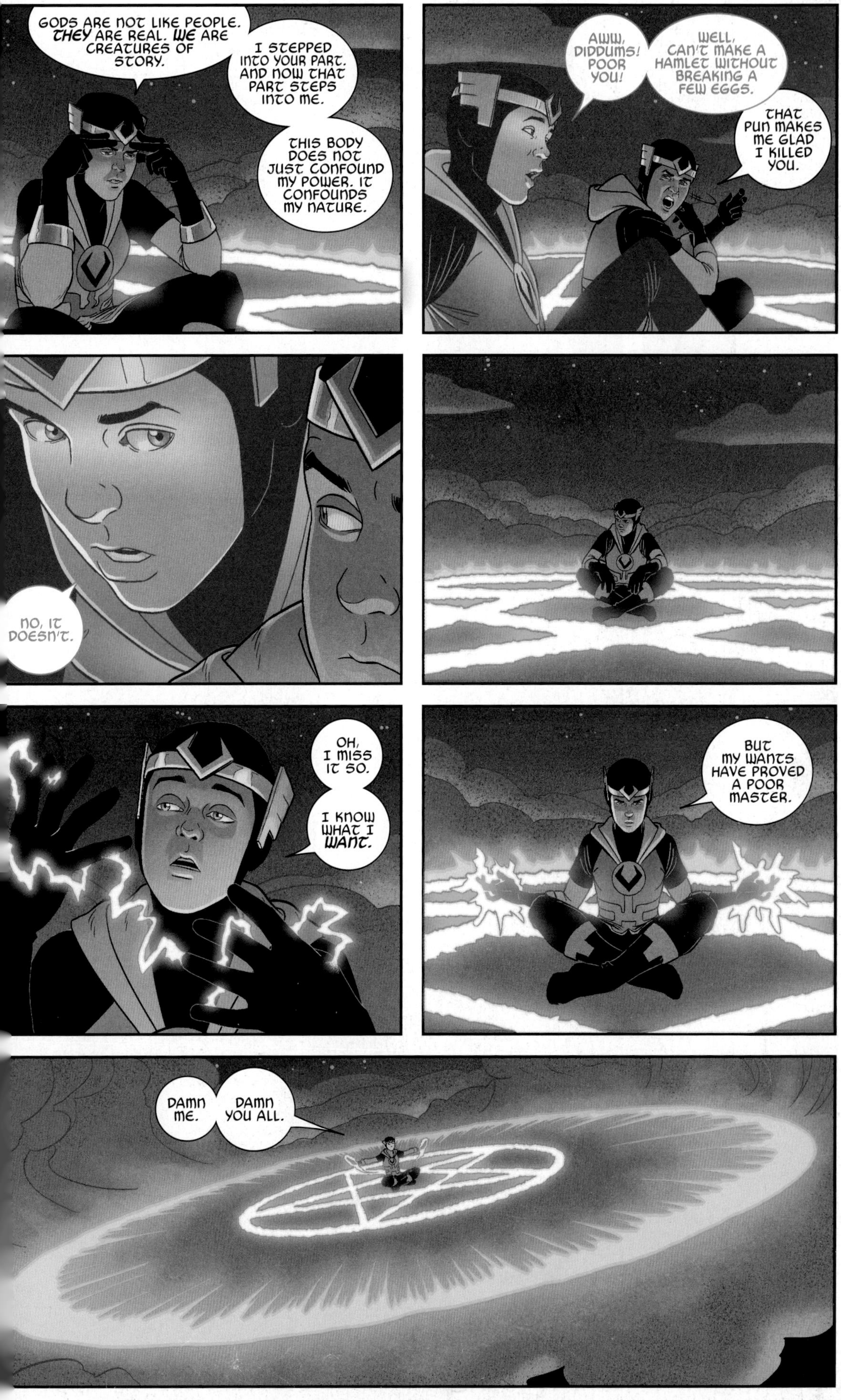
GODS ARE NOT LIKE PEOPLE. THEY ARE REAL. WE ARE CREATURES OF STORY.
I STEPPED INTO YOUR PART. AND NOW THAT PART STEPS INTO ME.
THIS BODY DOES NOT JUST CONFOUND MY POWER. IT CONFOUNDS MY NATURE.
AWW, DIDDUMS! POOR YOU!
WELL, CAN'T MAKE A HAMLET WITHOUT BREAKING A FEW EGGS.
THAT PUN MAKES ME GLAD I KILLED YOU.
NO, IT DOESN'T.
OH, I MISS IT SO.
I KNOW WHAT I WANT.
BUT MY WANTS HAVE PROVED A POOR MASTER.
DAMN ME.
DAMN YOU ALL.

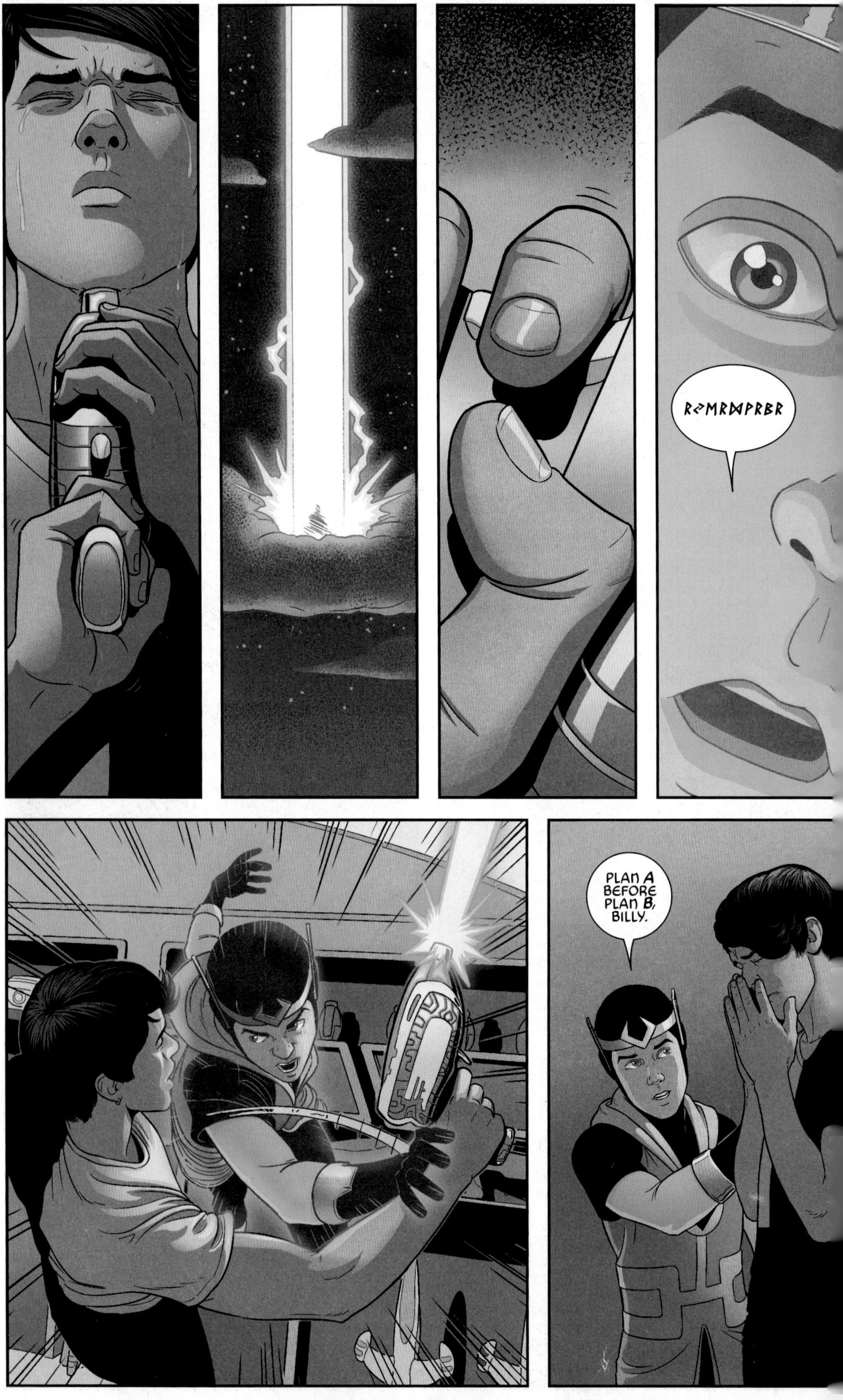
PLAN A BEFORE PLAN B, BILLY.

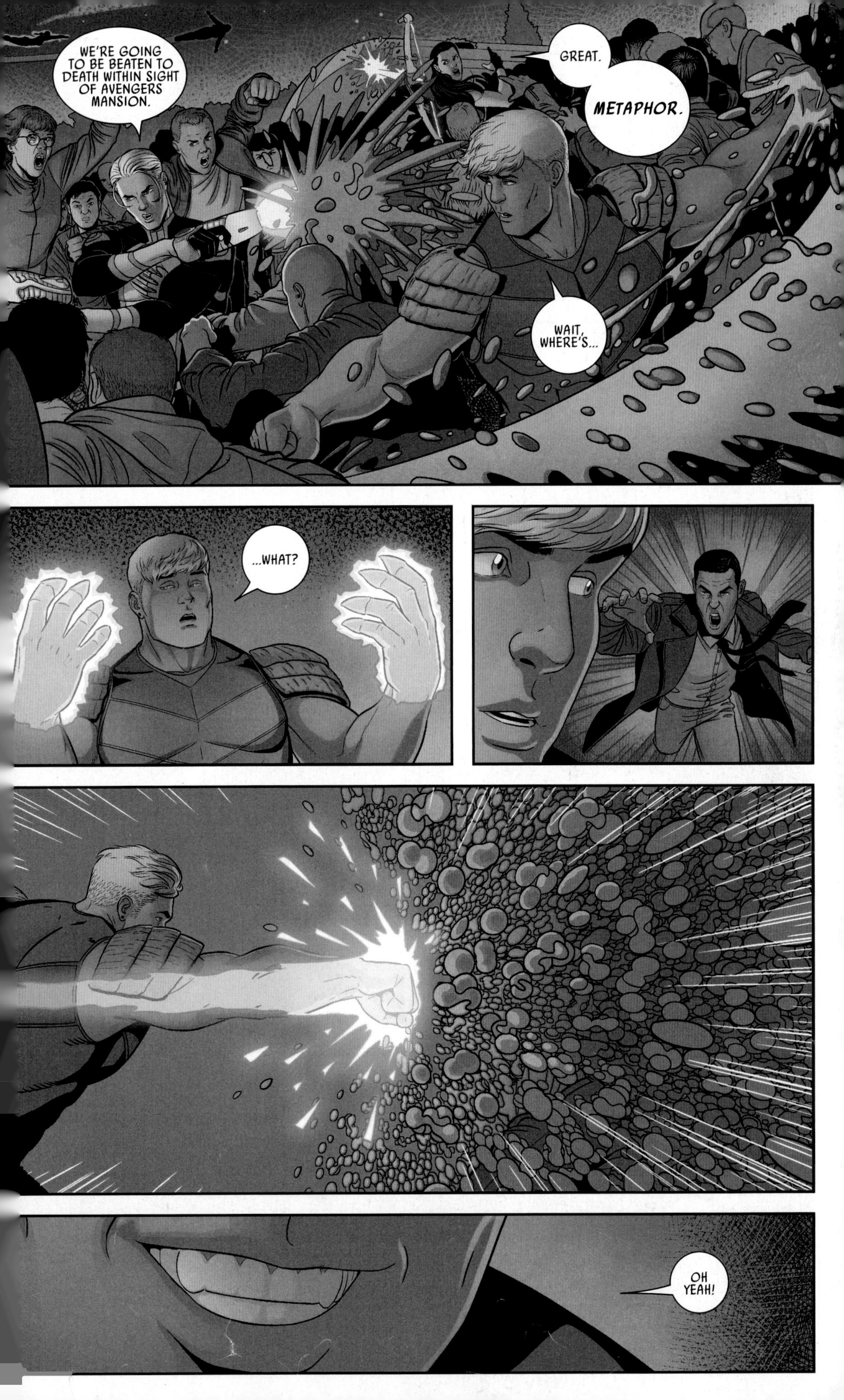
WE'RE GOING TO BE BEATEN TO DEATH WITHIN SIGHT OF AVENGERS MANSION.
GREAT.
METAPHOR.
WAIT, WHERE'S...
...WHAT?
OH YEAH!

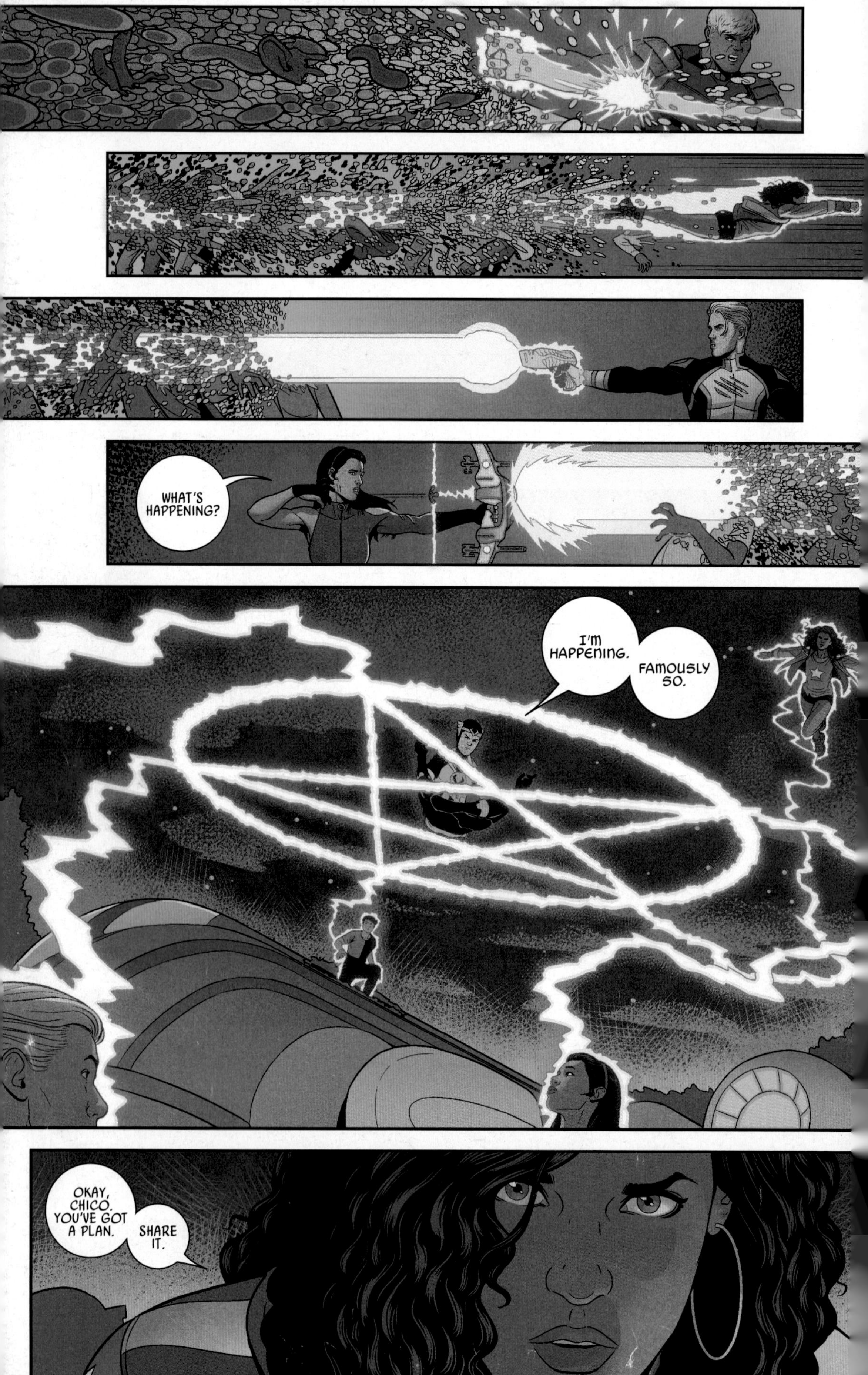
WHAT'S HAPPENING?
I'M HAPPENING.
FAMOUSLY SO.
OKAY, CHICO. YOU'VE GOT A PLAN.
SHARE IT.

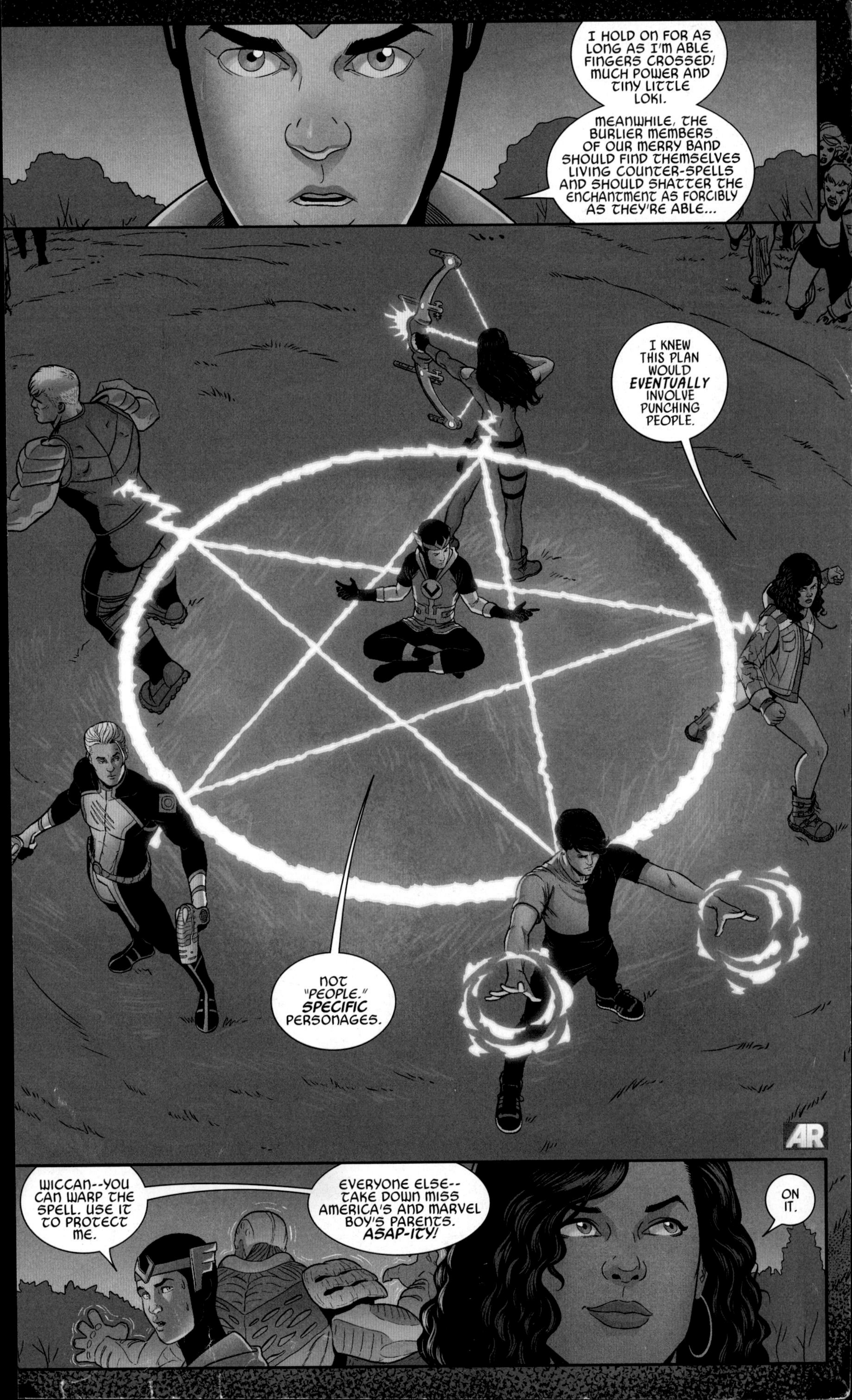
I HOLD ON FOR AS LONG AS I'M ABLE. FINGERS CROSSED! MUCH POWER AND TINY LITTLE LOKI.
MEANWHILE, THE BURLIER MEMBERS OF OUR MERRY BAND SHOULD FIND THEMSELVES LIVING COUNTER-SPELLS AND SHOULD SHATTER THE ENCHANTMENT AS FORCIBLY AS THEY'RE ABLE...
I KNEW THIS PLAN WOULD EVENTUALLY INVOLVE PUNCHING PEOPLE.
NOT "PEOPLE." SPECIFIC PERSONAGES.
AR
WICCAN--YOU CAN WARP THE SPELL. USE IT TO PROTECT ME.
EVERYONE ELSE--TAKE DOWN MISS AMERICA'S AND MARVEL BOY'S PARENTS. ASAP-ITY!
ON IT.

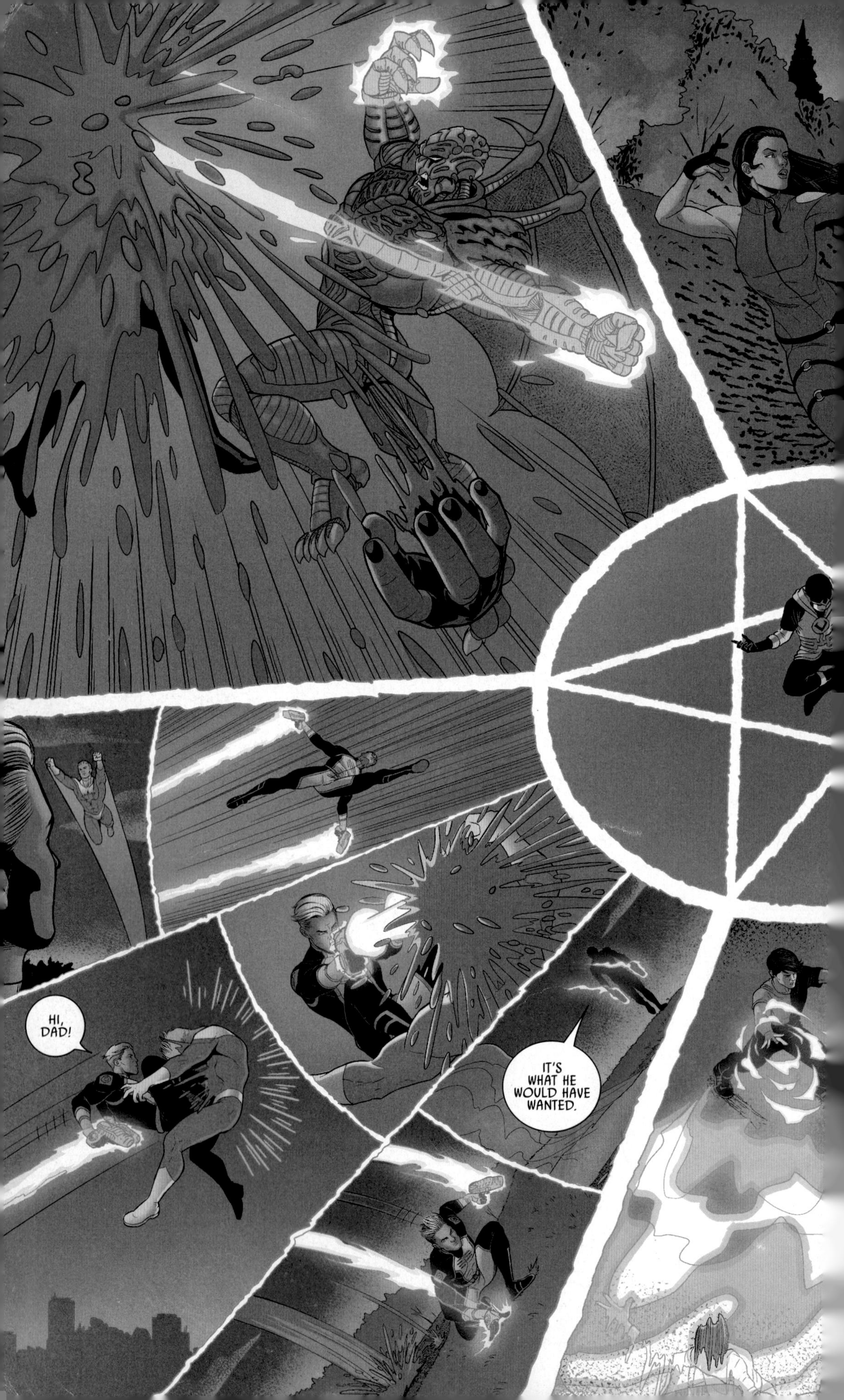
HI, DAD!
IT'S WHAT HE WOULD HAVE WANTED.

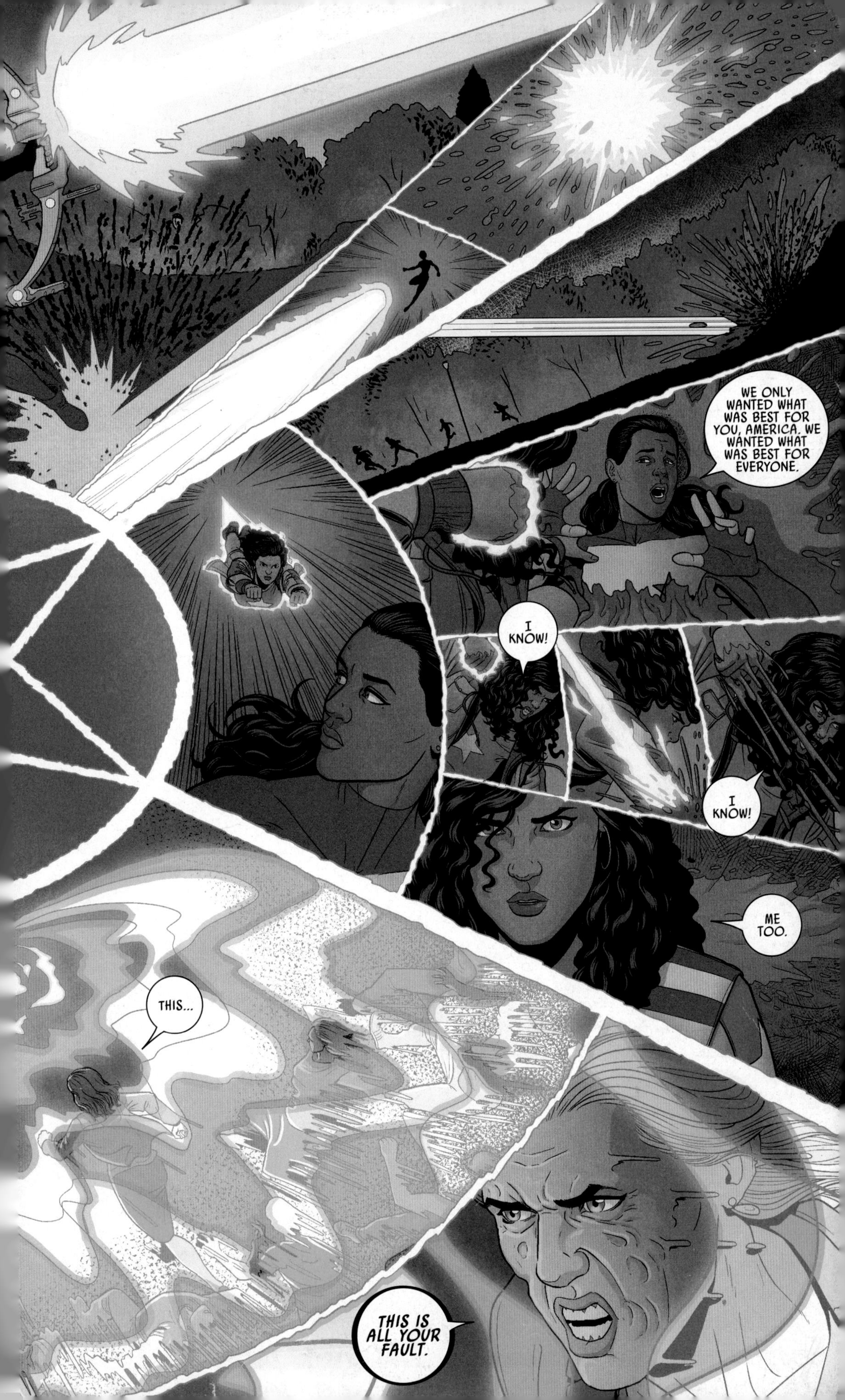
WE ONLY WANTED WHAT WAS BEST FOR YOU, AMERICA. WE WANTED WHAT WAS BEST FOR EVERYONE.
I KNOW!
I KNOW!
ME TOO.
THIS...
THIS IS ALL YOUR FAULT.

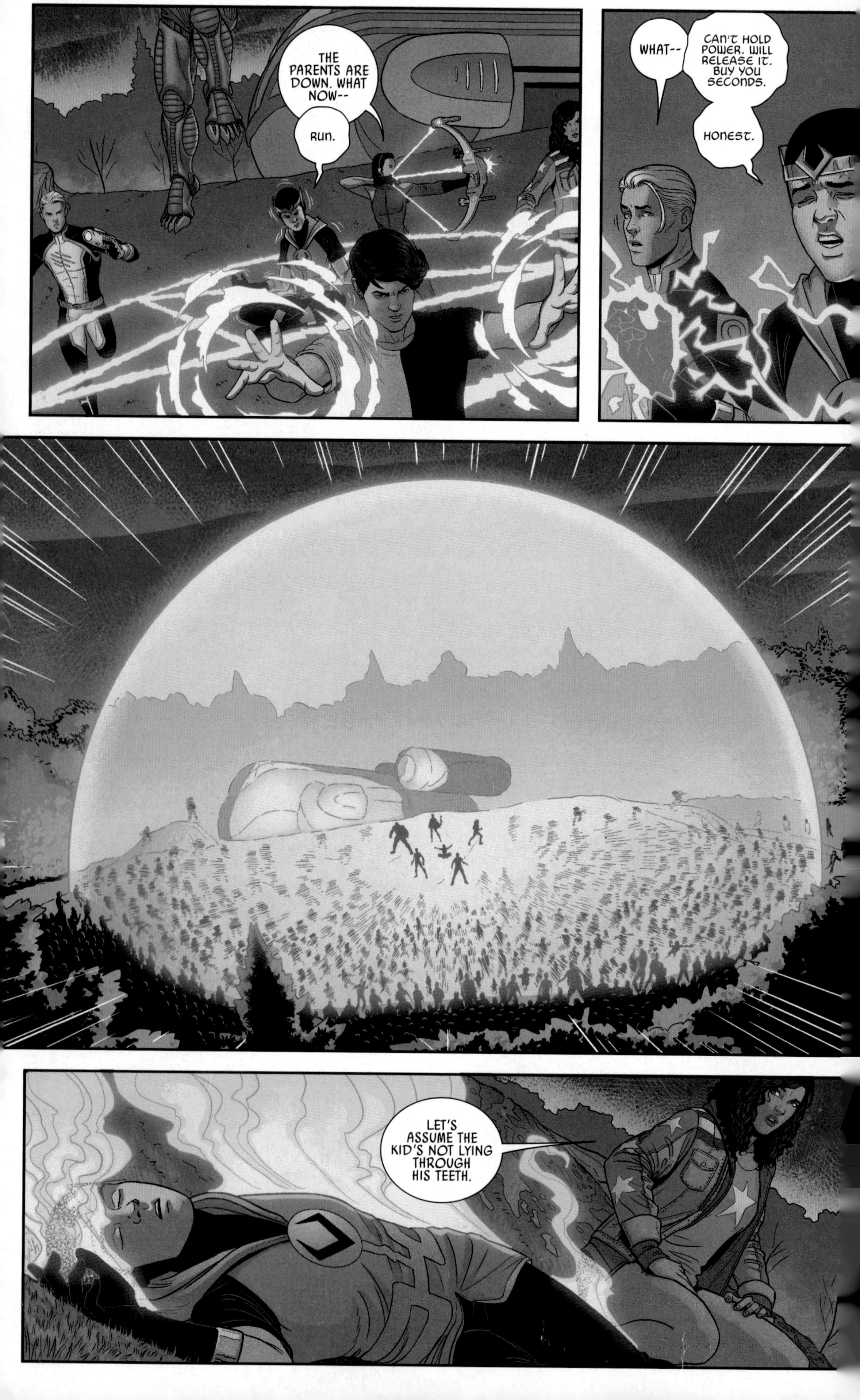
THE PARENTS ARE DOWN. WHAT NOW--
RUN.
WHAT--
CAN'T HOLD POWER. WILL RELEASE IT. BUY YOU SECONDS.
HONEST.
LET'S ASSUME THE KID'S NOT LYING THROUGH HIS TEETH.

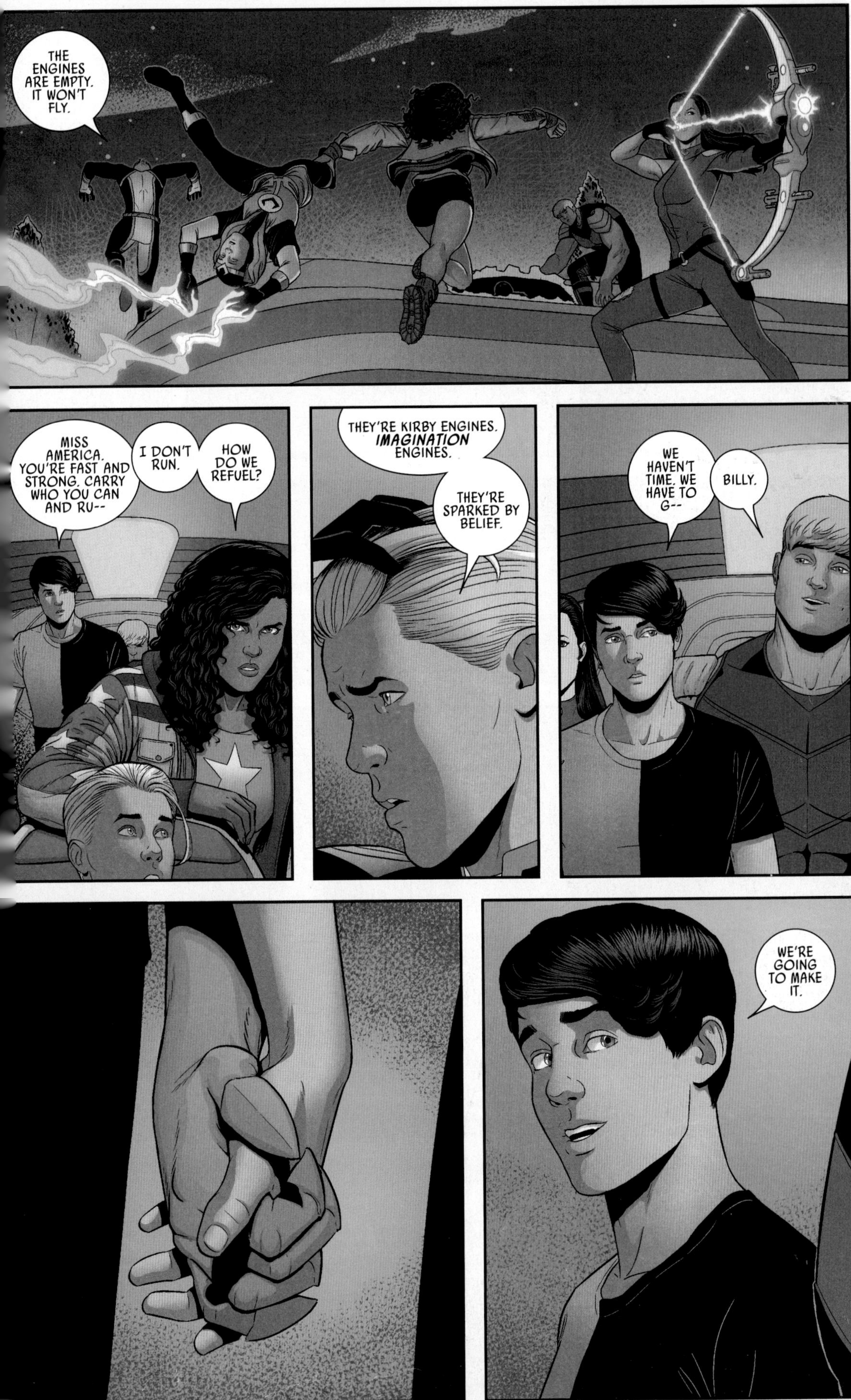
THE ENGINES ARE EMPTY. IT WON'T FLY.
MISS AMERICA. YOU'RE FAST AND STRONG. CARRY WHO YOU CAN AND RU--
I DON'T RUN.
HOW DO WE REFUEL?
THEY'RE KIRBY ENGINES. IMAGINATION ENGINES.
THEY'RE SPARKED BY BELIEF.
WE HAVEN'T TIME. WE HAVE TO G--
BILLY.
WE'RE GOING TO MAKE IT.

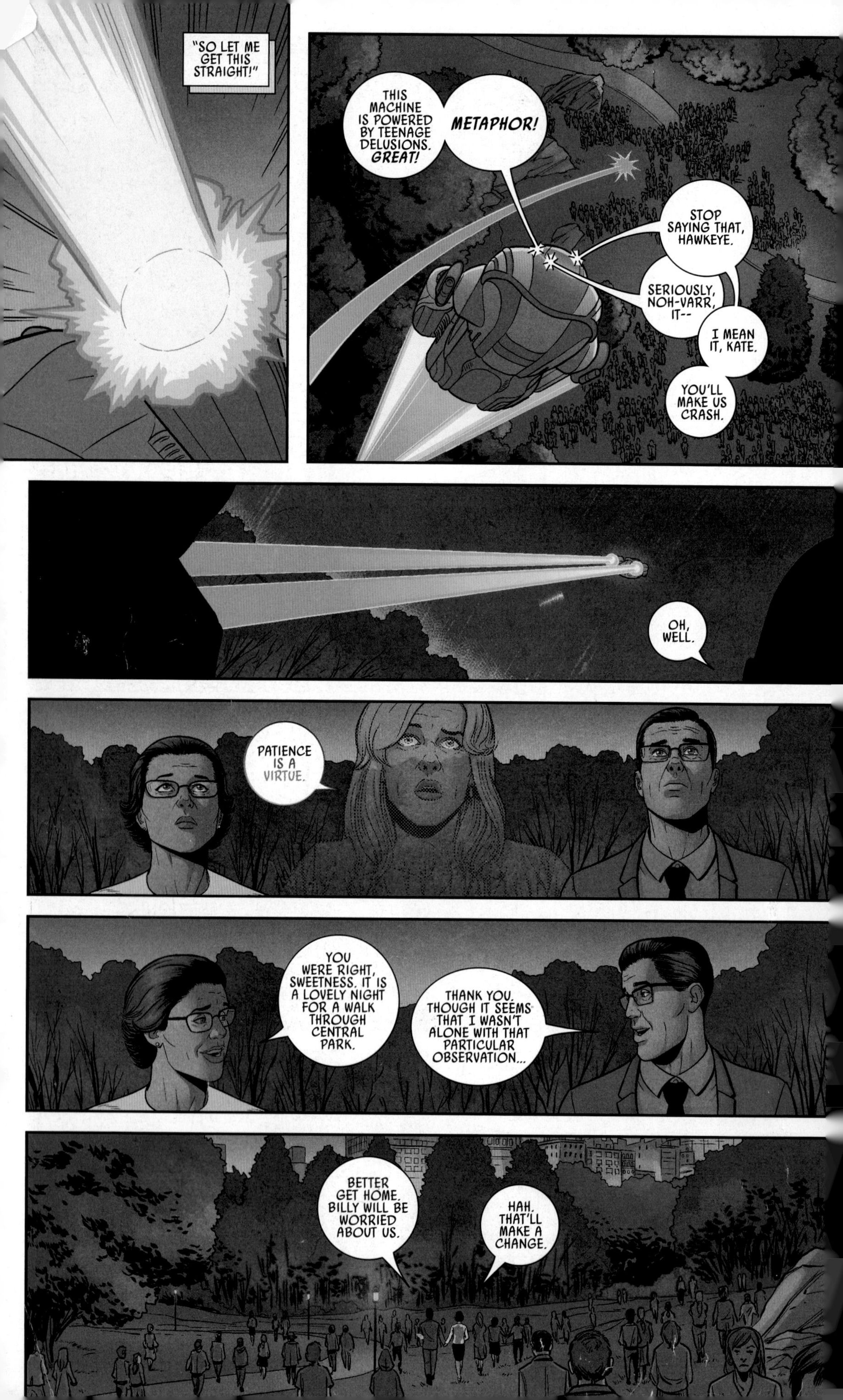
"SO LET ME GET THIS STRAIGHT!"
THIS MACHINE IS POWERED BY TEENAGE DELUSIONS. GREAT!
METAPHOR!
STOP SAYING THAT, HAWKEYE.
SERIOUSLY, NOH-VARR, IT--
I MEAN IT, KATE.
YOU'LL MAKE US CRASH.
OH, WELL.
PATIENCE IS A VIRTUE.
YOU WERE RIGHT, SWEETNESS. IT IS A LOVELY NIGHT FOR A WALK THROUGH CENTRAL PARK.
THANK YOU. THOUGH IT SEEMS THAT I WASN'T ALONE WITH THAT PARTICULAR OBSERVATION...
BETTER GET HOME. BILLY WILL BE WORRIED ABOUT US.
HAH. THAT'LL MAKE A CHANGE.

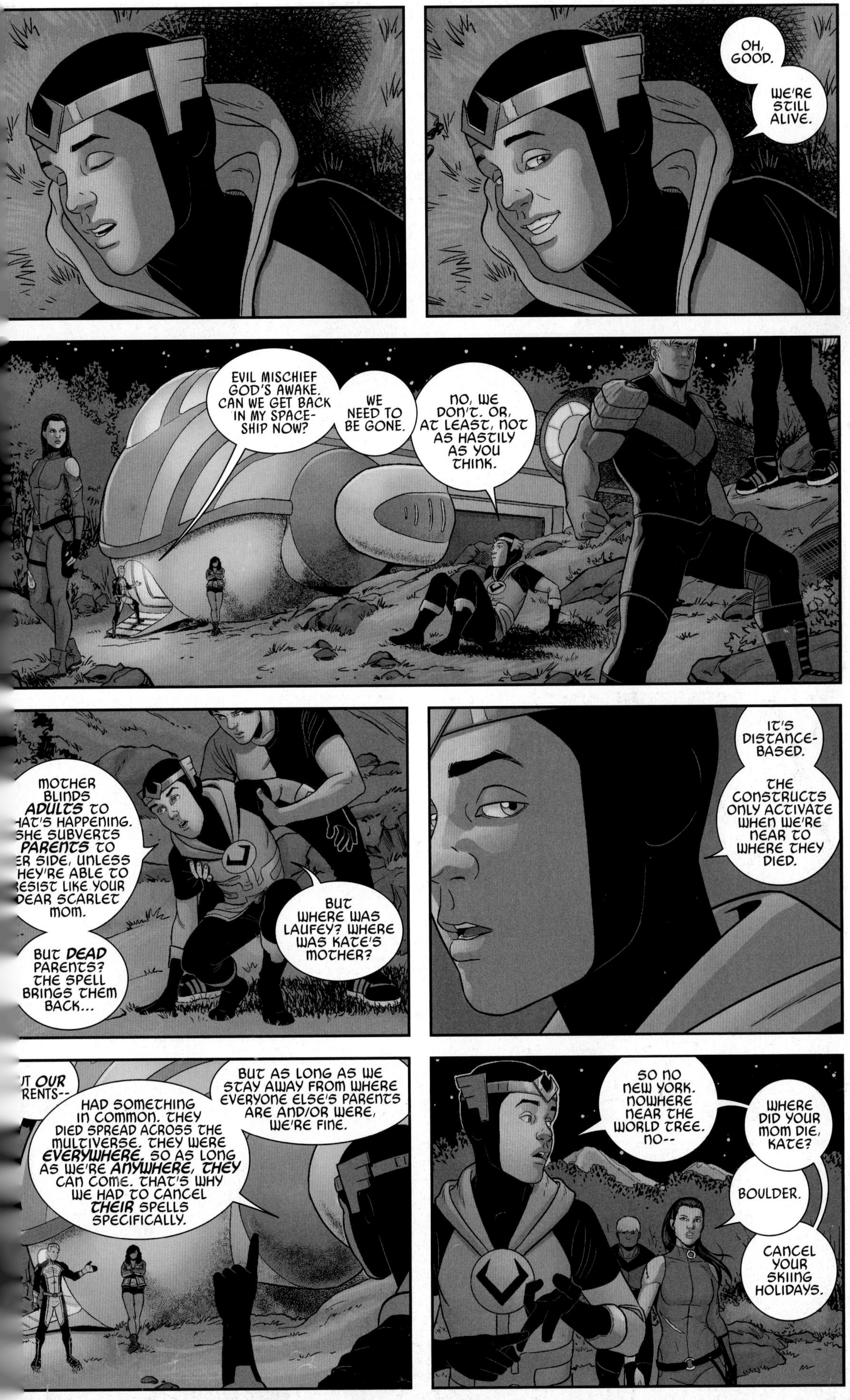
OH, GOOD.
WE'RE STILL ALIVE.
EVIL MISCHIEF GOD'S AWAKE. CAN WE GET BACK IN MY SPACE-SHIP NOW?
WE NEED TO BE GONE.
NO, WE DON'T. OR, AT LEAST, NOT AS HASTILY AS YOU THINK.
MOTHER BLINDS ADULTS TO HAT'S HAPPENING. HE SUBVERTS PARENTS TO ER SIDE, UNLESS HEY'RE ABLE TO ESIST LIKE YOUR DEAR SCARLET MOM.
BUT DEAD PARENTS? THE SPELL BRINGS THEM BACK...
BUT WHERE WAS LAUFEY? WHERE WAS KATE'S MOTHER?
IT'S DISTANCE-BASED.
THE CONSTRUCTS ONLY ACTIVATE WHEN WE'RE NEAR TO WHERE THEY DIED.
UT OUR RENTS--
HAD SOMETHING IN COMMON. THEY DIED SPREAD ACROSS THE MULTIVERSE. THEY WERE EVERYWHERE. SO AS LONG AS WE'RE ANYWHERE, THEY CAN COME. THAT'S WHY WE HAD TO CANCEL THEIR SPELLS SPECIFICALLY.
BUT AS LONG AS WE STAY AWAY FROM WHERE EVERYONE ELSE'S PARENTS ARE AND/OR WERE, WE'RE FINE.
SO NO NEW YORK. NOWHERE NEAR THE WORLD TREE. NO--
WHERE DID YOUR MOM DIE, KATE?
BOULDER.
CANCEL YOUR SKIING HOLIDAYS.

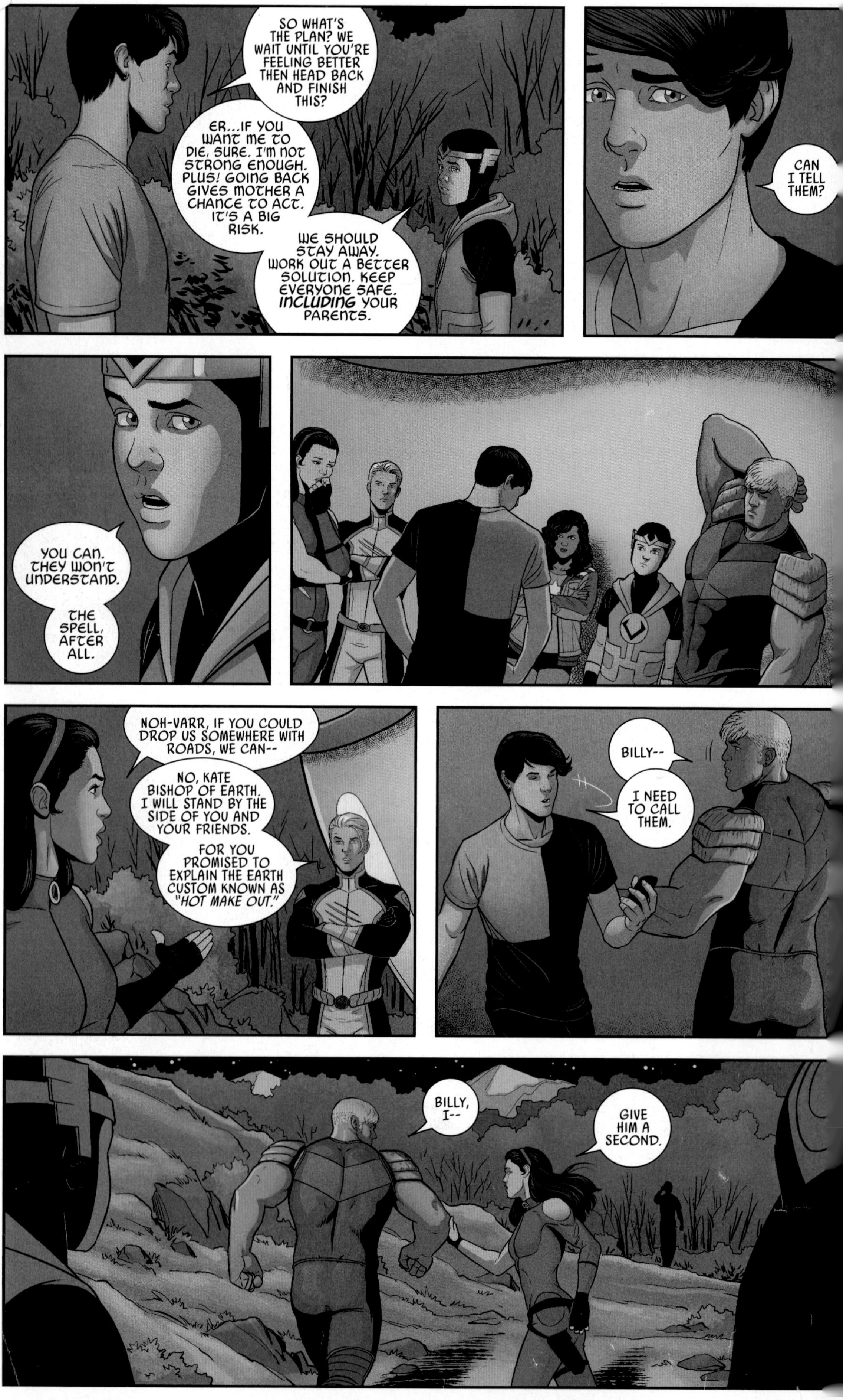
SO WHAT'S THE PLAN? WE WAIT UNTIL YOU'RE FEELING BETTER THEN HEAD BACK AND FINISH THIS?
ER...IF YOU WANT ME TO DIE, SURE. I'M NOT STRONG ENOUGH. PLUS! GOING BACK GIVES MOTHER A CHANCE TO ACT. IT'S A BIG RISK.
WE SHOULD STAY AWAY. WORK OUT A BETTER SOLUTION. KEEP EVERYONE SAFE. INCLUDING YOUR PARENTS.
CAN I TELL THEM?
YOU CAN. THEY WON'T UNDERSTAND.
THE SPELL, AFTER ALL.
NOH-VARR, IF YOU COULD DROP US SOMEWHERE WITH ROADS, WE CAN--
NO, KATE BISHOP OF EARTH. I WILL STAND BY THE SIDE OF YOU AND YOUR FRIENDS.
FOR YOU PROMISED TO EXPLAIN THE EARTH CUSTOM KNOWN AS "HOT MAKE OUT."
BILLY--
I NEED TO CALL THEM.
BILLY, I--
GIVE HIM A SECOND.

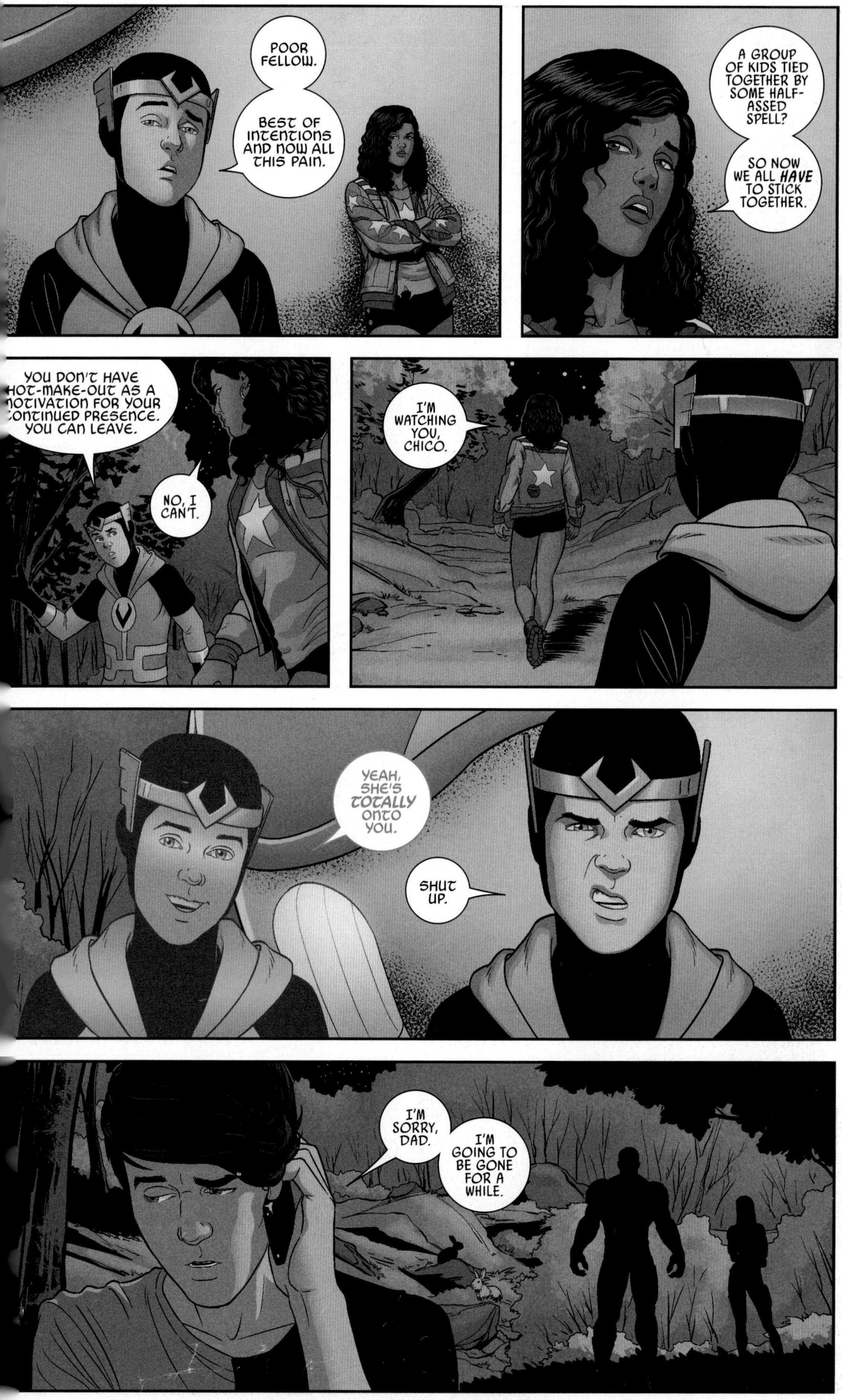
POOR FELLOW.
BEST OF INTENTIONS AND NOW ALL THIS PAIN.
A GROUP OF KIDS TIED TOGETHER BY SOME HALF-ASSED SPELL?
SO NOW WE ALL HAVE TO STICK TOGETHER.
YOU DON'T HAVE HOT-MAKE-OUT AS A MOTIVATION FOR YOUR CONTINUED PRESENCE. YOU CAN LEAVE.
NO, I CAN'T.
I'M WATCHING YOU, CHICO.
YEAH, SHE'S TOTALLY ONTO YOU.
SHUT UP.
I'M SORRY, DAD.
I'M GOING TO BE GONE FOR A WHILE.

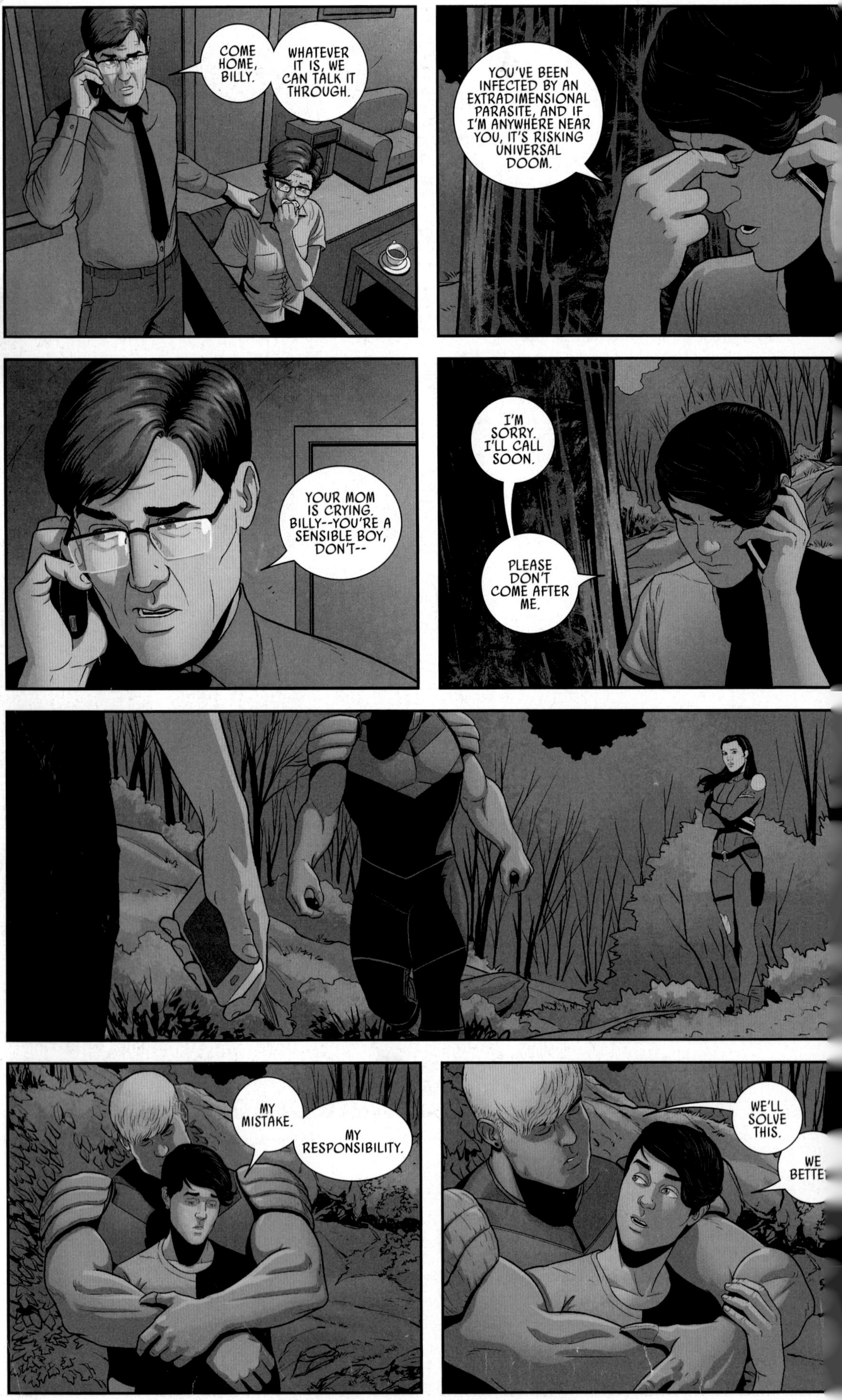
COME HOME, BILLY.
WHATEVER IT IS, WE CAN TALK IT THROUGH.
YOU'VE BEEN INFECTED BY AN EXTRADIMENSIONAL PARASITE, AND IF I'M ANYWHERE NEAR YOU, IT'S RISKING UNIVERSAL DOOM.
YOUR MOM IS CRYING. BILLY--YOU'RE A SENSIBLE BOY, DON'T--
I'M SORRY. I'LL CALL SOON.
PLEASE DON'T COME AFTER ME.
MY MISTAKE.
MY RESPONSIBILITY.
WE'LL SOLVE THIS.

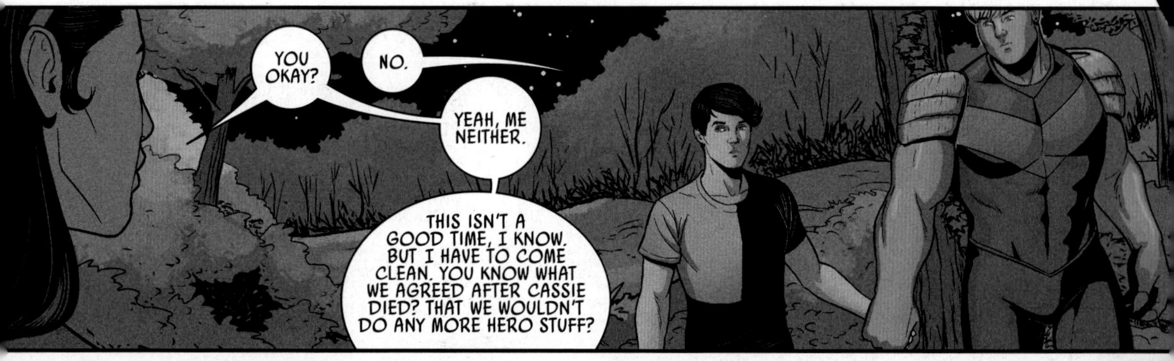
YOU OKAY?
NO.
YEAH, ME NEITHER.
THIS ISN'T A GOOD TIME, I KNOW. BUT I HAVE TO COME CLEAN. YOU KNOW WHAT WE AGREED AFTER CASSIE DIED? THAT WE WOULDN'T DO ANY MORE HERO STUFF?

YOU HAVE BEEN READING

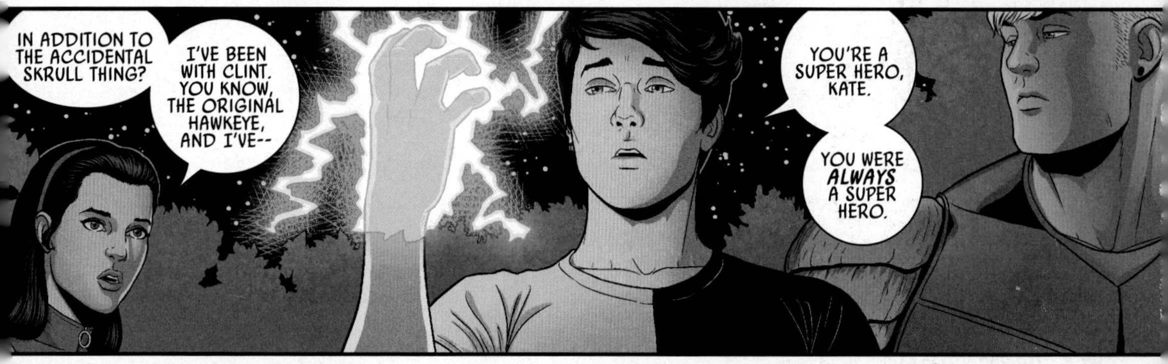
IN ADDITION TO THE ACCIDENTAL SKRULL THING?
I'VE BEEN WITH CLINT. YOU KNOW, THE ORIGINAL HAWKEYE, AND I'VE--
YOU'RE A SUPER HERO, KATE.
YOU WERE *ALWAYS* A SUPER HERO.

A MARVEL COMICS PUBLICATION

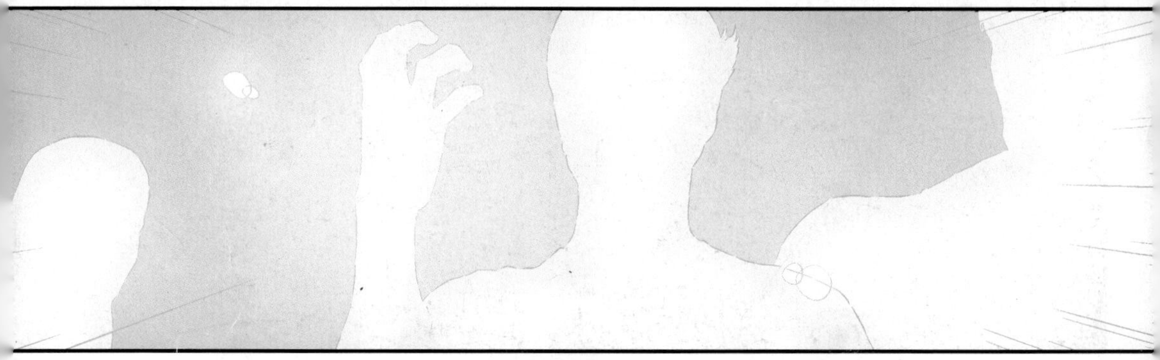

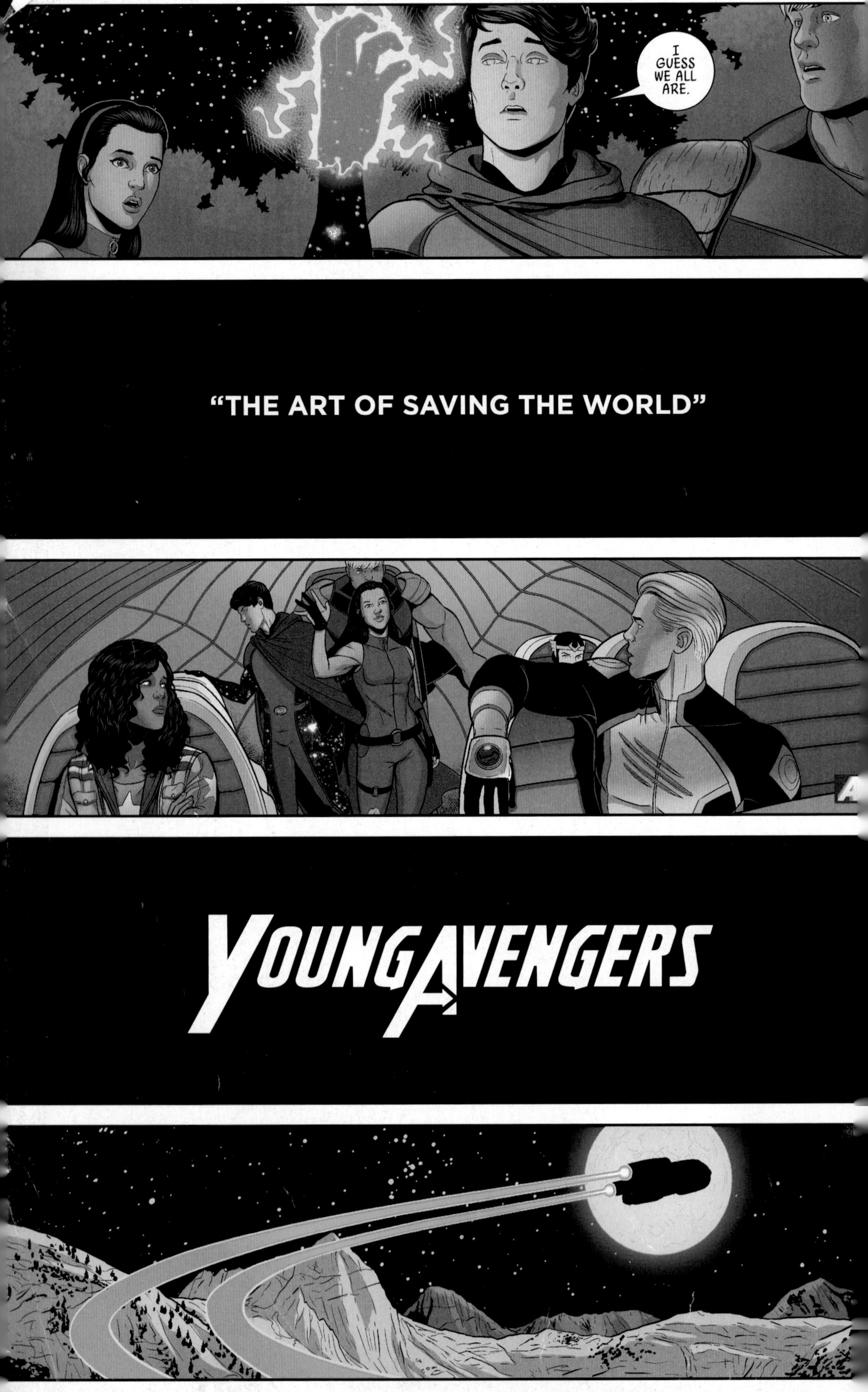
I GUESS WE ALL ARE.
“THE ART OF SAVING THE WORLD”
YOUNG AVENGERS

## #4 VARIANT
BY DAVID LAFUENTE & MORRY HOLLOWELL

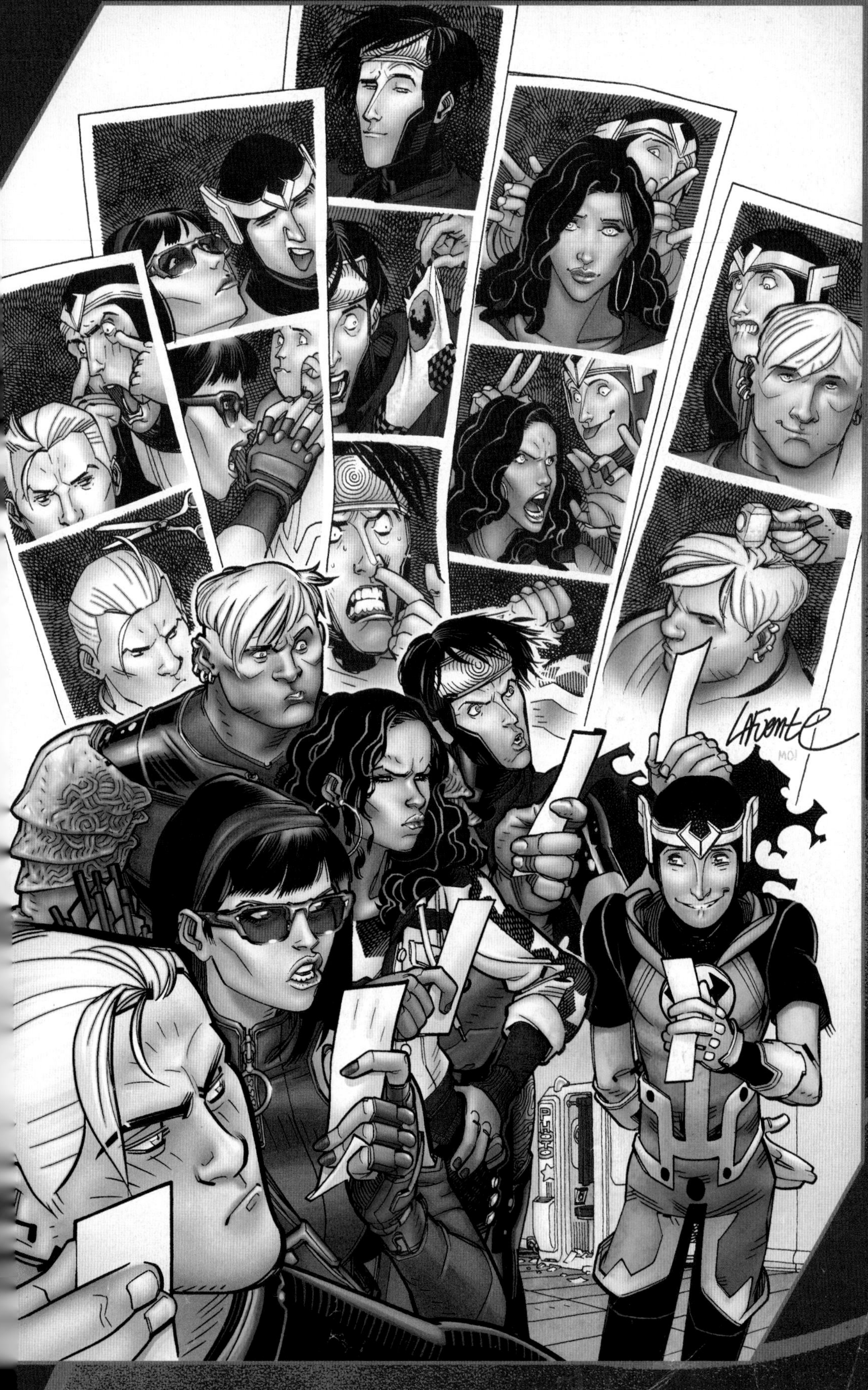
LAFUENTE
MO!

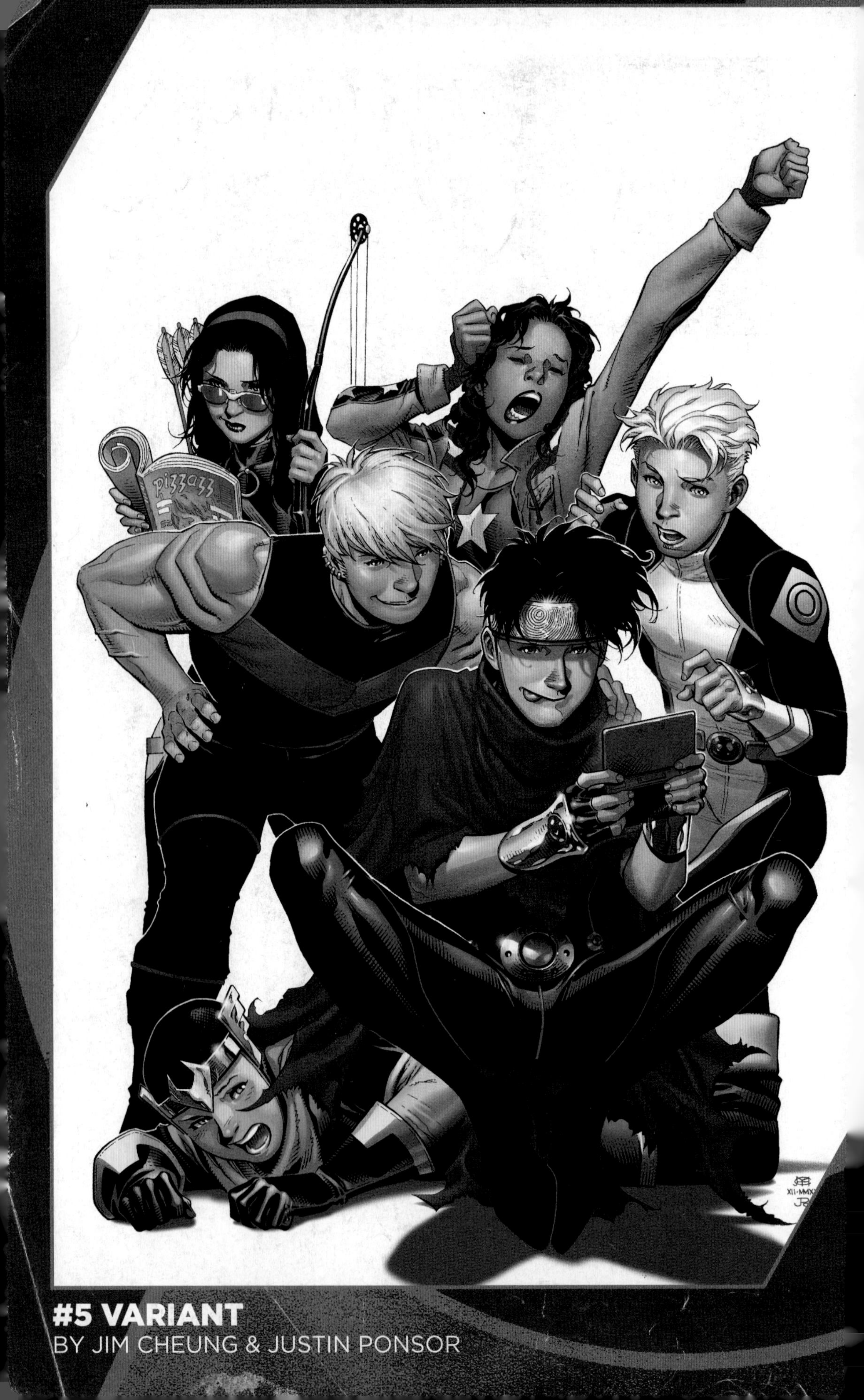
pizzazz

**#5 VARIANT**
BY JIM CHEUNG & JUSTIN PONSOR

## TO ACCESS THE FREE *MARVEL AUGMENTED REALITY APP* ...T ENHANCES AND CHANGES THE WAY YOU EXPERIENCE COMICS

1. **Download the app for free via**
   marvel.com/ARapp

2. **Launch the app on your camera-enabled**
   **Apple iOS® or Android™ device\***

3. **Hold your mobile device's camera ove**
   **any cover or panel with the AR grap**

4. **Sit back and see the future of comics**
   **in action!**

\*Available on most camera-enabled Apple iOS® and Android™ devices. Content subject to change and availability.

**YOUNG AVENGERS**

**AR INDEX**